Cassell Business Companions

GERMANY

Karsta Neuhaus and Margret Haltern

In association with
The British Chambers of Commerce

CASSELL

017940

Cassell
Villiers House, 41/47 Strand
London WC2N 5JE, England

387 Park Avenue South
New York, NY 10016–8810
USA

© 1991
ILT Verlag
Salzborn 9
4630 Bochum
Germany

First published 1991 under the title *Euro Business – German*
This revised edition first published in the UK 1992

British Library Cataloguing in Publication Data
Cassell Business Companions: Germany
  1. German language
  I. Title II. Haltern, Margret
  438.3421

  ISBN 0–304–33046–9

Typeset by Litho Link Ltd, Welshpool, Powys, Wales
Printed and bound in Great Britain by Biddles Ltd, Guildford and
King's Lynn

CONTENTS

INTRODUCTION

The realization of a Single European Market on 1 January 1993
will lead to increased attempts on the part of UK firms to compete
in foreign markets. This means making contact with potential
business partners abroad, first by telephone, fax and letter from
the UK office, followed by talks and negotiations face to face. In
other words, foreign language skills will play a major role in
determining the success or otherwise of such undertakings.

Conventional phrasebooks do not offer sufficient concrete help
for the complex needs of the business person operating in the
new trade arena. The aim of Cassell's new series of language
guides for European business is to meet this challenge by
providing a wide range of practical information in an easily
accessible form, creating a book which is an invaluable aid to
learning and an indispensable reference source.

Part I sets out the essential technical vocabulary and standard
phrases for different aspects of business with German companies:
Advertising/Buying and Selling/Insurance/Personnel/Contracts/
Accounts, *etc.*

This section is not intended as a substitute for technical
dictionaries, but rather as a useful aide-mémoire for the practised
negotiator. Moreover it will be especially useful to those
companies which do not have access to translation services or
trained interpreters. The vocabulary lists are complemented by
formulation aids and model letters which enable the user to
communicate in both the spoken and written language with
precision and competence.

A unique dimension to the text is the provision of a large
number of useful addresses which serves as a valuable source of
information for those conducting business abroad. Contact details
for official or institutional agencies are given alongside the topic
vocabulary (with translations where necessary).

Part II sets out the general language requirements for anyone
visiting a foreign country: Customs/Travel/Hotels/Banks, etc. A
special section on Small Talk examines those expressions which so

often prove essential in establishing first contact and in the
successful fostering of a business relationship.

Part III is a generous compendium of data including a glossary
of German job titles, abbreviations and key addresses for further
research purposes, plus information on the Single European
Market. An important section provides imformation on the former
GDR.

The Appendix incorporates a full bilingual glossary of technical
terms with pronunciations. A comprehensive index ensures that
you will find no difficulty in maximizing your use of this wide-
ranging guide to the essentials of business in German.

We should like to point out that the addresses and telephone
numbers were very carefully researched, but that telephone
numbers especially are often liable to change.

The authors wish you good luck and enjoyment in using the
language guide.

Karsta Neuhaus and Margret Haltern
Bochum

Notes on Signs, Symbols and Abbreviations Used in the Text

▼ Formulation aids for spoken and written contexts

✉ Model letters

■ Information on country and inhabitants

▶ Possible reactions from listeners

m masculine noun

f feminine noun

n neuter noun

pl plural noun

PART I

1

Market	Markt
buying motive	das Kaufverhalten
common market	Gemeinsamer Markt
to compete	konkurrieren
competition	die Konkurrenz
competitor	der Konkurrent
domestic market	der Binnenmarkt
highly competitive market	wettbewerbsintensiver Markt
market analysis	die Bedarfsanalyse
market research	die Marktforschung
market situation	die Marktlage
market survey	die Marktumfrage
marketing	der Absatz, der Vertrieb
marketing organization	die Absatzorganisation
monopoly	die Monopolstellung
price maintenance	die Preisbindung
questionnaire	der Fragebogen
sales potential	die Absatzmöglichkeit
sales territory	das Absatzgebiet
single market	europäischer Binnenmarkt
trend	der Trend

▼

Our products sell well.
Unsere Produkte finden guten Absatz.

We are putting our products on the market.
Wir bringen unsere Produkte auf den Markt.

We are launching a new product.
Wir bringen ein neues Produkt auf den Markt.

The addresses of all market research agencies in Germany are obainable from:

ADM
Arbeitskreis Deutscher
Marktforschungsinstitut e.V.
(Working Group of German Market
Research Agencies)
Papenkamp 2–6
D-2410 Mölln
Tel. 04542 801–0
Fax 84542 801201

Berufsverband Deutscher Markt- und
Sozialforscher e.V. (BVM)
(Professional Association of German
Market and Social Researchers)
Frankfurter Straße 22
D-6050 Offenbach/Main
Tel. 069 8001552
Fax 069 8003143

Die Lage der Weltwirtschaft und der deutschen Wirtschaft (The situation of the world economy and the German economy), a joint report of the five leading economic research institutes, published twice a year, can be ordered (on receipt of DM 5.00 plus postage) from:

Arbeitsgemeinschaft deutscher
wirtschaftswissenschaftlicher
Forschungsinstitute e.V.
(Association of German Economic Research
Institutes)
Poschingerstraße 5
D-8000 München 80
Tel. 089 9224-288
Fax 089 985369

Information on trade agencies is obtainable from:

> **Centralvereinigung Deutscher**
> **Handelsvertreter- und**
> **Handelsmaklerverbände (CDH)**
> **(Central Association of German Sales**
> **Representatives and Commercial**
> **Brokers)**
> **Geleiniusstraße 1**
> **D-5000 Köln 41**
> **Tel. 0221 514043**
> **Fax 0221 525767**

In addition there are 15 regional associations, the addresses of which are obtainable from:

> **British Chamber of Commerce in Germany**
> **Heumarkt 14**
> **D-5000 Köln 1**
> **Tel. 0221 234284/5**

> **German Chamber of Industry and**
> **Commerce in the UK**
> **16 Buckingham Gate**
> **London SW1E 6LB**

Part III contains a comprehensive list of addresses of the most important German Chambers of Industry and Commerce.

The following are the most important Statistical Offices:

> **Statistisches Bundesamt**
> **(Federal Statistical Office)**
> **Gustav-Stresemann-Ring 11**
> **D-6200 Wiesbaden**
> **Tel. 0611 75 1**
> **Fax 0611 753425**

Landesamt für Datenverarbeitung und
  Statistik Nordrhein-Westfalen
(Office of Data Processing and Statistics of
  the State of North Rhine-Westphalia)
Mauerstraße 51
D-4000 Düsseldorf
Tel. 0211 44971
Fax 0211 442006

Bayerisches Landesamt für Statistik und
  Datenverarbeitung
(Bavarian Office of Statistics and Data
  Processing)
Neuhauser Straße 51
D-8000 München
Tel. 089 2119 1
Fax 089 2119410

The addresses of all the other Statistical Offices can be obtained
from the Chambers of Industry and Commerce.

Statistisches Amt der Europäischen
  Gemeinschaft
(Statistical Office of the European
  Community)
rue Alcide de Gasperi
L-2920 Luxembourg
Tel. 00325 43011
Telex 3423 comeur lu

→1 Useful UK addresses can be found in Part III, 11.

2

Advertising	Werbung
advertisement	das Zeitungsinserat
advertising consultant	der Werbeberater
advertising gimmick, free gift	das Werbegeschenk

brochure, leaflet	**die Broschüre**
business reply card	**die Werbeantwort**
catalogue	**der Katalog**
circular	**das Rundschreiben**
commercial	**die Werbesendung,**
	der Werbespot
demonstration	**die Vorführung**
display material	**das Ausstellungsmaterial**
follow-up letter	**nachfassender Werbebrief**
free sample	**das Werbemuster**
handbill	**das Flugblatt**
in-depth knowledge of the trade	**fundierte Branchenkenntnisse**
instructions, leaflet, pamphlet	**das Merkblatt**
mail shot, mail circular	**die Postwurfsendung**
poster	**das Plakat**
prospectus, catalogue	**der Prospekt**
public relations	**die Öffentlichkeitsarbeit**
publicity agency	**die Werbeagentur**
publicity campaign	**die Werbekampagne**
publicity expenditure	**die Werbekosten**
sales promotional letter	**der Werbebrief**
sales promotion	**die Verkaufsförderung**
showroom	**der Ausstellungsraum**
training courses for salespersons	**die Schulungskurse für Verkäufer**
trial product sample	**das Produktmuster**

We specialize in . . .
Wir spezialisieren uns auf . . .

We trade/deal in . . .
Wir handeln mit . . .

We are well-known distributors.
Wir sind als Vertriebsorganisation bestens bekannt.

We are market leaders in the domestic market.
Wir sind marktführend auf dem Inlandmarkt.

We are manufacturers of . . .
Wir sind Hersteller von . . .

The new technology which we sell is very reliable.
Wir verkaufen eine zuverlässige neue Technologie.

We are retailers/wholesalers/importers/exporters in the . . . trade.
Wir sind Einzelhändler/Großhändler/Importeure/Exporteure in der . . . Branche.

We know the market well.
Wir verfügen über gute Kenntnis des Marktes.

We are a small/medium-sized firm.
Wir sind eine kleine/mittlere Firma.

We are an international company in the . . . sector, with annual sales of . . . and a range of well-established speciality products, many of which are the leading products on the market.
Wir sind eine internationale Firma, auf dem . . . Sektor tätig, mit einer jährlichen Verkaufsziffer von . . . und einer Auswahl von gut eingeführten Spezialprodukten, wovon viele zu den Marktführern zählen.

I'm in advertising.
Ich arbeite in der Werbung.

For promotional purposes.
Fur Werbezwecke.

**Zentralausschuß der Werbewirtschaft e.V.
(Central Committee of the German
   Advertising Industry)
Villichgasse 17
D-5300 Bonn 2
Tel. 0228 820920
Fax 0228 357583**

**Gesamtverband Werbeagenturen
   GWA e.V.
(Central Association of Advertising
   Agencies)
Friedensstraße 11
D-6000 Frankfurt/Main 1
Tel. 069 2560080
Fax 089 236883**

Deutscher Werbefachverband e.V. (DWF)
(German Professional Advertising
 Association)
c/o Norddeutscher Verband für Marketing
 und Kommunikation e.V.
Lange Laube 2
D-3000 Hannover 1
Tel. 0511 17277

→2 Useful UK addresses can be found in Part III, 11.

3

Fairs/Exhibitions	Messen/Ausstellungen
application	die Anmeldung
conditions of participation	die Teilnahmebedingungen
exhibit	das Ausstellungsstück
exhibition centre	das Messezentrum
exhibition regulations	die Messeordnung
exhibitor	der Aussteller
fair management	die Messeleitung
fair pass	der Messeausweis
floor plan	der Übersichtsplan
floor space	die Ausstellungsfläche
hall plan	der Hallenplan
hostess	die Messehostess
industrial fair	die Industriemesse
list of exhibitors	das Ausstellerverzeichnis
official catalogue	der Ausstellungskatalog
organizer (of a fair)	der Messeveranstalter
specialized fair	die Fachmesse
stand rental	die Standmiete
stand, stall, booth	der Messestand
trade fair	die Handelsmesse
visitor at a fair	der Messebesucher
to apply for space	anmelden (zu einer Messe)
to book exhibition space	Ausstellungsfläche mieten
to exhibit, to show	ausstellen (auf einer Messe)

to dismantle a stand	einen Stand abbauen
to open a fair	eine Messe eröffnen
to organize a fair	eine Messe veranstalten
to participate in a fair	sich an einer Messe beteiligen
to put up a stand	einen Stand aufbauen
to visit a fair	eine Messe besuchen

I work for . . .
Ich arbeite bei . . .

We make . . . and are interested in . . .
Wir produzieren . . . und sind interessiert an . . .

This is our latest model.
Dies ist unser neuestes Modell.

We've got some of our latest models here on our stand.
Hier auf unserem Stand haben wir einige unserer neuesten Modelle.

We are launching our product at this exhibition.
Wir führen unser Produkt auf dieser Messe ein.

We are introducing our product.
Wir stellen unser Produkt vor.

I'm sure there's a lot we can offer you.
Ich bin sicher, daß wir Ihnen eine Menge anbieten können.

Most customers appreciate the quality of our products.
Die meisten Kunden schätzen die Qualität unserer Produkte.

AUMA publications and the AUMA fairs programme provide all relevant information.

**Ausstellungs- und Messeausschuß der
  Deutschen Wirtschaft e.V. (AUMA)
(Exhibition and Trade Fair Committee of
  the German Economy)
Lindenstraße 8
D-5000 Köln 1
Tel. 0221 209070
Fax 0221 2090712**

The most important trade fair corporations are:

AMK Berlin
Ausstellung-Messe-Kongress-GmbH
(Exhibition-Trade Fair-Congress Company)
Messedamm 22
D-1000 Berlin 19
Tel. 030 30380
Fax 030 30382325
Telex 1 82 908

Deutsche Messe AG
(German Trade Fair PLC)
Messegelände
D-3000 Hannover 82
Tel. 0511 890
Fax 0511 8932626

Köln Messe
(Cologne Trade Fair)
Messeplatz 1
D-5000 Köln 21
Tel. 0221 8210
Fax 0221 8212574

Messe Düsseldorf GmbH
(Düsseldorf Trade Fair)
NOWEA
Postfach 320203
D-4000 Düsseldorf 30
Tel. 0211 456001
Fax 0211 4560668

Messe Frankfurt GmbH
(Frankfurt Trade Fair)
Ludwig-Erhard-Anlage 1
D-6000 Frankfurt 1
Tel. 069 75750
Fax 069 75756433

11

Münchner Messe- und
 Ausstellungsgesellschaft GmbH
 (Munich Trade Fair and Exhibition
 Company)
Theresienhöhe 13
D-8000 München 2
Tel. 089 51070
Fax 089 5107506

 Model Letter 2

4

Conferences and Meetings	Konferenzen und Sitzungen
agenda	die Tagesordnung
chairperson	der (die) Vorsitzende
unanimous(ly)	einstimmig
to attend a conference	an einer Konferenz teilnehmen
to bring forward a motion	einen Antrag stellen
to carry a motion	einen Antrag durchbringen
to clarify a position	einen Standpunkt klarstellen
to close a meeting	einen Sitzung schließen
to constitute a quorum	beschlußfähig sein
to decide on a motion	über einen Antrag entscheiden
to go into details	ins einzelne gehen
to keep the minutes	das Protokoll führen
to open the meeting	die Sitzung eröffnen
to outline	einen Überblick geben
to reject a motion	einen Antrag ablehnen
to vote for/against	abstimmen für/gegen

Some useful phrases:

Frankly, . . .	**Offen gesagt, . . .**
I am convinced that . . .	**Ich bin überzeugt, daß . . .**
I don't think so	**Ich glaube nicht**
I quite agree	**Ich bin der gleichen Meinung**
I think so	**Ich glaube schon/ich denke**
I'm afraid I couldn't go along with that	**Ich kann dem nicht zustimmen**
I'm afraid I don't agree	**Ich bin nicht Ihrer Meinung**
In my experience	**Nach meinen Erfahrungen**
May I bring up the question of	**Darf ich das Problem . . . zur Sprache bringen**
On the contrary	**Im Gegenteil**
On the one hand . . . on the other hand	**Einerseits . . . andererseits**
That's an important point	**Das ist ein wichtiger Punkt**
The main problem is . . .	**Das Hauptproblem ist . . .**
The pros and cons	**Das Für und Wider**
This sort of thing is in my line	**Das fällt in mein Fachgebiet**
To start with . . .	**Zu Beginn . . .**
To sum up, I can say that	**Zusammenfassend kann ich sagen**
Well, it depends	**Es kommt darauf an, je nachdem**
What do you think?	**Was denken Sie?**
What's your opinion?	**Was ist Ihre Meinung?**

**Bundesverband der
  Dolmetscher und Übersetzer e.V.
(Federal Association of Interpreters and
  Translators)**

Rüdigerstraße 79a
D-5300 Bonn 2
Tel. 0228 345000
Fax 0228 344290

International Verband der
    Konferenzdolmetscher
(International Association of Conference
    Interpreters)
Regionalgruppe Deutschland
(Regional Group Germany)
Bergstraße 4
D-6900 Heidelberg
Tel. 06221 44504
Fax 06221 402296

The Chamber of Industry and Commerce will also help you to find
an interpreter or a local translation bureau.

→3 Useful UK addresses can be found in Part III, 11.

5

Product Descriptions	Produkt-bezeichnungen
a limited number of	eine begrenzte Auswahl von
a wide range of	eine große Auswahl von
bulk goods	die Massengüter
capital goods	die Investitionsgüter
commodity, goods, merchandise	die Güter, die Ware, die Handelsware
consumer goods	die Verbrauchsgüter
finished goods	die Fertigfabrikate
item	der Posten (Ware)
label	das Etikett
model, pattern, specimen	das Musterstück
operating instructions	die Gebrauchsanweisung
pattern	das Muster, die Vorlage, das Modell

product liability	die Produkthaftung
quantity	die Menge
raw materials	die Rohstoffe
sample	das Muster, die Probe
sample collection	die Musterkollektion
sample of no commercial value	Muster ohne Wert
semi-finished goods	die Halbfertigfabrikate
series production	die Serienfertigung
shortage	die Fehlmenge
single-part production	die Einzelfertigung
special design	die Sonderanfertigung

Some classifications:

blend (coffee, tea)	die Mischung (Kaffee, Tee)
brand	die Marke
grade	die Sorte, die Güteklasse
quality	die Qualität
– commercial quality	– handelsübliche Qualität
– fair average quality (f.a.q.)	– Durchschnittsware
– first-class quality	– erstklassige Qualität
– outstanding quality	– hervorragende Qualität
– poor quality	– schlechte Qualität
– second-rate quality	– zweite Wahl
– standard quality	– Standardqualität
registered trade mark	eingetragenes Warenzeichen
size	die Größe

You inform your customer:

Our product . . .	Unser Produkt . . .
. . . is in accordance with the German safety regulations	. . . entspricht den deutschen Sicherheitsvorschriften
. . . is in accordance with the highest technical standards	entspricht den höchsten technischen Standards
. . . is carefully manufactured	. . . ist sorgfältig hergestellt
. . . is maintenance-free	. . . ist wartungsfrei
. . . is reliable	. . . ist zuverlässig

15

. . . is fully adjustable to all XY systems	. . . ist an alle XY Systeme anpassbar
. . . is easy and safe	. . . ist einfach und sicher
. . . to handle, to operate	. . . zu bedienen
. . . to assemble	. . . zu montieren
. . . to repair	. . . zu reparieren

This is what you may hear in German:

Gibt es darauf Garantie?
Does it come with a guarantee?

Darauf sind zwei Jahre Garantie.
The guarantee lasts for two years.

Die Garantie ist abgelaufen.
The guarantee has run out.

Ist es benutzerfreundlich?
Is it user-friendly?

Könnten Sie bitte erklären, wie es funktioniert?
Could you please explain how it works?

Bundesverband deutscher Patentanwälte e.V.
(Federal Association of German Patent Lawyers)
Webergasse 3
D-7300 Eßlingen
Tel. 0711 356539/359619
Fax 0711 359903

Europäisches Patentamt
(European Patent Office)
Erhardtstraße 27
D-8000 München
Tel. 089 23990
Fax 089 23994465

Deutsches Patentamt
(German Patent Office)
Zweibrückenstraße 12
D-8000 München 2
Tel. 089 21951
Fax 089 2221

DIN Deutsches Institut für Normung e.V.
Deutsches Informationszentrum für
  Technische Regeln (DITR)
(German Institute of Standardization
German Information Centre for
  Technical Norms)
Burggrafenstraße 6
D-1000 Berlin 30
Tel. 030 2601260
Fax 030 2601231

VdTÜV
Verband der Technischen
  Überwachungsvereine e.V.
(Federation of Engineering Control
  Associations)
Kurfürstenstraße 56
D-4300 Essen 1
Tel. 0201 81110
Fax 0201 8111120

Stiftung Warentest
(Product Test Foundation)
Lützowplatz 11–13
D-1000 Berlin 30
Tel. 030 69011
Fax 030 6901400

6

Buying and Selling	Kaufen, Verkaufen
accepted in the trade	handelsübich
buyer	der Käufer
commission agent	der Kommissionär
commission merchant, dealer	der Kommissionskaufmann
customer	der Kunde
distribution network	das Vertriebsnetz, die Vertriebs-organization
exporter	der Exporteur
franchised dealer	der Vertragshändler
hire-purchase	der Ratenkauf
importer	der Importeur
profit margin	die Gewinnspanne
purchase	der Kauf
purchasing power	die Kaufkraft
representative, commercial agent	der Vertreter, der Handelsvertreter
retailer	der Einzelhändler
sales	die Verkäufe, der Absatz
sales on commission	der Kommissionsverkauf
seller	der Verkäufer
sub-dealer	der Unter-Händler
supplier	der Lieferant
trade	der Handel
trade custom	die Handelsusance
trade mark-up	die Handelsspanne
trade relations	die Handelsverbindungen
trader, merchant	der Händler, der Kaufmann
turnover	der Umsatz
wholesale dealer	der Großhändler
to bargain	handeln, feilschen
to buy, to purchase	kaufen
– to buy at best price	– bestens kaufen
– to buy secondhand	– aus zweiter Hand kaufen
to find a ready market	sich gut verkaufen lassen
to lease	pachten, mieten

to rent	**mieten, vermieten, verpachten**
to sell	**verkaufen**
– to sell at a loss	**– mit Verlust verkaufen**
– to sell direct	**– direkt verkaufen**
– to sell off	**– ausverkaufen (das Lager räumen)**
to trade	**Handel treiben**
to trade in	**in Zahlung geben**

Sales are up by 10%.
Der Verkauf ist um 10% gestiegen.

On a sales or return basis.
Verkauf mit Rückgaberecht.

The goods are out of stock.
Die Waren sind ausverkauft.

You may hear the following in German:

Inlandverkauf
home sales

Exporte
export sales

Zunahme/Rückgang der Umsatzerlöse
increase/decrease in sales

> **Bundesverband des Deutschen Exporthandels e.V.**
> **(Federal Association of German Export Trade)**
> **Gotenstraße 21**
> **D-2000 Hamburg 1**
> **Tel. 040 23601624**
> **Fax 040 23601610**
>
> **Bundesverband des deutschen Groß- und Außenhandels e.V.**

19

(Federal Association of German Wholesale
and Export Trade)
Kaiser-Friedrich-Straße 13
D-5300 Bonn 1
Tel. 0228 260040
Fax 0228 2600455

These organizations deal with current questions on the Single
European Market, co-operation with EC associations, foreign
trade law, customs law, international tax law.

Hauptgemeinschaft des Deutschen
Einzelhandels e.V.
(Central Association of German Retail
Traders)
Sachsenring 89
D-5000 Köln 1
Tel. 0221 33980
Fax 0221 3398119

→4 Useful UK addresses can be found in Part III, 11.

7

Inquiry, Offer, Prices	Anfrage, Angebot, Preise
buying conditions	die Einkaufsbedingungen
detailed information about	ausführliche Informationen über
latest catalogue	neuester Katalog
list of products	das Warenverzeichnis
price list	die Preisliste
references	die Referenzen
selection of samples	die Auswahlmustersendung
selling conditions	die Verkaufsbedingungen
specification	detaillierte Aufstellung
terms	die Bedingungen

to be interested in	**interessiert sein an**
to inform	**informieren**
to refer to	**sich wenden an**
estimate	**der Kostenvoranschlag**
offer, proposal	**das Angebot**
– bid	**– das Kaufangebot (das Gebot)**
– binding offer	**– verbindliches Angebot**
– offer without engagement	**– freibleibendes Angebot**
– quotation	**– das Angebot mit Preisangabe**
– written offer	**– schriftliches Angebot**
proforma invoice	**die Proforma-Rechnung**
tender	**die Ausschreibung**
to accept an offer	**ein Angebot annehmen**
to make a firm offer	**fest anbieten**
to offer subject to confirmation	**freibleibend anbieten**
to revoke an offer	**ein Angebot widerrufen**
to submit an offer	**ein Angebot unterbreiten**
all-in price	**der Preis, alles inbegriffen**
at half price	**zum halben Preis**
buying price	**der Einkaufspreis**
competitive price	**konkurrenzfähiger Preis**
consumer price	**der Verbraucherpreis**
fair price	**angemessener Preis**
favourable price	**günstiger Preis**
fixed price	**fester Preis**
list price	**der Listenpreis**
lump sum	**der Pauschalbetrag**
price deduction	**der Preisnachlaß**
price increase	**die Preiserhöhung**
producer's price	**der Erzeugerpreis**
retail price	**der Einzelhandelspreis**
selling price	**der Verkaufspreis**
special price	**der Sonderpreis**
subscription price	**der Bezugspreis**
surcharge	**der Preisaufschlag**
unit price	**der Stückpreis**
wholesale price	**der Großhandelspreis**

to adjust prices	**Preise ausgleichen**
to beat prices	**Preise unterbieten**
to quote prices	**Preise angeben**
cash discount	**der Barzahlungsrabatt**
discount	**das Skonto, der Rabatt**
quantity discount	**der Mengenrabatt**
special discount	**der Sonderrabatt**
trade discount	**der Handelsrabatt**

We see from your advertisement in . . . that you are producers of . . .
Wir ersehen aus Ihrer Anzeige in . . ., daß Sie . . . produzieren.

We have heard of your products.
Wir haben von Ihren Produkten gehört.

Your name was given to us by . . .
Ihr Name wurde uns genannt von . . .

We saw your stand at the Hanover Fair.
Wir sahen Ihren Stand auf der Hannover Messe.

We would like to have further details about . . .
Wir hätten gerne nähere Einzelheiten über . . .

We require for immediate delivery . . .
Wir benötigen bei sofortiger Lieferung . . .

We are in the market for . . ./we require . . .
Wir haben Bedarf an . . .

Would you please quote your best price and terms of payment?
Würden Sie uns bitte Ihren günstigsten Preis und Ihre Zahlungsbedingungen angeben.

Full information regarding export prices and discounts for regular orders would be appreciated.
Wir würden gerne ausführliche Information über Exportpreise und Diskonte bei regelmäßiger Auftragserteilung erhalten.

We are prepared to place a trial order.
Wir sind bereit, einen Probeauftrag zu erteilen.

Please find enclosed our price list, as requested.
Wunschgemäß senden wir Ihnen als Anlage unsere Preisliste.

We are sending you our illustrated catalogue under separate cover.
Wir senden Ihnen mit getrennter Post unseren bebilderten Katalog.

We can make you a firm offer for . . .
Wir können Ihnen ein festes Angebot machen über . . .

Our offer is firm subject to acceptance by . . .
Unser Angebot ist fest bei Annahme bis zum . . .

We give a trade discount of 20% on our catalogue prices.
Wir gewähren einen Händlerrabatt von 20% auf unsere Katalogpreise.

Packing included.
Einschließlich Verpackung.

The price quoted is fob London.
Der Preis versteht sich fob London.

Recommended price.
Unverbindlicher Richtpreis.

No extra charge.
Kein Aufpreis.

Prices are subject to change without notice.
Preisänderungen vorbehalten.

Subject to prior sale.
Zwischenverkauf vorbehalten.

Prices are subject to revision according to the following price revision formula:
Die Preise unterliegen einer Preisgleitung gemäß folgender Preisgleitklausel:

We assure you that your order will be carried out to your complete satisfaction.
Wir versichern Ihnen, daß Ihr Auftrag zu Ihrer vollen Zufriedenheit ausgeführt wird.

 Model Letters 3, 4

8

Order and Acknowledgement
Auftrag und Auftragsbestätigung

acknowledgement of order	die Auftragsbestätigung
advance order	die Vorausbestellung
initial order	die Erstbestellung
order	der Auftrag
order book	das Auftragsbuch
order form	der Bestellschein
order number	die Auftragsnummer
orders on hand	der Auftragsbestand
repeat order	die Nachbestellung
to enter/book an order	eine Bestellung vormerken
to execute an order	einen Auftrag ausführen
to place an order	einen Auftrag erteilen
as per your order/in accordance with your order	laut Ihrer Bestellung

We thank you for your quotation and have pleasure in placing our order for . . .
Wir danken Ihnen für Ihr Angebot und freuen uns, Ihnen einen Auftrag über . . . zu erteilen.

Kindly supply the following goods at your earliest convenience.
Bitte liefern Sie folgende Waren möglichst bald.

The delivery dates stipulated in our order must be strictly adhered to.
Die in unserer Bestellung genannten Liefertermine müssen genauestens eingehalten werden.

Your careful attention to our instructions would be appreciated.
Wir wären Ihnen für die genaue Beachtung unserer Anweisungen dankbar.

This order is subject to our General Terms and Conditions.
Diese Bestellung unterliegt unseren Allgemeinen Geschäftsbedingungen.

Please confirm this order in due course.
Bitte bestätigen Sie diesen Auftrag zu gegebener Zeit.

We acknowledge receipt of your order for ...
Wir bestätigen den Eingang Ihres Auftrags über ...

The order will be carried out in accordance with your instructions.
Der Auftrag wird weisungsgemäß ausgeführt werden.

 Model Letter 5

9

Sales Contract	Kaufvertrag
agreement	die Vereinbarung
commercial settlement of a dispute	die Streitfallregelung
contract clause	die Vertragsklausel
contract of sale	der Kaufvertrag
contracting parties	vertragsschließende Parteien
deadlines	die Vertragsfristen für Leistungen
dispute	der Streitfall (bei Verträgen)
fulfilment of contract	die Vertragserfüllung
guarantee, warrant	der Garantievertrag, die Bürgschaft
hire-purchase	der Abzahlungskauf
maturity date of contract	der Vertragsfälligkeitstag
penalties	die Vertragsstrafen
period of contract	die Vertragsdauer
sale on trial	der Kauf auf Probe
sale or return	der Kauf mit Rückgaberecht
seller's warranties	die Gewährleistungspflicht
terms of contract	die Vertragsbedingungen

as per contract . . .	laut Vertrag . . .
the contract expires	**der Vertrag läuft aus**
the contract is null and void	**der Vertrag ist null und nichtig**
to amend a contract	**einen Vertrag ändern**
to become contractual	**vertraglich festschreiben**
to cancel a contract	**einen Vertrag stornieren, kündigen**
to certify a contract	**einen Vertrag beglaubigen**
to contract/to enter into a contract	**einen Vertrag abschließen**
to extend a contract	**einen Vertrag verlängern**
to negotiate the conditions of a contract	**die Vertragsbedingungen aushandeln**

▼

We reserve title to the goods delivered pending payment in full.
Wir behalten uns das Eigentum an den gelieferten Waren bis zur vollständigen Bezahlung vor.

In the event of litigation, the courts in Bochum shall have exclusive jurisdiction.
Gerichtsstand Bochum.

This is what you may read in German:

Wir geben Ihnen das Vorkaufsrecht.
We will give you first option.

Wir arbeiten mit 10%.
We work on 10%.

Contacts to German solicitors and specialized lawyers can be established through:

> **Deutscher Anwaltsverein**
> **(German Law Society)**
> **Adenauer Allee 196**
> **D-5300 Bonn 1**
> **Tel. 0228 26070**
> **Fax 0228 260746**

10

Production	Produktion
after-sales service	der Kundendienst
assembly	die Montage
assembly instructions	die Montageanleitung
assembly line	das Fließband
assembly-line production	die Fließfertigung
direct labour	die Fertigungslöhne
engineering	technische Planung
industrial plant	der Industriebetrieb
industrial production	industrielle Produktion
industrial standard	die Industrienorm
machine shop	die Werkstatt (Betrieb)
maintenance contract	der Wartungsvertrag
one-off production, individual construction	die Einzelfertigung
operations scheduling	die Arbeitsvorbereitung
output	die Produktionsleistung
production	die Produktion
production period	die Produktionszeit
production programme	das Produktionsprogramm
production schedule	der Fertigungsplan
quality control	die Qualitätskontrolle
series production	die Serienherstellung
service	die Dienstleistung
servicing manual	die Wartungsanleitung
subcontractor, supplier	die Zulieferfirma
tool	das Werkzeug
workshop	die Werkstatt
to make, to produce, to manufacture	herstellen
to streamline (production)	rationalisieren, modernisieren

11

Storage   Lagerhaltung

stock	der Lagerbestand
stock clerk/warehouseman	der Lagerverwalter
stock control	die Lagerbestandskontrolle
stock rotation	der Lagerumschlag
warehouse	das Lagerhaus
warehouse company	die Lagerhausgesellschaft
to have in stock	vorrätig haben
to store, to stock	lagern
to take stock	die Inventur aufnehmen

▼

Our stock is running low.
Unser Lagerbestand geht zur Neige.

12

Packing and Marking   Verpackung und
                                Markierung

export packing	die Exportverpackung
package	das Packstück, das Kollo
packaging	die Einzelverpackung
packing	die Verpackung
packing at cost price	die Verpackung zum Selbstkostenpreis
packing list	die Packliste
seaworthy packing	seemäßige Verpackung
special packing	die Sonderverpackung
wrapping	die Umhüllung, die Verpackung
gross weight	das Bruttogewicht
net weight	das Nettogewicht

tare	die Tara, das Verpackungsgewicht

barrel	das Faß
can, metal container	der Kanister
cardboard box, carton	die Schachtel
case	die Kiste
container	der Container
crate	die Lattenkiste
pallet	die Palette
returnable container	der Leihbehälter
sack, bag	der Sack
skid	der Schlitten

Shipping marks: / Versandmarkierungen:

made in . . ./country of origin	das Ursprungsland
marks	die Kurzmarkierung des Empfängers
order number	die Auftragsnummer
package numbers	die Kollonummern
port of destination	der Bestimmungshafen
weight and measurements	das Gewicht und die Abmessungen

Caution marks: / Vorsichtsmarkierungen:

Bottom	Unten
Glass – Fragile	Glas – Zerbrechlich
Handle with Care	Vorsicht
Inflammable	Entzündbar
Keep Dry	Vor Nässe Schützen
Keep in Cool Place	Kühl Aufbewahren
Lift Here	Hier Anheben
Poison	Gift
Radioactive	Radioaktive Substanz
Store Away from Heat	Vor Hitze Schützen
Top	Oben
Use No Hooks	Keine Haken

29

13

Transport and Delivery

Transport und Lieferung

air cargo, air freight	die Luftfracht
Bill of Lading (B/L)	das Konnossement
(non-negotiable) n.n. copy of B/L	(nicht begebbare Kopie)
bulk haulage	der Massengütertransport
carriage	der Gütertransport, die Anfuhr, die Abfuhr
Community Transport Procedure (CTP)	Gemeinschaftliches Versandverfahren
consignee	der Empfänger einer Sendung
consignment, shipment	die Warensendung
consignor, shipper	der Absender einer Sendung
country of destination	das Bestimmungsland
date of shipment	das Versanddatum
deadline	die Lieferfrist, äußerster Termin
delivery note	der Lieferschein
dispatch department	die Versandabteilung
dispatch note	die Versandanzeige
forwarder, carrier	der Spediteur
freight, cargo, carriage	die Fracht
freight/forwarding charges	die Frachtkosten
freight rate	die Frachtrate
– freight collect	– Fracht gegen Nachnahme
– freight included	– Fracht inbegriffen
long hauls	der Güterfernverkehr
lot	die Warenpartie
notify address	die Avisierungsanschrift
piggyback service	der Huckepackverkehr
place of destination	der Bestimmungsort
place of dispatch	der Versandort
roll-on/roll-off service	der RoRo-Verkehr
shipping documents	die Warenbegleitpapiere
– air waybill	– der Luftfrachtbrief
– consignment note, waybill	– der Frachtbrief
– duplicate consignment note	– das Frachtbriefdoppel

– Forwarding Agent's Certificate of Receipt (FCR)	**– die Spediteurübernahme-bescheinigung**
– railway consignment note	**– der Eisenbahnfrachtbrief**
short hauls	**der Güternahverkehr**
suppliers, contractors	**die Lieferfirma**
supply contract	**der Liefervertrag**
transport	**der Transport**
– air transport	**– der Lufttransport**
– rail transport	**– der Transport per Schiene**
– road transport	**– der Transport auf der Straße**
– water transport	**– der Wassertransport**
transshipment, reloading	**die Umladung**
to deliver	**ausliefern, zustellen**
to deliver within the specified time	**liefern, innerhalb der Lieferzeit**
to dispatch, to send off, to effect delivery	**senden, abschicken, die Lieferung durchführen**
to load, to unload	**laden, ausladen**
to ship, to forward	**versenden, befördern**
to specify the delivery route	**den Versandweg angeben**
to supply, to furnish a customer with goods	**liefern, beliefern**
in transit	**unterwegs, auf dem Transit**
via (Dover)	**über (Dover)**

The delivery can be effected, e.g.:

carriage paid	**frei Haus**
freight paid	**frachtfrei**
freight forward	**unfrei, Fracht zu Lasten des Empfängers**
ex-warehouse	**ab Lager**

31

Incoterms

International Commercial Terms are a set of international rules for the interpretation of trade terms, published as ICC Publication Number 460, 1990 edition, by:

> **ICC Publishing S.A.**
> **International Chamber of Commerce**
> **38 cours Albert 1er**
> **F-75008 Paris**

Incoterms 1990

EXW	Ex works (. . . named place)	**EXW**	**Ab Werk (. . . benannter Ort)**
FCA	Free Carrier (. . . named place)	**FCA**	**Frei Frachtführer (. . . benannter Ort)**
FAS	Free alongside ship (. . . named port of shipment)	**FAS**	**Frei Längsseite Seeschiff (. . . benannter Verschiffungshafen)**
FOB	Free on board (. . . named port of shipment)	**FOB**	**Frei an Bord (. . . benannter Verschiffungshafen)**
CFR	Cost and freight (. . . named port of destination)	**CFR**	**Kosten und Fracht (. . . benannter Bestimmungshafen)**
CIF	Cost, insurance and freight (. . . named port of destination)	**CIF**	**Kosten, Versicherung und Fracht (. . . bennannter Bestimmungshafen)**
CPT	Carriage paid to (. . . named place of destination)	**CPT**	**Frachtfrei (. . . benannter Bestimmungsort)**
CIP	Carriage and insurance paid to (. . . named place of destination	**CIP**	**Frachtfrei Versichert (. . . benannter Bestimmungsort)**

DAF	Delivered at frontier (. . . named place)	**DAF**	**Geliefert Grenze (. . . benannter Ort)**
DES	Delivered ex ship (. . . named port of destination)	**DES**	**Geliefert AB Schiff (. . . benannter Bestimmungshafen)**
DEQ	Delivered ex quay (duty paid) (. . . named port of destination)	**DEQ**	**Geliefert ab Kai (Verzollt) (. . . benannter Bestimmungshafen**
DDU	Delivered duty unpaid (. . . named place of destination)	**DDU**	**Geliefert Unverzollt (. . . benannter Ort)**
DDP	Delivered duty paid (. . . named place of destination)	**DDP**	**Geliefert Verzollt (. . . benannter Ort)**

▼

Delivery can be effected at the earliest possible date.
Lieferung kann so bald wie möglich erfolgen.

Delivery immediately after receipt of order.
Lieferung sofort nach Eingang der Bestellung.

We forwarded today by order and for account of . . .
Wir sandten Ihnen heute im Auftrag und für Rechnung . . .

We inform you that the goods have been dispatched by rail today.
Wir teilen Ihnen mit, daß die Waren heute per Bahn versandt wurden.

We hope that the consignment will reach you safely.
Wir hoffen, daß die Sendung wohlbehalten bei Ihnen ankommt.

**Bundesverband des Deutschen
Güterfernverkehrs (Bdf) e.V.
(Federal Association of German
Long-distance Haulage)
Breitenbachstraße 1**

D-6000 Frankfurt
Tel. 069 79190
Fax 069 7919265

Bundesverband Spedition und Lagerei e.V.
(Federal Association of the Forwarding
   Trade and Warehousing Business)
Weberstraße 77
D-5300 Bonn 1
Tel. 0228 210095
Fax 0228 213537

**Bundesverband der deutschen
   Binnenschiffahrt e.V.**
(Federal Association of Inland Waterway
   Carriers)
Dammstraße 15–17
D-4100 Duisburg 13
Tel. 0203 800060
Fax 0203 8000621

Verband Deutscher Reeder e.V.
(Association of German Shipowners)
Esplanade 6
D-2000 Hamburg 36
Tel. 040 350970
Fax 040 35097211

→5 Useful UK addresses can be found in Part III, 11.

14

Complaints	Mängelrügen
adjustment	die Regulierung der Beschwerde
circumstances beyond our control	unvorhersehbare Umstände
claim	**der Anspruch**
compensation	**der Schadenersatz**

complaint	die Beschwerde, die Mängelrüge
defect	der Mangel, der Defekt
defective goods	mangelhafte Ware
delay	die Verzögerung
fault	der Fehler
faulty material	fehlerhaftes Material
hidden defect	versteckter Mangel
non-conformity with sample	die Nichtübereinstimmung mit Muster
poor quality	schlechte Qualität
replacement	die Ersatzlieferung
substitute	die Ersatzlieferung
well-founded complaint	begründete Beschwerde
to allow a claim	eine Beschwerde anerkennen
to compensate	entschädigen
to complain about	sich beschweren über
to demand compensation	Schadenersatz verlangen
to exchange the goods	die Ware umtauschen
to grant an allowance	einen Preisnachlaß gewähren
to refund	erstatten
to refuse a claim	eine Beschwerde ablehnen
to take the goods back	die Ware zurücknehmen

When dealing with this subject orally, you could begin as follows:

▼

I don't like to complain, but I have had a lot of trouble with . . .
Ich beschwere mich nicht gerne, aber ich habe eine Menge Ärger gehabt mit . . .

I'm sorry, but I'm not at all satisfied with . . .
Leider bin ich überhaupt nicht zufrieden mit . . .

I'm very annoyed about . . .
Ich bin sehr ärgerlich über . . .

I'm not the sort of person who normally complains, but . . .
Normalerweise beschwere ich mich nicht, aber . . .

I'm disappointed with . . .
Ich bin enttäuscht über . . .

I'm sorry to hear . . .
Es tut mir leid zu hören . . .

I'm sorry about this, it's our fault.
Es tut mir leid, es ist unser Fehler.

I'll look into the matter immediately.
Ich werde mich sofort um die Angelegenheit kümmern.

I'll find out what happened.
Ich werde herausfinden, was passiert ist.

Can I see the guarantee?
Kann ich den Garantieschein sehen?

The following phrases are used for written complaints:

▼

We are sorry to inform you . . .
Wir müssen Ihnen leider mitteilen . . .

We are disappointed with the execution of our order.
Wir sind enttäuscht über die Ausführung unseres Auftrags.

On checking the items we noticed . . .
Bei Prüfung der Artikel bemerkten wir . . .

The quality of the goods does not correspond with that of the sample.
Die Qualität Ihrer Waren entspricht nicht dem Muster.

The goods were damaged in transit.
Die Ware wurde auf dem Transport beschädigt.

The damage seems to have been caused by inadequate packing.
Der Schaden ist anscheinend auf unsachgemäße Verpackung zurückzuführen.

We were promised delivery by the end of the month.
Die Lieferung wurde uns zum Monatsende zugesagt.

We are placing the defective goods at your disposal.
Wir stellen Ihnen die mangelhaften Waren zur Verfügung.

Please send us replacements for the damaged goods.
Bitte senden Sie uns Ersatz für die beschädigten Waren.

We must apologize for not having dispatched the goods in time.
Wir müssen uns entschuldigen, Ihnen die Waren nicht rechtzeitig gesandt zu haben.

We regret not having carried out your order properly.
Wir bedauern, Ihren Auftrag nicht ordentlich ausgeführt zu haben.

A new consignment has been sent off to you today.
Eine neue Lieferung ist heute an Sie abgegangen.

Please return the goods at our expense.
Bitte senden Sie die Waren auf unsere Kosten zurück.

We will take all possible steps to ensure that such a mistake does not occur again.
Wir werden dafür Sorge tragen, daß sich ein solcher Fehler nicht wiederholt.

Please accept our apologies for the trouble caused.
Wir bitten um Entschuldigung für den entstandenen Ärger.

We regret to inform you that we cannot assume any liability.
Leider müssen wir Ihnen mitteilen, daß wir keine Haftung Übernehmen können.

 # Model Letters 6, 7, 8

15

Insurance	Versicherung
beneficiary	**der Begünstigte**
claim	**der Schadensfall**
coverage	**die Deckung**
credit insurance	**die Kreditversicherung**
damage	**der Schaden**
insurance	**die Versicherung**
insurance certificate	**das Versicherungszertifikat**
insurance company	**die Versicherungsgesellschaft**
insurance policy	**die Versicherungspolice**

insurance against loss on the exchange rate	die Kursverlustversicherung
liability	die Haftung
policy holder	der Versicherungsinhaber
premium	die Prämie
third-party insurance, liability insurance	die Haftpflichtversicherung
transportation insurance	die Transportversicherung
underwriter	der Versicherer
to cover a risk	ein Risiko abdecken
to settle a claim	einen Schadensfall regulieren
to take out insurance	eine Versicherung abschließen
to underwrite a risk	ein Risiko versichern

Transport insurance can be taken out in accordance with the terms 'Allgemeine Deutsche Binnentransport-Versicherungsbedingungen' (ADB, 1963).

Insurance is frequently taken out under the terms of ADS (Allgemeine Deutsche Seeversicherungsbedingungen) Güterversicherung 1973, Fassung 1984, or, on an international level, under the Institute Cargo Clauses, e.g.

Clause A   full cover/all risks (volle Deckung)
Clause B   stranding cover (Strandungsfalldeckung)

> **Deutscher Transport-Versicherungs-Verband e.V.**
> **(German Association of Transport Insurance Companies)**
> **Rödingsmarkt 16**
> **D-2000 Hamburg 11**
> **Tel. 040 362426**
> **Fax 040 362196**
>
> **Gesamtverband der Deutschen Versicherungswirtschaft e.V.**
> **(Central Association of the German Insurance Industry)**
> **Ebertplatz 1**

D-5000 Köln 1
Tel. 0221 77640
Fax 0221 7764153

Verein deutscher Versicherungsmakler e.V.
(Association of German Insurance Brokers)
Katharinenstraße 4
D-2000 Hamburg 11
Tel. 040 3605–255
Fax 040 367788

Bundesaufsichtsamt für das
  Versicherungswesen
(Federal Supervisory Board for the
  Insurance Industry)
Ludwigkirchplatz 3–4
D-1000 Berlin 15
Tel. 030 88931
Fax 030 8893494

→6 Useful UK addresses can be found in Part III, 11.

16

Invoicing and Payment	Rechnungsstellung und Zahlung
advance payment	die Vorauszahlung
commercial invoice	die Handelsrechnung
consular invoice	die Konsularrechnung
date of invoice	das Rechnungsdatum
down-payment	die Anzahlung
invoice	die Rechnung
invoice amount	der Rechnungsbetrag
item	der Rechnungsposten
invoice number	die Rechnungsnummer
part-payment/interim payment	die Teilzahlung
payment of the balance	die Restzahlung
payment on account	die Abschlagszahlung
payment, settlement	die Zahlung

39

remittance	die Überweisung
statement of account	der Kontoauszug
terms of payment	die Zahlungsbedingungen
total (sum) amounting to £/DM	die Gesamtsumme über £/DM
as per invoice	laut Rechnung
brought forward (b/f)	Übertrag
E & OE (errors and omissions excepted)	Irrtum vorbehalten

Some usual terms of payment:

3% for cash	3% Skonto bei Barzahlung
3 months' credit	3 Monate Ziel
10 days 2% (2% off for payment within 10 days)	2% innerhalb von 10 Tagen
30 days net	30 Tage netto
cash with order (CWO)	Barzahlung bei Auftragserteilung
cash on delivery (COD)	Barzahlung bei Lieferung, Nachnahme
cash against documents (CAD), documents against payment (D/P)	Kasse gegen Dokumente
documents against acceptance (D/A)	Dokumente gegen Akzept
payment against bank guarantee	Zahlung gegen Bankgarantie
payment by acceptance	Zahlung durch Akzept
payment by cheque	Zahlung durch Scheck
payment by irrevocable confirmed documentary letter of credit (L/C)	Zahlung durch unwiderrufliches bestätigtes Dokumenten akkreditiv
payment by sight draft	Zahlung durch Sichttratte

payment on receipt of goods (ROG)	**Zahlung bei Erhalt der Ware**

The **Dokumentenakkreditiv** (Documentary Letter of Credit) plays an important role in exports: as a method of payment it protects both buyer and seller. Payment under a confirmed irrevocable L/C is the safest method of payment in foreign trade.

Normally the following shipping documents have to be presented under the terms of the credit:

air waybill	**der Luftfrachtbrief**
bill of lading	**das Konnossement**
certificate of origin	**das Ursprungszeugnis**
commercial invoice	**die Handelsrechnung**
freight note	**der Frachtbrief**
insurance certificate	**das Versicherungszertifikat**

The International Chamber of Commerce, Paris, has published sets of rules governing documentary credits. The guidelines entitled 'Uniform Customs and Practice for Documentary Credits, 1983' Revision are used by the banks and banking associations of virtually every country and territory in the world.

to balance an account	**ein Konto ausgleichen**
to charge	**berechnen, belasten**
to credit	**eine Gutschrift erstellen**
to draw a cheque	**einen Scheck ausstellen**
to invoice, to bill	**berechnen, Rechnung erstellen**
to pay, to make payment, to effect payment	**zahlen**
to pay on the due date	**bei Fälligkeit zahlen**
to pay cash	**bar zahlen**
to pay in advance	**im voraus zahlen**
to pay under reserve	**unter Vorbehalt zahlen**
to remit	**überweisen**
to transfer	**überweisen**
without charge	**ohne Berechnung**

▼

Please remit the sum of £ . . .
Bitte überweisen Sie die Summe von £ . . .

I have an account with XY Bank.
Ich habe ein Konto bei der XY Bank.

We transferred £ . . . to your account yesterday.
Wir überwiesen gestern £ . . . auf Ihr Konto.

The amount of £ . . . will be paid to your account with XY Bank.
Der Betrag von £ . . . wird auf Ihr Konto bei der XY Bank gezahlt.

We have drawn a cheque for DM . . . on XY Bank.
Wir haben einen Scheck über DM . . . auf die XY Bank ausgestellt.

We have accepted your draft and will honour it at maturity/when it is due.
Wir haben Ihre Tratte akzeptiert und werden sie bei Fälligkeit einlösen.

Please credit this amount to our account.
Bitte schreiben Sie diesen Betrag unserem Konto gut.

We enclose a cheque covering your invoice no . . .
Zum Ausgleich Ihrer Rechnung Nr . . . fügen wir einen Scheck bei.

Please send us your official receipt.
Bitte senden Sie uns eine Empfangsbestätigung.

The banking system in Germany has some special features. While the private-sector banks, co-operative banks and public-sector banks differ in the priorities they set in their business policies, there is no division of functions.
The commercial banks (universal banks of the continental European type) may be grouped into:

● the private commercial banks
● the public-sector banks (savings banks and their central institutions)
● the co-operative banks (commercial and agricultural credit co-operatives and their central banks).

In addition, there are a great many specialist banks (mortgage banks, instalment credit institutions, postal giro and postal savings offices).

> **Deutsche Bundesbank (German Federal Bank)**
> **Wilhelm-Epstein-Straße 14**
> **D-6000 Frankfurt/Main 50**
> **Tel. 069 1581**

Some banking associations:

Bundesverband deutscher Banken e.V.
(Federal Association of German Banks)
Mohrenstraße 35–41
D-5000 Köln 1
Tel. 0221 16630

Deutscher Sparkassen- und Giroverband
e.V.
(German Savings Banks Association)
Simrockstraße 4
D-5300 Bonn 1
Tel. 0228 2040

Bundesverband der Deutschen
Volksbanken u. Raiffeisenbanken e.V.
(Association of German Urban and
Agricultural Co-operative Banks)
Heussallee 5
D-5300 Bonn 1
Tel. 0228 5090

Verband deutscher Hypothekenbanken
e.V.
(Association of German Mortgage Banks)
Holbeinstraße 17
D-5300 Bonn 2
Tel. 0228 372026

A publication in English, entitled *The Banking System in Germany*, is available from the Bundesverband deutscher Banken e.V., Köln.

See also Part II, 5.

 **Model Letters 9, 10**

17

Outstanding Accounts

Außenstände

additional period of time	die Nachfrist
amount overdue	überfälliger Betrag
arrears	rückständige Beträge
assignment of a debt	die Forderungsabtretung
bill overdue	überfälliger Wechsel
collection agency	das Inkassobüro
debt, claim	die Forderung
– bad debt	– uneinbringliche Forderung
– doubtful debt	– zweifelhafte Forderung
default interest	die Verzugszinsen
due date	der Rückzahlungstermin
dunning letter	der Mahnbrief
extension	die Verlängerung (Kredit)
factoring	die Darlehensgewährung gegen Forderungsabtretung
outstanding accounts	die Außenstände
overdue	überfällig
payee	der Zahlungsempfänger
period of limitation	die Verjährung
prolongation	Verlängerung (Wechsel)
recourse	der Regress
reminder	das Erinnerungsschreiben
security	die Sicherheit
transfer of title for the purpose of securing a debt	die Sicherungsübereignung
to bounce (of a cheque)	platzen (Scheck)
to control	überwachen
to demand payment	zur Zahlung auffordern
to fall due	fällig werden
to grant an extension	einen Aufschub gewähren
to object to something	Widerspruch erheben
to overdraw an account	ein Konto überziehen
to prolong, to extend	verlängern
to remind somebody of something	erinnern an

business reputation	geschäftlicher Ruf
credit inquiry	die Auskunftseinholung
credit standing	die Kreditwürdigkeit
estimated annual turnover	geschätzter Jahresumsatz
financial standing	die Vermögenslage
honest	ehrlich, rechtschaffen
reliability	die Zuverlässigkeit
solvency	die Zahlungsfähigkeit
strictly confidential	streng vertraulich
without obligation	unverbindlich

▼

Looking through our books we find that a balance of . . . is still open.
Bei Durchsicht unserer Bücher haben wir festgestellt, daß ein Saldo von . . . offensteht.

Our statement of account has obviously been overlooked.
Sie haben sicherlich unseren Kontoauszug übersehen.

May we remind you that your payment has been overdue since 31 July?
Dürfen wir Sie erinnern, daß Ihre Zahlung seit dem 31. Juli überfällig ist?

Our invoice of . . . is still unpaid.
Unsere Rechnung vom . . . ist noch unbeglichen.

Your account is overdrawn/unbalanced.
Ihr Konto ist überzogen/offen.

Please send your cheque by . . .
Bitte senden Sie Ihren Scheck bis zum . . .

Messrs . . . have given us your name as a trade reference.
Fa . . . hat uns Ihren Namen als Handelsreferenz genannt.

Do you think it would be justifiable to grant them a credit of up to . . .?
Ist ein Kredit bis zur Höhe von . . . vertretbar?

They have always met their obligations promptly.
Dir Firma ist ihren Zahlungsverpflichtungen stets pünktlich nachgekommen.

This information is given in strictest confidence and without any obligation on our part.
Diese Auskunft wird streng vertraulich und ohne jede Haftung erteilt.

For information concerning the standing and reputation of your business partner you can refer to a credit enquiry agency which will supply you with information subject to payment. The best-known are:

> **Schimmelpfeng**
> **Hahn-Straße 31–35**
> **D-6000 Frankfurt 71**
> **Tel. 069 663030**
> **Fax 069 66303175**

> **Verband der Vereine Creditreform e.V.**
> **(Association of Credit Reform Societies)**
> **Hellersbergstraße 12**
> **D-4040 Neuss 1**
> **Tel. 02101 1090**
> **Fax 02101 109140**

Mahnbescheid (Summary Court Notice to pay a debt)

On certain preconditions and with regard to rightful claims in DM it is possible in Germany to obtain a legally effective judicial order for execution (Vollstreckungsbescheid) through the Local First Instance Court (Amtsgericht). On the basis of this order a compulsory execution can be levied (Zwangsvollstreckung). The method is of great importance in Germany.

British applicants may refer to:

> **Amtsgericht Schöneberg**
> **(District Court Schöneberg)**
> **Grunewaldstraße 66–67**
> **D-1000 Berlin 62**

 Model Letters 11, 12, 13, 14

18

Bankruptcy/ Liquidation

Konkurs

affidavit	eidesstattliche Erklärung
attachment (seizure of goods)	die Pfändung
bankruptcy, liquidation	der Konkurs
composition	der Vergleich
compromise	der (außergerichtliche) Vergleich
compulsory sale	der Zwangsverkauf
creditor	der Gläubiger
debtor	der Schuldner
dispute	der Streit
insolvency	die Zahlungsunfähigkeit
lawsuit, litigation	der Prozeß, der Rechtsstreit
lawyer	der Jurist (gen.), der Rechtsanwalt
official receiver (OR)	der Konkursverwalter
receiving order	der Konkurseröffnungsbeschluß
reservation of title	der Eigentumsvorbehalt
solicitor	der Rechtsanwalt
trustee	der Konkursverwalter
to bring an action against . . .	eine Klage einreichen gegen . . .
to file for bankruptcy	Konkurs anmelden
to go bankrupt	Konkurs machen

Contact with German solicitors can be made through:

> **Deutscher Anwaltsverein**
> **(German Law Society)**
> **Adenauer Allee 196**
> **D-5300 Bonn 1**
> **Tel. 0228 26070**
> **Fax 0228 260746**

→7 Useful UK addresses can be found in Part III, 11.

19

Accounting — Buchhaltung

account	das Konto
accountant, bookkeeper	der Buchhalter
accounting, bookkeeping	die Buchhaltung
amortization instalment	die Tilgungsrate
annual financial statement	der Jahresabschluß
auditing	das Prüfungswesen
balance	der Saldo
book value	der Buchwert
budgetary accounting	die Finanzplanung
call money	das Tagesgeld
cash flow	der Finanzmittelfluß
credit note	die Gutschriftsanzeige
debit note	die Lastschriftsanzeige
entry	die Buchung
expenditure	die Ausgaben
inventory	die Inventur
ledger	das Hauptbuch
liquidity	die Liquidität
mortgage	die Hypothek
order book	das Auftragsbuch
overdraft credit	der Überziehungskredit
percentage	der Prozentsatz
profitability	die Rentabilität
receipts	die Einnahmen
result	das Ergebnis
short-term/medium-term/ long-term credit	kurz-/mittel-/langfristiger Kredit
statistics	die Statistik
valuation	die Bewertung
voucher	der Beleg
yield	die Rendite
to book	buchen
to book in conformity	gleichlautend buchen
to calculate	rechnen
to cancel	stornieren

to carry forward (the balance)	**vortragen (Saldo)**
to certify	**bescheinigen**
to close an account	**ein Konto schließen**
to open an account	**ein Konto eröffnen**

Bundesverband der Bilanzbuchhalter e.V.
(Federal Association of Accountants)
Friedrich-Ebert-Allee 73–75
D-5300 Bonn
Tel. 0228 239790
Fax 0228 230619

20

Balance Sheet — Bilanz

accruals	**die Rückstellungen**
assets	**die Aktiva**
balance sheet	**die Bilanz**
borrowed capital	**das Fremdkapital**
chartered accountant	**der Wirtschaftsprüfer**
current assets	**das Umlaufvermögen**
equity capital	**das Eigenkapital**
finished products/goods	**fertige Erzeugnisse**
fixed assets	**das Anlagevermögen**
inventories	**die Vorräte**
legal reserves	**die gesetzliche Rücklagen**
liabilities	**die Passive**
liquid funds	**flüssige Mittel**
loan	**das Darlehn**
notes payable	**die Wechselverbindlichkeiten**
raw materials	**die Rohstoffe**
receivables	**die Forderungen**
share	**die Aktie**
trade payables	**die Verbindlichkeiten aus Lieferungen und Leistungen**
work in progress	**unfertige Erzeugnisse**

If you have any queries with regard to rendering of accounts and preparing a balance sheet you can contact:

**Institut der Wirtschaftsprüfer in
Deutschland e.V.
(Institute of Chartered Accountants in
Germany)
Tersteegenstraße 14
D-4000 Düsseldorf 30
Tel. 0211 45610
Fax 0211 4541097**

See at the end of Part I, pp. 66–9, for the layout of the 'Balance Sheet' according to 'Bilanzrichtliniengesetz' (Accounting and Reporting Legislation. Adoption of the 4th, 7th, and 8th EC Directives).

21

Statement of Earnings	Gewinn- und Verlustrechnung
administration expenses	**die Verwaltungskosten**
after-tax profit	**der Gewinn nach Steuern**
compound interest	**der Zinseszins**
depreciations	**die Abschreibungen**
dividend	**die Dividende**
gross profit	**der Bruttoerttrag**
interests	**die Zinsen**
operating expense and income	**betrieblicher Aufwand und Ertrag**
pre-tax profit	**der Gewinn vor Steuern**
profit and loss account	**das Gewinn- und Verlustkonto**
rate of interest	**der Zinssatz**
sales	**die Umsatzerlöse**
to write off	**abschreiben**

See at the end of Part I, pp. 70–1, for the layout of the Profit and Loss Account according to 'Bilanzrichtliniengesetz' (Accounting and Reporting Legislation, Adoption of the 4th, 7th, and 8th EC Directives).

22

Annual Report	Geschäftsbericht
annual general meeting of the shareholders	die Jahreshauptversammlung
annual report	der Geschäftsbericht
bookings	die Auftragseingänge
business development, growth	die Geschäftsentwicklung
capital structure	die Kapitalverhältnisse
development of a product	die Entwicklungstätigkeit
economic position	wirtschaftliche Lage
expected growth	voraussichtliche Entwicklung
indebtedness	die Verschuldung
investment	die Investition
production	die Produktion
research	die Forschungstätigkeit
return, yield	der Ertrag
revenues	die Erlöse
subsidy	die Subvention
trading result	das Betriebsergebnis
year under review	das Berichtsjahr

23

Costs and Calculation	Kosten und Kalkulation
all-in costs	die Gesamtkosten
at cost	zum Selbstkostenpreis
at your/our expense	auf Ihre/unsere Kosten
calculation	die Kalkulation
capacity usage ratio	der Ausnutzungsgrad
capital gains tax	die Kapitalertragssteuer
capital transfer tax	die Kapitalverkehrsteuer
church tax	die Kirchensteuer
corporation tax	die Körperschaftssteuer
cost effective	kostenwirksam

cost free/free of charge	**kostenlos**
cost price	**die Selbstkosten**
cost-covering	**kostendeckend**
costs	**die Kosten**
direct material	**das Fertigungsmaterial**
direct wages	**die Fertigungslöhne**
excise tax	**die Verbrauchssteuer**
expenditure, expenses	**die Ausgaben**
extras	**die Nebenkosten**
fixed costs	**die Fixkosten**
income tax	**die Einkommensteuer**
inheritance tax	**die Erbschaftssteuer**
liable for tax	**steuerpflichtig**
marginal costs	**die Grenzkosten**
net worth tax	**die Vermögenssteuer**
no hidden extras	**keine versteckten Kosten**
overhead charges	**die Gemeinkostenzuschläge**
overhead costs	**die Gemeinkosten**
production costs	**die Herstellungskosten**
profit mark-up	**der Gewinnzuschlag**
real property transfer tax	**die Grunderwerbssteuer**
refund of costs	**die Kostenerstattung**
royalty	**die Lizenzgebühr**
selling expenses	**die Vertriebskosten**
surtax	**die Zusatzsteuer**
tax	**die Steuer**
tax allowance	**die Steuervergünstigung**
tax consultant	**der Steuerberater**
tax exemption	**der Steuerfreibetrag**
tax-favoured	**steuerbegünstigt**
tax-free	**steuerfrei**
trade tax (levied by local authorities)	**die Gewerbesteuer**
turnover tax	**die Umsatzsteuer**
unit cost	**die Stückkosten**
VAT (value added tax)	**die Mehrwertsteuer**
variable costs	**variable Kosten**
volume of production	**der Beschäftigungsgrad**
wage tax	**die Lohnsteuer**
wealth tax	**die Vermögenssteuer**
zero-rated	**ohne Mehrwertsteuer**

Value added tax in EC countries

	lower %	standard %	higher %
Belgien	6 and 17	19	25 and 33
Dänemark	—	22	—
Deutschland	7	14	—
Frankreich	5.5 and 7	18.6	33.3
Griechenland	6	18	36
Großbritannien	0	17.5	—
Holland	5	19	—
Irland	0 and 10	23	—
Italien	2 and 9	18	38
Luxemburg	3 and 6	12	—
Portugal	0 and 8	17	30
Spanien	6	12	33

Contacts with German tax consulting firms can be established through:

**Deutscher Steuerberaterverband
(Association of German Tax
  Consultants)
Bertha-von-Suttner-Platz 25
D-5300 Bonn 1
Tel. 0228 653773
Fax 0228 630362**

24

Personnel Matters	Personalangelegen-heiten
application	die Bewerbung
apprentice, trainee	der Lehrling, der Azubi
boss	der Chef
chairman (-woman)	der (die) Generaldirektor(in)
clerk	kaufmännische(r) Angestellte(r)

co-determination, workers' participation in management	die Mitbestimmung
contract of employment	der Anstellungsvertrag
curriculum vitae	der Lebenslauf
dismissal	die Entlassung
education, training	die Erziehung, die Ausbildung
employee	der (die) Angestellte, der (die) Beschäftigte
employee	der Arbeitnehmer
employer	der Arbeitgeber
executive	die Führungskraft, leitende(r) Angestellte(r)
expert	der Fachmann
financial controller	der (die) Leiter(in) des Finanzwesens
flexible working hours, flexitime	Gleitzeit
foreign language secretary	der (die) Fremdsprachen- sekretär(in)
foreman	der (die) Meister(in)
fringe benefits	zusätzliche Vergütung an Arbeitnehmer (in addition to wages or salary)
full-time worker	die Vollarbeitskräfte
interview	das Einstellungsgespräch
job	die Stellung
management	die Unternehmensleitung
manager	der (die) Leiter(in), der (die) Geschäftsführer(in)
managing director	geschäftsführendes Vorstandsmitglied
master (craftsman)	der (die) Meister(in)
on-the-job training	dis Ausbildung am Arbeitsplatz
part-time workers	die Teilzeitkräfte
payroll	die Lohnabrechnung, die Personalliste
pension fund	die Pensionskasse
personal data sheet	der Kurz-Lebenslauf
personal secretary	die Chefsekretärin
personnel manager	der Personalleiter

plant manager	der (die) Werksleiter(in)
probation period	die Probezeit
professional experience	berufliche Erfahrung
profit sharing	die Gewinnbeteiligung
promotion	die Beförderung
proxy	der (die) Handlungsbevoll-mächtigte
purchasing manager, chief buyer	der (die) Leiter(in) des Einkaufs
qualification	die Eignung, die Qualifikation
questionnaire	der Fragebogen
references	die Referenzen
rise	die Gehaltserhöhung
salary	das Gehalt
sales manager	der (die) Leiter(in) des Verkaufs
school leaving certificate	das Schulabgangszeugnis
secretary (to XY)	der (die) Sekretär(in) (von XY)
shift work	die Schichtarbeit
skilled worker	der (die) Facharbeiter(in)
superannuation fund	die Pensionskasse
superior	der (die) Vorgesetzte
temporary staff	das Aushilfspersonal
testimonial	das Zeugnis des Arbeitgebers
trade union	die Gewerkschaft
typist	die Schreibkraft
unemployment	die Arbeitslosigkeit
unskilled worker	der (die) Hilfsarbeiter(in)
vacancy, opening	offene Stelle
vocational training	die Berufsausbildung
wage(s)	der Lohn, die Löhne
workforce, staff, personnel	die Belegschaft
working hours	die Arbeitszeit
works council member	das Betriebsratsmitglied
to apply for	sich bewerben um
to attend an evening course	einen Abendkurs besuchen
to employ, to engage, to take on	einstellen
to give notice	kündigen
to manage	leiten, führen, verwalten
to serve an apprenticeship	eine Lehre absolvieren

55

| to train, to instruct | beruflich ausbilden |
| to work overtime | Überstunden machen |

In an interview you may be asked:

Würden Sie mir bitte etwas über Ihre Ausbildung und Ihren persönlichen Hintergrund erzählen.
Will you please tell me about yourself and your educational background?

Welche Fremdsprachen haben Sie gelernt?
What foreign languages have you learned/studied?

Können Sie mit einem Computer umgehen?
Are you computer-literate?

Warum möchten Sie sich verändern?
Why do you want to leave your present job?

Wann können Sie bei uns anfangen?
When can you start working for us?

Welche Position bekleiden Sie in Ihrer Firma?
What position do you hold in your present job?

Vorstandsmitglied	member of the board, director
Geschäftsführer	managing director
Direktor	manager/head of . . .
Prokurist	holder of procuration (no equivalent)
	ppa . . . (signature of holder)
Abteilungsleiter	department manager/head
Handlungsbevollmächtigter	holder of commercial authority (no counterpart in the UK), ranking below 'Prokurist'
	i.V. . . . (signature of holder)
Sachbearbeiter	person in charge of . . .
Gruppenleiter	group manager

▼

With reference to your advertisement in yesterday's . . ., I would like to apply for the position of . . . in your company.
Unter Bezugnahme auf Ihre Anzeige in der gestrigen . . . möchte ich mich um die Stelle als . . . in Ihrer Firma bewerben.

I am familiar with export and import procedures.
Ich bin mit Export- und Importverfahren vertraut.

I am very interested in working in the UK because . . .
Ich bin sehr daran interessiert in UK zu arbeiten, weil . . .

I have a good working knowledge of English.
Ich habe gute Englischkenntnisse.

I enclose a CV with details of my practical training and experience.
Ich füge einen Lebenslauf mit Einzelheiten über meine berufliche Ausbildung und Erfahrung bei.

Please find enclosed copies of testimonials by . . .
In der Anlage finden Sie Zeugnisse der Firmen . . .

My present position is subject to three months' notice.
Ich habe drei Monate Kündigungszeit.

> **Bundesanstalt für Arbeit**
> **(Federal Labour Office)**
> **Regensburger Straße 104**
> **D-8500 Nürnberg 30**
> **Tel. 0911**
>
> **Zentralstelle für Arbeitsvermittlung**
> **(Central Employment Exchange)**
> **Feuerbachstraße 42–46**
> **D-6000 Frankfurt/Main**
> **Tel. 069 71110**

 Model Letter 15

25

Data Processing	Datenverarbeitung
blank, space	die Leerstelle, das Füllzeichen
cable connection	der Kabelanschluß
calculator (pocket-)	der Rechner (Taschen-)
carry over	der Übertrag

central processing unit (CPU)	**die Zentraleinheit**
communication line	**die Datenübertragungsleitung**
daisy-wheel	**das Typenrad, das Schreibrad**
database	**die Datenbank**
data flowchart	**der Datenflußplan**
data transfer	**der Datenaustausch**
density	**die Speicherdichte**
direct memory access	**direkter Zugriff**
disk	**die Diskette**
disk operating system (DOS)	**das Plattenbetriebssystem**
disk storage	**der Magnetplattenspeicher**
display	**die Anzeige (Bildschirm)**
drive (disk)	**das Laufwerk**
electronic data processing	**die Datenverarbeitung (EDV)**
electronic mail	**elektronische Post**
– fax	**– Telefax**
– teletex	**– Teletex**
– telex	**– Telex**
electronic mailbox	**elektronischer Briefkasten**
to erase	**löschen**
file	**die Datei**
floating point	**das Gleitkomma**
hard disk	**die Festspeicherplatte**
input	**die Dateneingabe**
interface	**die Schnittstelle**
keyboard	**die Tastatur**
listing	**die Listen**
magnetic head	**der Magnetkopf**
magnetic tape	**das Magtnetband**
manual	**das Handbuch**
mask, picture	**die Maske**
master file	**die Stammdatei**
memory	**der Speicher**
memory protection	**der Speicherschutz**
office automation	**die Büroautomatisierung**
operating system	**das Betriebssystem**
output	**die Datenausgabe**
paper feed	**der Papiervorschub**
password, keyword	**das Kennwort**
plotter	**elektronisches Zeichengerät**
plug-compatible	**steckerkompatibel**

power supply	die Stromversorgung
private line	die Standleitung
programming language	die Programmiersprache
random access memory (RAM) working storage	der Arbeitsspeicher
read-only memory (ROM)	der Festspeicher
remote printer	der Drucker
scanner	der Bildabtaster
screen, monitor	der Bildschirm
service	die Wartung
shift key	die Umschalttaste
slot	der Anschluß (der Stecker-)
software	das Programm
source program	das Ursprungs-/Quellprogramm
spreadsheet	die Kalkulationstabelle
subroutine	das Unterprogramm
tape library system	das Magnetband-Bibliotheksystem
tape drive unit	das Magnetbandgerät
tariff zone	die Tarifzone
teleprocessing	die Datenfernverarbeitung
text- (word-) processing system	das Textverarbeitungssystem
transmission channels	die Übertragungswege
update	der Änderungsdienst
user identification	die Benutzeridentifikation
utility	das Dienstprogramm
wire printer	der Nadeldrucker
write head	der Schreibkopf
write lock, file protection	der Schreibschutz

Does the computer run IBM-compatible software?
Arbeitet der Computer mit IBM kompatiblen Programmen?

Can I use 3½ or 5¼ disks?
Kann ich 3½" oder 5¼" Disketten benutzen?

Can I run colour and graphics software on the PC?
Kann ich mit Farb- oder Graphikprogrammen auf dem PC arbeiten?

59

Are there single or twin disk drives?
Hat der PC ein oder zwei Diskettenlaufwerke?

Can I use any IBM-compatible monochrome or colour monitor?
Kann ich jeden IBM kompatiblen Mono- oder Farbbildschirm benutzen?

Can I choose foreground or background colours?
Kann ich Vordergrund- oder Hintergrundfarben auswählen?

Can I use any type of PC monitor provided it has a standard 9-pin D connector?
Kann ich jeden Bildschirm benutzen, vorausgesetzt, er hat einen Standard D Stecker mit 9 Polen?

Can I use the modem for commercial information services?
Kann ich das Modem für geschäftliche Informationsdienste nutzen?

Does the computer include a built-in communication modem?
Verfügt der PC über ein eingebautes Kommunikationsmodem?

Does the keyboard have all the special function keys?
Hat die Tastatur alle Spezialfunktionen?

Does the price include manual, word processor, software disks?
Schließt der Preis Handbuch, Textverarbeitungsprogramm, Programmdisketten als Zubehör ein?

26

Co-operation and Business Partnerships

Zusammenarbeit und Geschäftsbeteiligungen

acquisition	**der Erwerb**
agent, representative	**der Vertreter**
asset deal	**der Kauf der Einzelwirt-schaftsgüter der Zielgesell-schaft**

branch	die Zweigniederlassung, die Filiale
commission	die Provision
commission agent	der Zwischenhändler
consortium	das Konsortium
division	die Konzerngruppe
franchise	die Konzession
general agency	die Generalvertretung
group, concern	der Konzern
head office, headquarters	die Zentrale
joint venture	das Beteiligungsunternehmen/ die Gelegenheitsgesellschaft
legally protected	gesetzlich geschützt
letter of intent	die Absichtserklärung
merger	die Fusion, der Zusammenschluß
parent company, holding	die Muttergesellschaft
patented	patentiert
registered office	der Geschäftssitz
royalties	die Lizenzgebühren
share deal	der Kauf der Geschäftsanteile der Zielgesellschaft
sole proprietorship	die Einzelfirma
subject to payment of royalties	lizenzpflichtig
subsidiary	die Tochtergesellschaft
take-over	die Übernahme einer Gesellschaft
under patent law	patentrechtlich
venture capital	das Wagnis-/Beteiligungskapital
to acquire a licence	eine Lizenz erwerben
to apply for a patent	ein Patent anmelden
to do business	Geschäfte tätigen
to entrust a firm with the agency	die Vertretung übertragen
to establish, to found	gründen
to exploit a patent	ein Patent verwerten
to grant sole selling rights	das Alleinverkaufsrecht vergeben
to join a firm	in eine Firma eintreten
to manufacture under licence	in Lizenz herstellen
to merge	fusionieren

to run a business	**ein Geschäft betreiben**
to sell as sole agent	**vertreiben als Alleinvertreter**
to sell goods on commission	**Waren in Kommission verkaufen**
to set up a business	**sich selbständig machen**

▼

We are looking for representatives to sell our products.
Wir suchen Handelsvertreter für den Verkauf unserer Produkte.

Please state the terms on which you are willing to act as our representative.
Bitte teilen Sie uns die Bedingungen mit, zu denen Sie bereit sind, als unser Vertreter zu arbeiten.

You will be paid 3% commission on all sales.
Wir zahlen Ihnen 3% Provision auf alle Verkäufe.

Some types of firms

AG (Aktiengesellschaft)
Joint stock company with the following boards:
Hauptversammlung (general meeting of shareholders),
Aufsichtsrat (supervisory board), Vorstand (board of
management). The capital stock is acquired by sale of
shares to the public. The shares are freely transferable.
Annual accounts and audits have to be published.

GmbH (Gesellschaft mit beschränkter Haftung)
Joint stock company, at least two partners, a minimum
nominal capital of DM 50,000. Shares are not quoted on
the stock exchange. Accounts and audits have to be
published.

GbR (Gesellschaft bürgerlichen Rechts)
Partnership without legal name, at least two partners,
formed to carry on business. Each partner is fully liable
for the debts of the firm.

OHG (offene Handelsgesellschaft)
Partnership with legal name, at least two partners.
Partners have an unlimited liability to the full extent of
their property.

KG (Kommanditgesellschaft)

Partnership under legal name. At least one partner's liability is limited to the amount of money he has put into the firm, and at least one partner must have unlimited liability.

Einzelkaufmann

Sole proprietorship. The sole trader's liability is unlimited.

If you are putting your products on the German market and need support you can refer to:

Bundesverband deutscher
Unternehmensberater (BdU) e.V.
(Federal Association of German
Management Consultants)
Friedrich-Wilhelm-Straße 2
D-5300 Bonn 1
Tel. 0228 238055
Fax 0228 230625

Bundeskartellamt
(Federal Monopolies and Mergers
Commission)
Mehringdamm 129
D-1000 Berlin 61
Tel. 030 69011
Fax 030 6901400

Responsible for all questions on the admissibility of mergers under German law.

World Trade Center
Ruhrgebiet
Sparkassenstraße 1
D-4650 Gelsenkirchen
Tel. 0209 22097/22098
Fax 0209 144285

Contacts in foreign trade can be arranged for medium-sized and small enterprises. Provides services and office accommodation, secretarial services, translation services, advice and analyses.

63

**Kommunalverband Ruhrgebiet
(Ruhr District Municipal Associations)
Kronprinzenstraße 35
D-4300 Essen 1
Tel. 0201 20690
Fax 0201 2069500**

Contacts can be established with research and transfer institutions and certain industries in the Ruhr area.

**Deutscher Industrie- und Handelstag
(Association of German Chambers of
Industry and Commerce)
Adenauerallee 148
D-5300 Bonn
Tel. 0228 1040
Fax 0228 104663**

Informative material on all aspects of the market, financing instruments, innovation and transfer of technology, arranging cooperations and joint ventures.

**Deutscher Handwerkskammertag
(Association of German Chambers of
Crafts)
Referat Außenwirtschaft
(Foreign Trade Department)
Johanniterstraße 1
D-5300 Bonn 1
Tel. 0228 545 211/276
Fax 0228 545205**

Informative material and advice on all matters concerning craft.

The German Chamber of Industry and Commerce also publishes requests and offers for representation from Great Britain and Germany in its periodical *British German Trade*, published twice a month.

Requests for cooperations, joint ventures and licensing are also published.

**British Chamber of Commerce in Germany
Heumarkt 14
D-5000 Köln 1
Tel. 0221 234284/5**

Further information on the European Single Market can be found in Part III, 8.

→**8** Useful UK addresses can be found in Part III, 11.

27

Business Letter	Geschäftsbrief
address	die Adresse
date	das Datum
care of (c/o)	per Adresse (per Adr.)
enclosure	die Anlage (Anl.)
for the attention of	zu Händen von . . . (z.Hd.)
printed letterhead	gedruckter Briefkopf
(our/your) reference	das Diktat-/Akten-/
	Bezugszeichen
signature	die Unterschrift
subject line (placed above the salutation line)	Betreff (Betr . . .)

The standard layout and customary salutation phrases are illustrated in a model letter in Part III, 1.

 **Model Letter 1**

28

Presentation of Balance Sheet

Assets

Unpaid Capital, called up
Expenses incurred in connection with the start-up or expansion of the business

A Fixed Assets
I *Intangible Assets*
  1 Licences, trade marks and patents, etc., as well as licences to such rights and assets
  2 Goodwill
  3 Advances paid on intangible assets

II *Tangible Assets*
  1 Land, rights similar to land, and buildings, including buildings on property owned by others
  2 Technical equipment and machinery
  3 Other equipment, office furniture and equipment
  4 Advances paid on fixed assets, and assets under construction

III *Financial Assets*
  1 Shares in group companies.
  2 Loans to group companies
  3 Participating interests of 25% or more
  4 Loans to entities with which the enterprise is linked by virtue of participating interests of 25% or more
  5 Other investments – long term
  6 Other loans

B Current Assets
I *Inventories*
  1 Raw materials and supplies
  2 Work in progress; incompleted projects
  3 Finished goods and goods for resale
  4 Advance payments on stocks

II *Receivables and Other Current Assets*
  1 Trade receivables
  2 Amounts due from group companies
  3 Receivables from entities with which the enterprise is linked by virtue of participating interests of 25% or more
  4 Other current assets

III *Securities*
  1 Shares in group companies
  2 Treasury stock
  3 Other securities

IV *Checks, Cash, Deposits with Federal Bank and with Bank of Federal Postal System, Deposits with Commercial Banks*

C Pre-paid Expenses
Excess of Liabilities over Assets to the extent not covered by Shareholders' Equity

Gliederung der Bilanz

Aktiva

Ausstehende Einlagen, davon eingefordert
Aufwendungen für die Ingangsetzung (Erweiterung) des
Geschäftsbetriebes

A Anlagevermögen
I *Immaterielle Vermögensgegenstände*
  1 Konzessionen, gewerbliche Schutzrechte und ähnliche Rechte und
    Werte, sowie Lizenzen an solchen Rechten
  2 Geschäfts- oder Firmenwert
  3 Geleistete Anzahlungen

II *Sachanlagen*
  1 Grundstücke, grundstücksgleiche Rechte und Bauten einschließlich
    der Bauten auf fremden Grundstücken
  2 Technische Anlagen und Maschinen
  3 Andere Anlagen, Betriebs- und Geschäftsausstattung
  4 Geleistete Anzahlungen und Anlagen im Bau

III *Finanzanlagen*
  1 Anteile an verbundenen Unternehmen
  2 Ausleihungen an verbundene Unternehmen
  3 Beteiligungen
  4 Ausleihungen an Unternehmen, mit denen ein
    Beteiligungsverhältnis besteht
  5 Wertpapiere des Anlagevermögens
  6 Sonstige Ausleihungen

B Umlaufvermögen
I *Vorräte*
  1 Roh-, Hilfs- und Betriebsstoffe
  2 Unfertige Erzeugnisse, unfertige Leistungen
  3 Fertige Erzeugnisse und Waren
  4 Geleistete Anzahlungen

II *Forderungen und sonstige Vermögensgegenstände*
  1 Forderungen aus Lieferungen und Leistungen
  2 Forderungen gegen verbundene Unternehmen
  3 Forderungen gegen Unternehmen, mit denen ein
    Beteiligungsverhältnis besteht
  4 Sonstige Vermögensgegenstände

III *Wertpapiere*
  1 Anteile an verbundenen Unternehmen
  2 Eigene Anteile
  3 Sonstige Wertpapiere

IV *Schecks, Kassenbestand, Bundesbank- und Postgiroguthaben,*
    Guthaben bei Kreditinstituten

C Rechnungsabgrenzungsposten
  Nicht durch Eigenkapital gedeckter Fehlbetrag.

Liabilities and Shareholders' Equity

A Shareholders' Equity
I *Share Capital*
II *Capital Reserve*
III *Earnings Reserve*
    1   Legal reserve
    2   Reserve for treasury stock
    3   Statutory reserves
    4   Other earnings reserves
IV *Retained Earnings/Accumulated Deficit brought forward from previous year*
V *Net Income/Loss for the year*
Special reserves, to be taxed in later years

B Accruals
    1   Accruals for pensions and similar obligations
    2   Accrued taxes
    3   Other accruals

C Liabilities
    1   Debenture loans (convertible)
    2   Amounts due to banks
    3   Advance payments received
    4   Trade payables
    5   Notes payable
    6   Amounts due to group companies
    7   Amounts owed to entities with which the enterprise is linked by virtue of participating interests of 25% or more
    8   Other liabilities:
       taxes
       in respect of social security

D Deferred Income

Contingencies and Commitments
Discounted notes, guarantees, guarantees given on notes and loans, other warranties, pledges on company assets to secure another party's liabilities, other contingencies and commitments.

Passiva

A Eigenkapital
I *Gezeichnetes Eigenkapital*
II *Kapitalrücklage*
III *Gewinnrücklagen*
    1 Gesetzliche Rücklage
    2 Rücklage für eigene Anteile
    3 Satzungsmäßige Rücklagen
    4 Andere Gewinnrücklagen
IV *Gewinn-/Verlustvortrag*

V *Jahresüberschuß/-fehlbetrag*
Sonderposten mit Rücklagenanteil

B Rückstellungen
    1 Rückstellungen für Pensionen und ähnliche Verpflichtungen.
    2 Steuerrückstellungen
    3 Andere Rückstellungen

C Verbindlichkeiten
    1 Anleihen (davon konvertibel)
    2 Verbindlichkeiten gegenüber Kreditinstituten
    3 Erhaltene Anzahlungen auf Bestellungen
    4 Verbindlichkeiten aus Lieferungen und Leistungen
    5 Verbindlichkeiten aus der Annahmen gezogener und der
      Ausstellung eigener Wechsel
    6 Verbindlichkeiten gegenüber verbundenen Unternehmen
    7 Verbindlichkeiten gegenüber Unternehmen, mit denen ein
      Beteiligungsverhältnis besteht
    8 Sonstige Verbindlichkeiten:
      davon aus Steuern
      davon im Rahmen der sozialen Sicherheit

D Rechnungsabgrenzungsposten

Haftungsverhältnisse
Verbindlichkeiten aus der Begebung und Übertragung von Wechseln,
Bürgschaften, Wechsel- und Schuldbürgschaften, Gewährleistungs-
verträgen, Haftungsverhältnisse aus der Bestellung von Sicherheiten für
fremde Verbindlichkeiten sowie sonstige Haftungsverhältnisse

29

Presentation of Statement of Earnings

1 **Sales**
2 Increase or decrease of finished goods and work in progress
3 Other capitalized labour, overheads and materials
4 Other operating income
5 Materials:
   (a) raw materials, supplies and purchased goods
   (b) purchased services (e.g. utilities, subcontracting costs, etc.)
6 Personnel costs:
   (a) wages and salaries
   (b) social security and pension contributions, pensions
7 Depreciation, amortization and special provisions:
   (a) on intangible and tangible assets, and on capitalized business start-up or expansion costs
   (b) on current assets to the extent usual provisions made by corporations are exceeded
8 Other operating expenses
9 Income from participating interests of 25% or more, income from group companies
10 Income from group companies' other securities and long-term financial investments
11 Other interest and similar income from group companies
12 Writedown of financial assets and of securities included in current assets
13 Interest and similar expenses to group companies
14 **Results of ordinary operations**
15 Extraordinary income
16 Extraordinary expenses
17 **Extraordinary, net**
18 Taxes on income
19 Other taxes
20 **Net income/loss for the year**

Income and expenses arising from profit and loss pooling arrangements and similar contract are to be presented as separate line items.

Gliederung der Gewinn- und Verlustrechnung

1 **Umsatzerlöse**
2 Erhöhung oder Verminderung des Bestandes an fertigen und unfertigen Erzeugnissen
3 Andere aktivierte Eigenleistungen
4 Materialaufwand
5 (a) Aufwendungen für Roh-, Hilfs- und Betriebsstoffe und für bezogene Waren
 (b) Aufwendungen für bezogene Leistungen
6 Personalaufwand:
 (a) Löhne und Gehälter
 (b) soziale Abgaben und Aufwendungen für Altersversorgung und Unterstützung, davon für Altersversorgung
7 Abschreibungen:
 (a) auf immaterielle Vermögensgegenstände des Anlagevermögens und Sachanlagen sowie auf aktivierte Aufwendungen für die Ingangsetzung und Erweiterung des Geschäftsbetriebes
 (b) auf Vermögensgegenstände des Umlaufvermögens, soweit diese die in der Kapitalgesellschaft üblichen Abschreibungen überschreiten
8 Sonstige betriebliche Aufwendungen
9 Erträge aus Beteiligungen, davon aus verbundenen Unternehmen
10 Erträge aus anderen Wertpapieren und Ausleihungen des Finanzanlagevermögens, davon aus verbundenen Unternehmen
11 Sonstige Zinsen und ähnliche Erträge, davon aus verbundenen Unternehmen
12 Abschreibungen auf Finanzanlagen und auf Wertpapiere des Umlaufvermögens
13 Zinsen und ähnliche Aufwendungen, davon an verbundene Unternehmen
14 **Ergebnis der gewöhnlichen Geschäftstätigkeit**
15 Außerordentliche Erträge
16 Außerordentliche Aufwendungen
17 **Außerordentliches Ergebnis**
18 Steuern vom Einkommen und Ertrag
19 Sonstige Steuern
20 **Jahresüberschuß/-fehlbetrag**

Erträge und Aufwendungen aus Verlustübernahme und aufgrund einer Gewinngemeinschaft, eines Gewinnabführungs- oder eines Teilgewinnabführungsvertrages sind gesondert auszuweisen.

PART II

1

First Contacts

1.1 Greeting someone and saying goodbye

Good morning	**Guten Morgen**
Good afternoon	**Guten Tag**
Good evening	**Guten Abend**
Good night	**Gute Nacht**
Hello	**Hallo**
Are you Mrs Kern by any chance?	**Sind Sie zufällig Frau Kern?**
▶ Yes, that's me	▶ **Ja**
Nice to meet you/how nice to see you	**Schön, Sie zu sehen**
Did you have a good journey/trip?	**Hatten Sie eine gute Reise?**
How was your flight?	**Wie war Ihr Flug?**
How long are you planning to stay?	**Wie lange möchten Sie bleiben?**
Are you enjoying your stay?	**Fühlen Sie sich hier wohl?**
How are you?	**Wie geht's?**
▶ Fine, thanks and you?	▶ **Danke, gut und Ihnen?**
▶ Not too bad, thanks	▶ **Ganz gut**

If you are not feeling at all well, you can respond to the question 'Wie geht's?' by saying: 'Nicht sehr gut.'

Goodbye/bye-bye	**Auf Wiedersehen**
Cheerio	**Tschüss**
Have a good trip/safe journey	**Gute Reise**
See you soon	**Bis bald**

I'll see you later	**Bis später**
See you tomorrow	**Bis morgen**
Take care	**Alles Gute**
All the best	**Alles Gute**
▶ The same to you	▶ **Danke gleichfalls**
Have a nice time	**Viel Vergnügen**
I'm afraid I must go now	**Ich muß jetzt leider gehen**
Thank you very much for . . .	**Vielen Dank für . . .**
Thank you very much for making my stay so pleasant	**Vielen Dank für den angenehmen Aufenthalt**
It was very nice	**Es war sehr schön**
I've enjoyed talking to you	**Es war schön, mit Ihnen zu reden**
It's been a useful meeting	**Es war ein nützliches Treffen**
Pleased to have met you	**Es war schön, Sie kennenzulernen**
I'll give you a ring soon	**Ich rufe bald an**
I'll be in touch	**Ich werde mich melden**
Please give my regards to your wife	**Grüßen Sie bitte Ihre Frau von mir**

1.2 Communication

Do you speak English?	**Sprechen Sie Englisch?**
I don't speak much German	**Ich spreche nur ein wenig Deutsch**
I'm afraid my German isn't very good	**Mein Deutsch ist leider nicht sehr gut**
I'm English	**Ich bin Engländer(in)**
I don't understand	**Ich verstehe Sie nicht**

Don't speak so fast, please	**Sprechen Sie bitte nicht so schnell**
Could you speak more slowly, please?	**Könnten Sie bitte langsamer sprechen?**
Could you repeat that, please?	**Wiederholen Sie es bitte**
I'm afraid I didn't quite understand	**Ich habe des leider nicht richtig verstanden**
I'm sorry, I can't follow you; would you write it down please?	**Ich kann Ihnen nicht folgen, schreiben Sie es bitte auf**
Could you spell it, please?	**Buchstabieren Sie es bitte**
Could you translate that for me, please?	**Können Sie das bitte für mich übersetzen?**
What does it mean?	**Was heißt das?**
▶ Oh, I see	▶ **Ich verstehe**
How do you pronounce the word?	**Wie spricht man das Wort aus?**
How do you say . . . in German?	**Was heißt . . . auf Deutsch?**

If you do not know the exact German equivalent to an English word and wish to paraphrase something, you can say:

Es ist eine Art von . . .	It's a kind of . . ./sort of . . .

1.3 Introductions

My name's . . .	**Ich heiße . . .**
May I introduce . . .	**Darf ich Ihnen . . . vorstellen**
This is my wife	**Dies ist meine Frau**
my husband	**mein Mann**
my son/daughter	**mein Sohn/meine Tochter**
my (boy)friend/(girl)friend	**mein Freund/meine Freundin**

my colleague	**mein Kollege**
a colleague of mine	**ein(e) Kollege(in) von mir**
our chief engineer	**unser leitender Ingenieur**

■ Please note:

As a rule German people will give their surnames in formal introductions – and not their first names. When being introduced and when greeting and saying goodbye to someone they will nearly always shake hands. In business circles it is not common to address people by their first names; it would be advisable to let your German business partner make the choice.

If you are not well acquainted with someone, you should always use 'Sie' and not 'du'. 'Du' is used for friends, relatives and children; young people up to the age of about twenty-five also tend to prefer 'du' when speaking to one another.

In fact 'Sie' and 'Herr'/'Frau' do not sound quite as distant and uncordial as 'Mr' and 'Mrs' in English, and the use of 'du' and first names implies a much closer intimacy than the use of first names in Britain.

When talking to someone of equal rank and profession, you may find yourself being addressed as 'Herr Kollege' or 'Frau Kollegin'. Nowadays 'Fräulein' (Miss) is only used for young unmarried girls and, as a rule, when addressing waitresses. For correspondence 'Fräulein' is very seldom used. 'Frau' is preferred instead, irrespective of whether the addressee is married or not.

The following are examples of various ways of introducing yourself or another person:

Ich möchte Ihnen gerne Herrn Schmidt vorstellen.
▶ **Guten Tag, Herr Schmidt. Sehr erfreut.**

Darf ich Ihnen Frau Müller vorstellen?
▶ **Guten Tag, Frau Müller. Schön, Sie kennenzulernen.**

Das ist Herr Meier, unser tüchtiger Einkäufer.
▶ **Sehr angenehm.**

Kennen Sie Fräulein Naumann, meine Sekretärin schon?
▶ **Wie schön, Sie nach den vielen Telefonaten selber kennenzulernen.**

If you want to introduce yourself, you may say:

Guten Tag, mein Name ist Fox.
▶ **Angenehm, Kaminski.**

You may also hear the following short form:

Guten Tag, Kaminski.

1.4 Appointments and arranging to meet someone

I'm . . ./I'm from . . .	**Ich bin . . ./ich komme aus . . .**
I work for . . .	**Ich arbeite bei . . .**
May I speak to . . .?	**Kann ich mit . . . sprechen?**
I've got an appointment with . . .	**Ich habe eine Verabredung mit . . .**
Nice to meet you/Pleased to meet you	**Es ist schön, Sie kennenzulernen**
When?/At what time?	**Wann?**
At two o'clock	**Um zwei Uhr**
From two to three	**Von zwei bis drei Uhr**
Between two and three	**Zwischen zwei und drei**
In an hour's time	**In einer Stunde**
Not before seven	**Nicht vor sieben Uhr**
Not after nine	**Nicht nach neun (Uhr)**
It's (too) late	**Es ist (zu) spät**
It's (too) early	**Es ist (zu) früh**
I'm sorry I'm late	**Es tut mir leid, daß ich zu spät komme**
Have you been waiting long?	**Warten Sie schon lange?**

What you might hear in German:

Zu wem möchten Sie?	Who would you like to speak to?
Mit wem sind Sie verabredet?	With whom have you arranged an appointment?
Haben Sie einen Termin?	Have you got an appointment?
Dürfte ich Ihren Namen haben?	May I have your name, please?
Wen darf ich melden?	Who shall I say is here?
Zimmer 493, vierter Stock links	Room 493, 4th floor, on the left
Frau Meyer-Sebelin wird Sie gleich abholen, bitte warten Sie hier einen Moment	Mrs Meyer-Sebelin will be along in a minute; please wait here for a moment
Herein	Come in!
Herr Degener erwartet Sie	Herr Degener is expecting you
Wie schön, Sie zu sehen!	How nice to see you!
Wie schön, daß Sie kommen konnten	I'm glad you could come
Darf ich Ihnen den Mantel abnehmen?	Let me take your coat
Bitte setzen Sie sich	Please do sit down
Darf ich Ihnen etwas zu trinken anbieten?	May I get (offer) you a drink?
Darf ich Sie zu einer Tasse Kaffee einladen?	May I invite you for a cup of coffee?
Rauchen Sie?/Zigarette?	Do you smoke?/Cigarette?
▶ **Nein, danke, ich rauche nicht**	▶ No, thank you I don't smoke
Macht es Ihnen etwas aus, wenn ich rauche?	Do you mind if I smoke?
▶ **Nein**	▶ That's fine/Go ahead
▶ **Ich fände es besser, wenn Sie nicht rauchen würden**	▶ I'd rather you didn't

Haben Sie Feuer?	Have you got a light?
▶ **Bitte**	▶ Here you are
Hatten Sie eine gute Reise?	Did you have a good journey?
Seit wann sind Sie schon hier?	How long have you been here?
▶ **Seit zwei Tagen**	▶ For two days
Ist dies Ihre erste Reise nach Berlin?	Is this your first trip to Berlin?
▶ **Wir waren vor zwei Jahren schon einmal hier**	▶ We came here two years ago
Gefällt es Ihnen hier?	Do you like it here?
▶ **Ja**	▶ Yes, I do
Wo sind Sie untergebracht?	Where are you staying?
▶ **Ich wohne im Hotel . . .**	▶ I'm staying at the . . . Hotel
Ich hoffe, daß Ihr Hotel in Ordnung ist	I hope you're satisfied with your hotel
Vielleicht können wir zusammen zu Mittag (Abend) essen?	Perhaps we could have lunch (dinner) together?
Haben Sie morgen Zeit?	Are you free tomorrow?
▶ **Ja, sehr schön, ich habe Zeit**	▶ Yes, that's fine, I'm free then
▶ **Ja, ich komme gerne**	▶ Yes, I'd love to come
Möchten Sie nächste Woche essen gehen?	Would you like to go for a meal next week?
▶ **Ja, gerne**	▶ Yes, I'd love to
Ich würde Ihnen gerne die Abteilung zeigen	I'd like to show you round the department
▶ **Das ist sehr nett von Ihnen**	▶ That's very kind of you
Ich könnte Ihnen die Stadt etwas zeigen	I could show you something of the town
Wie wär's mit Montag?	What about Monday?
▶ **Wunderbar**	▶ That's fine
▶ **Lassen Sie mich mal sehen . . .**	▶ Let me check first . . .
▶ **Ich werde den Termin schriftlich bestätigen**	▶ I'll write and confirm that date

▶ Ich werde versuchen, es einzurichten
▶ Ich kann leider nicht
▶ Ich kann es leider nicht einrichten, ich habe schon etwas anderes vor

▶ I'll try and make it
▶ Sorry, I can't
▶ I'm sorry, I can't make it; I've already arranged something else

Bis später/bis Sonntag

See you later/on Sunday

■ Please note:

As in English, answering a question with a mere 'Yes' or 'No' does not sound very communicative, so here are a few suggestions:

Gefällt es Ihnen hier?
▶ **Ja, sehr gut**

Wollen wir heute abend gemeinsam essen gehen?
▶ **Ja, gerne**

Haben Sie heute abend Zeit?
▶ **Leider nicht**

A number of ways of answering in the affirmative and in the negative:

Yes, of course	**Ja, natürlich**
With pleasure	**Mit Vergnügen**
Perhaps	**Vielleicht**
I'm afraid not	**Ich fürchte, nein**
Certainly not	**Auf keinen Fall**

1.5 Asking and telling the time

What's the time, please?	**Wie spät ist es?**
It's about/exactly . . . two o'clock	**Es ist ungefähr/genau . . . zwei Uhr**

	written as:	spoken as:
a quarter past twelve	**12.15 Uhr**	**viertel nach zwölf**

81

ten past twelve	**12.10 Uhr**	**zehn (Minuten) nach zwölf**
half past twelve	**12.30 Uhr**	**halb eins**
twenty to one	**12.40 Uhr**	**zwanzig (Minuten) vor eins**
a quarter to one	**12.45 Uhr**	**viertel vor eins**

Drei Uhr

Zwanzig nach zwölf

Fünf nach halb vier

Viertel vor eins

Viertel nach zehn

Halb zehn

■ Please note:

3.30 a.m./p.m. is not, as in English, regarded as thirty minutes past three but as thirty minutes to four, half an hour before four: **'halb vier'**.

The 24-hour clock is used in travel timetables.

'15.30 Uhr' (fünfzehn Uhr dreißig) is 3.30 p.m.
'21.10 Uhr' (einundzwanzig Uhr zehn) is 9.10 p.m.
'12.25 Uhr' (zwölf Uhr fünfundzwanzig) is 12.25 p.m.
'0.25 Uhr' (null Uhr fünfundzwanzig) is 12.25 a.m.

The 24-hour clock is used more often than in the UK.

In southern and eastern Germany you will also hear the following:

'ein Viertel vier'	3.15 h. or 15.15 Uhr
'dreiviertel vier'	3.45 h. or 15.45 Uhr

Remember the time difference for Britain and Germany and also the different summer times in the two countries – Great Britain: GMT, i.e. CET minus one hour, summer time between March and October. In Germany, summer time between March and September.

General expressions:

during the day	**tagsüber**
in the morning	**morgens**
at noon	**mittags**
in the evening	**abends**
at night	**nachts**
at midnight	**um Mitternacht**
today/yesterday/tomorrow	**heute/gestern/morgen**
the day before yesterday	**vorgestern**
the day after tomorrow	**übermorgen**
daily	**täglich**
hourly	**stündlich**

at any time	**jederzeit**
this morning/tonight	**heute morgen/heute abend**
last week	**letzte Woche**
every week	**jede Woche**
two weeks ago/two years ago	**vor zwei Wochen/vor zwei Jahren**
in two days' time	**in zwei Tagen**
in two weeks/in a fortnight	**in zwei Wochen/in vierzehn Tagen**
for two days	**seit zwei Tagen**
I've been staying here for two days	**Ich bin seit zwei Tagen hier**
I'm staying here for two weeks	**Ich werde zwei Wochen hier bleiben**
since 8 o'clock	**seit acht Uhr**
1992	**neunzehnhundertzweiundneunzig**

In Part III you will find a list of days of the week, months and public holidays.

The date:

What's the date today?	**Den wievielten haben wir heute?**
Today's January the 25th	**Heute haben wir den fünfundzwanzigsten Januar**
On July the 6th of this year/last year/next year	**Am 6. Juli (am sechsten Juli) dieses Jahres/des vergangenen/des nächsten Jahres**
Until the first of January	**Bis zum 1. Januar**
In your letter of May the fifth	**In Ihrem Brief vom 5. Mai**

The letter was posted on the thirtieth of March	**Der Brief wurde am 30 März (am dreißigsten) abgeschickt**
The 10th of this month	**Der 10. d.M.**
The 10th of last month	**Der 10. des vergangenen Monats**

■ Please note:

There are a number of ways of writing the date in German:

written as:	spoken as:
15. April 1990	**fünfzehnter April 1990**
15.4 90/15.04.90	**fünfzehnter vierter neunzig** or **der fünfzehnte Vierte neunzig**

Part III contains a list of ordinal numbers which will be useful when stating the date.

2

Everyday Topics

2.1 The weather

Talking about the weather is a popular way of getting into conversation with someone. You may hear such sentences as:

Ein schöner Tag	It's a beautiful day
Schöner Tag heute, nicht wahr?	Nice day today, isn't it?
Schrecklicher Tag, nicht?	It's an awful day, isn't it?
Es wird regnen	It's going to rain
Es wird schön bleiben	It's going to stay fine
Wie ist das Wetter in England?	What's the weather like in England?

85

Wie wird das Wetter morgen?	What's the weather going to be like tomorrow?
Es ist ziemlich neblig	It's quite foggy
Die Temperatur ist über/unter dem Gefrierpunkt	The temperature is above/

It is better not to talk too much on this topic otherwise there is the risk of being regarded as a boring conversationalist.

In Part III.5 there is a conversion table for Fahrenheit and Celsius (centigrade) temperatures.

2.2 General questions

Where is . . ./where are . . .?	**Wo ist . . ./wo sind . . .?**
▶ There is . . ./there are . . .	▶ **Dort ist . . ./dort sind**
Is there . . ./are there . . .	**Gibt es . . .?**
Who?	**Wer?**
What?	**Was?**
Which/what kind of . . .	**Welcher?**
Whose?	**Wessen?**
Where?	**Wo?**
Where from?	**Woher?**
Where (to)?	**Wohin?**
When?	**Wann?**
For how long?	**Wie lange?**
Since when?/How long?	**Seit wann?**
Why?	**Warum?**
How?	**Wie?**
Pardon?/I beg your pardon?	**Wie bitte?**

What would you like?	**Was wünschen Sie?**
How much does it cost?	**Was kostet das?**
How much do I owe you?	**Was schulde ich Ihnen?**
Have you got . . .?	**Haben Sie . . .?**
What does that mean?	**Was heißt das?**
What's that?	**Was ist das?**
Who's that?	**Wer ist das?**
When do you open/close?	**Wann öffnen/schließen Sie?**
How do I get to . . .?	**Wie komme ich nach . . .?**
Excuse me, can you tell me where I can find . . .	**Entschuldigen Sie bitte, können Sie mir sagen, wo . . . ist**
a department store?	**ein Kaufhaus?**
a tourist information office?	**ein Fremdenverkehrsbüro?**
a toilet?	**eine Toilette?**
How do I get to . . .?	**Wie komme ich zu . . .?**
Where's the British Embassy, please?	**Wo ist die englische Botschaft, bitte?**

Embassy of
The United Kingdom of Great Britain
and Northern Ireland
Friedrich Ebert-Allee 77
D-5300 Bonn
Tel: 0228/234061

2.3 Apologizing

I'm (so) sorry/Sorry	**Entschuldigen Sie bitte**
I'm very sorry (about it)	**Es tut mir sehr leid**
▶ It's all right	▶ **Es macht nichts**
▶ It was my fault	▶ **Es war mein Fehler**

I'm afraid it's not possible, I (do) apologize	**Es ist leider nicht möglich, ich bedaure es außerordentlich**
I'm sorry to hear that	**Es tut mir leid, das zu hören**
I'm sorry, I didn't notice	**Entschuldigen Sie bitte, es war ein Versehen**
My apologies for being late	**Entschuldigen Sie bitte, daß ich zu spät komme**
Excuse my saying so, but . . .	**Es ist mir unangenehm, aber ich muß Ihnen sagen, daß . . .**

■ Please note:

If you want to speak to a stranger in the street, it is more polite to begin sentences with 'Entschuldigen Sie bitte'.

Excuse me, please	**Entschuldigen Sie bitte** (when asking for information)
Excuse me, can I park here?	**Entschuldigen Sie bitte, kann ich hier parken?**
Excuse me, do you happen to know if there's a bank near here?	**Entschuldigen Sie bitte, wissen Sie zufällig, ob es hier in der Nähe eine Bank gibt?**

2.4 Requesting and thanking

Can you do me a favour, please? ▶ Certainly	**Können Sie mir bitte einen Gefallen tun?** ▶ **Natürlich**
Excuse me, I wonder if you could help me?	**Können Sie mir vielleicht helfen?**
I'm sorry to trouble you, but could you . . .?	**Entschuldigen Sie bitte die Störung, aber könnten Sie . . .?**
May I? ▶ Yes, certainly	**Erlauben Sie?** ▶ **Ja, bitte**

Do you mind if I open the window?	**Kann ich bitte das Fenster öffnen?**
May I ask you a question?	**Darf ich Sie etwas fragen?**
Can I help you?	**Kann ich Ihnen helfen?**
▶ Can you tell me . . ., please?	▶ **Können Sie mir sagen . . .?**
▶ Can you show me . . ., please?	▶ **Können Sie mir zeigen . . .?**
▶ I need . . .	▶ **Ich brauche**
▶ I'd rather . . ./I'd prefer . . .	▶ **Ich möchte lieber . . .**
Please hurry up, it's urgent	**Bitte beeilen Sie sich, es ist eilig**
Pardon?/I beg your pardon?	**Wie bitte?**
There/here you are	**Bitte (sehr)** (when giving something to someone)
Thank you	**Danke**
Thank you very much (indeed)	**Vielen Dank**
Thank you for your trouble	**Vielen Dank für Ihre Mühe**
Thank you for showing me round the factory/shop	**Danke, daß Sie mich durch die Fabrik/Werkstatt geführt haben**
It's been a useful meeting, thank you	**Es war eine erfolgreiche Besprechung, danke**
That's very kind of you, thank you	**Danke, das ist sehr freundlich von Ihnen**
You've been very helpful	**Sie waren mir eine große Hilfe**
Thank you for all your help	**Vielen Dank für Ihre Hilfe**
▶ Don't mention it	▶ **Keine Ursache**
▶ My pleasure	▶ **Es war mir eine Freude**
▶ That's quite all right	▶ **Nicht der Rede wert**
▶ You're welcome	▶ **Nichts zu danken/Keine Ursache**

■ Please note:

When making a request, you should not forget to add 'bitte' – it sounds more polite. There are various nuances of expression for requesting something.

89

To ask the time, for example, you could say:

Wie spät ist es, bitte?
Entschuldigen Sie bitte, wie spät ist es?
Können Sie mir bitte sagen, wie spät es ist?
Entschuldigen Sie bitte, können Sie mir sagen, wie spät es ist?

2.5 Personal data

What's your name, please?
▶ My name's . . .

Wie heißen Sie?
▶ **Ich heiße . . .**

When were you born?
▶ I was born on . . .

Wann sind Sie geboren?
▶ **Ich bin am . . . geboren**

How old are you?
▶ I'm . . . years old
▶ I'm over . . ./under . . .

Wie alt sind Sie?
▶ **Ich bin . . . Jahre alt**
▶ **Ich bin über . . ./unter . . .**

Are you married?
▶ I'm married/single/divorced/
  a widow/widower

Sind Sie verheiratet?
▶ **Ich bin verheiratet/ledig/**
  geschieden/verwitwet

Do you have any children?

Haben Sie Kinder?

Are you here on business?
▶ Yes, I am

Sind Sie geschäftlich hier?
▶ **Ja**

Where do you come from?

Woher kommen Sie?

Which part of England do you
come from?

Aus welcher Gegend Englands
kommen sie?

Where do you live?

Wo wohnen Sie?

Please fill in this form

Bitte füllen Sie dieses Formular
aus

What profession are you in?

Was sind Sie von Beruf?

What do you do for a living?

Was machen Sie beruflich?

May I ask you what you do?
▶ I work in an office
▶ I'm a businesswoman/
  businessman

Darf ich fragen, was Sie tun?
▶ **Ich bin Angestellte(r)**
▶ **Ich bin Geschäftsfrau/**
  Geschäftsmann

▶ I'm responsible for/in charge of the export department	▶ **Ich bin zuständig für die Exportabteilung**
▶ I'm head of research	▶ **Ich bin Leiter(in) der Forschungsabteilung**
▶ I'm a sales manager	▶ **Ich bin Verkaufsleiter(in)**

What line of business are you in?	**In welcher Branche arbeiten Sie?**
▶ I'm in computers	▶ **Ich arbeite in der Computerbranche**

Who do you work for?	**Für wen arbeiten Sie?**
▶ I work for . . .	▶ **ich arbeite für . . .**

I'm over here for the Trade Fair	**Ich bin zur Messe hergekommen**
How are you getting on?	**Wie kommen Sie voran?**
What kind of hobbies do you have?	**Was für Hobbies haben Sie?**
Are you interested in golf?	**Interessieren Sie sich für Golf?**
Do you do any sport?	**Treiben Sie Sport?**
Do you speak any foreign languages?	**Sprechen Sie Fremdsprachen?**

Part III, 1 contains a standard curriculum vitae (Model letter 15).

3

Travel

3.1 Customs and Immigration

entry	**die Einreise**
border	**die Grenze**
customs/customs officer	**das Zollamt/Zollbeamt(er)in**
customs clearance	**die Zollabfertigung**

customs control	**die Zollkontrolle**
customs declaration	**die Zollerklärung**
customs declaration form	**das Zollerklärungsformular**
duty/duty-free/dutiable	**der Zoll/zollfrei/zollpflichtig**
import duty/export duty	**der Einfuhr-/Ausfuhr-Zoll**

I'm travelling with my family	**Ich reise mit meiner Familie**
I'm here on business	**Ich bin geschäftlich hier**
I'm here on holiday	**Ich bin zum Urlaub hier**
I'm staying for three weeks	**Ich bleibe drei Wochen**
I've been here before	**Ich war schon früher hier**
I'm not going to work in Germany	**Ich werde nicht in Deutschland arbeiten**
These are only personal belongings	**Dies sind nur persönliche Gegenstände**
These are samples	**Dies sind Muster**
These are presents	**Dies sind Geschenke**
This is my suitcase	**Dies ist mein Koffer**
This is not mine	**Dies ist nicht meiner**
I've nothing to declare	**Ich habe nichts zu verzollen**
I'm declaring these bottles of whisky	**Ich muß diese Flaschen Whisky angeben**

At the border you might hear or read the following sentences in German:

Anmeldepflichtige Waren	Goods to declare
Nicht anmeldepflichtige Waren	Nothing to declare
Kann ich Ihren Paß sehen?	Can I see your passport, please?
Ihre Reisedokumente bitte	Your travel documents, please
Haben Sie Ihre Landungskarte ausgefüllt?	Have you filled in your landing card?

Was ist der Zweck Ihres Besuchs?	What's the purpose of your visit?
▶ **Ich bin geschäftlich hier**	▶ I'm here on business
Wie lange werden Sie bleiben?	How long are you going to stay?
Ist dies Ihr erster Aufenthalt in Deutschland?	Is this your first visit to Germany?
Bundesrepublik Deutschland	Federal Republic of Germany
Bürger(innen) aus EG Ländern	Citizens of EC Countries
Dann können Sie durchgehen	You can go through, then
Haben Sie etwas zu verzollen?	Have you got anything to declare?
Ist dies Ihr Koffer?	Is this your suitcase?
Öffnen Sie bitte den Kofferraum	Open your boot, please
Was ist hier drin?	What's in here?
Sie dürfen 200 Zigaretten mitnehmen	You're allowed 200 cigarettes
Dafür müssen Sie Zoll bezahlen	You'll have to pay duty on this

■ Please note:

Details of customs regulations will not be given in this chapter as they would be outside the scope of this language guide. Should you have any questions concerning customs you can write to the following address:

> **HM Customs and Excise**
> **Dorset House**
> **Stamford Street**
> **London SE1 9PS**

You can also make inquiries at the London Chamber of Commerce and Industry:

> **London Chamber of Commerce and Industry**
> **69 Cannon Street**
> **London EC4N 5AB**
> **Tel: 071-248 4444**
> **extension: 3008/9/10**

The 'Customs and Trade Procedures' department will provide helpful information on the following areas:
Customs procedures/documents/ clearance/controls of imports/ exports UK/foreign/temporary movements.

The British Chamber of Commerce and Industry will, of course, be able to offer you further help:

> **British Chamber of Commerce and Industry**
> **Heumarkt 14**
> **D-5000 Köln 1**
> **Tel: 0221/234284-5**

The following provides useful background information:
Zollsätze im Ausland und Internationaler Anzeiger für Zollwesen, Brüssel
(Customs Rates Abroad and International Advertiser for Customs, Brussels)

Published by Bundesamt für Außenhandels-Informationen (BfAI) (Federal Office of Foreign Trade), Postfach 10 80 07, D-5000 Köln 1

3.2 Planes

Can you help me, please?	**Können Sie mir bitte helfen?**
Where's the office of . . . Airline?	**Wo ist das Büro der . . . Fluglinie?**

I'd like to book a flight to Düsseldorf, please	**Ich möchte einen Flug nach Düsseldorf buchen**
A single flight/return flight	**Einfacher Flug/Hin- und Rückflug**
When's the next plane to . . .?	**Wann fliegt die nächste Maschine nach . . .**
I'd like to fly to . . .	**Ich möchte nach . . . fliegen**
Can I fly direct from here?	**Kann ich direkt fliegen?**
Do I have to change planes?	**Muß ich umsteigen?**
Is there a connection to . . .?	**Gibt es einen Anschluß nach . . .?**
Is there a stop-over?	**Gibt es eine Zwischenlandung?**
Are there any seats available?	**Gibt es noch Plätze?**
Where can I confirm the return flight?	**Wo kann ich den Rückflug bestätigen?**
I'd like a seat by the window	**Ich möchte einen Platz am Fenster**
Non-smoking section	**Nichtraucher-Abteilung**
What is the flight number?	**Welche Nummer hat der Flug?**
When does the plane take off?	**Wann startet die Maschine?**
Will we arrive on time?	**Werden wir pünktlich ankommen?**
How long will the flight be delayed?	**Wie lange wird sich der Flug verzögern?**
Has the plane already landed?	**Ist die Maschine schon gelandet?**
Will meals be served during the flight?	**Wird während des Fluges eine Mahlzeit serviert?**
How much does my suitcase weigh?	**Wieviel wiegt mein Koffer?**
What's the charge for excess baggage?	**Was kostet Übergepäck?**

I'll take this hand luggage with me	**Ich nehme dies als Handgepäck mit**
I feel sick. Could you bring me something for airsickness?	**Mir ist übel. Haben Sie ein Mittel dagegen?**
My suitcase has got lost	**Mein Koffer ist verloren gegangen**
My suitcase has been damaged	**Mein Koffer ist beschädigt**
Could you send this suitcase to the following address, please?	**Bitte schicken Sie den Koffer an die folgende Adresse**

You might read and hear the following at German airports:

Ankommende Flüge	Incoming Flights
Ankunft/Abflug	Arrivals/Departures
Ausfuhrerklärung	Export Declaration
Auskunftsschalter	Information Desk
Autovermietung	Car Hire
Bitte Anschnallen	Fasten Your Seatbelts Please
Bordkarte	Boarding Card
Buchungen	Reservations
Businessklasse	Business Class
Erste Klasse	First Class
Flughafen	Airport
Fluglinie	Airline
Flugsteig	Gate
Gepäckannahme	Baggage Check-in
Gepäckausgabe	Baggage Reclaim
Gepäckermittlung	Baggage Tracing
Gültig	Valid
Letzter Aufruf	Last Call
Notausgang	Emergency Exit
Ortszeit	Local Time
Planmäßiger Flug	Scheduled Flight
Sperrgepäck	Bulky Luggage
Start	Take-off
Touristenklasse	Economy Class
Zollfreie Waren	Duty-free
Zwischenlandung	Stop-over

Achtung Bitte	Attention Please
Alle Transitpassagiere des Lufthansafluges 123 nach Berlin werden dringend gebeten, sich sofort/ umgehend zum Flugsteig 57 zu begeben	All Lufthansa Transit passengers continuing their flight to . . . are now requested to proceed immediately/urgently to Gate 57
Letzter Aufruf für Lufthansaflug 123 von London nach Düsseldorf Flugsteig B 53	Last call for Lufthansa Flight 123 from London to Dusseldorf Gate B 53
Sie können eine Stunde vor dem Abflug einchecken	Check-in is one hour before take-off
Haben Sie Handgepäck?	Have you got any hand luggage?
Ich kann Sie auf die Warteliste setzen	I can put you on the waiting list
Der Flug ist verschoben	The flight is/has been delayed
Wir haben eine Verspätung von 40 Minuten	We're 40 minutes late
Der Flug wurde gestrichen	The flight has been cancelled

INTERNATIONAL AIRPORTS

✈ HAMBURG

✈ BREMEN

✈ HANNOVER

✈ BERLIN

✈ MÜNSTER

✈ DÜSSELDORF

✈ LEIPZIG

✈ KÖLN/BONN

✈ FRANKFURT/MAIN

✈ NÜRNBERG

✈ STUTTGART

✈ MÜNCHEN

■ Please note:

Direct flights by Lufthansa or British Airways 1990

	BHX	BRS	DUB	GLA	LHR/LGW	MAN
Berlin					○	
Bremen					○	
Düsseldorf	○	○	○	○	○	○
Frankfurt	○		○		○	○
Hamburg	○				○	○
Hannover					○	○
Köln/Bonn	○				○	
Leipzig					○	
München	○		○		○	○
Münster						○
Nürnberg					○	
Stuttgart					○	

BHX = Birmingham; BRS = Bristol; DUB = Dublin;
GLA = Glasgow; LHR = London Heathrow;
LGW = London Gatwick; MAN = Manchester

There are also direct flights from Great Britain to various regional airports in Germany.

It is almost impossible to find a porter at an airport. However, you will be able to get a trolley, for which you often have to insert a coin, as at Düsseldorf Airport (DM 2.00).

On the whole there are excellent connections between airports and city centres, for example by fast local commuter trains (S-Bahn) in Düsseldorf, Frankfurt or München, buses in Köln and Hamburg, or Airport Express trains linking Düsseldorf, Köln, Bonn and Frankfurt.

Here are several useful phone numbers of airports and airlines:

London Heathrow Airport
Bath Road
Heathrow
Middlesex
Tel: 081-759 4321

99

London Gatwick Airport
Horley
Surrey
Tel. (0293) 535353

British Airways
Victoria Station
London SW1W 9SJ
Tel. 081-897 4000

Lufthansa offices in Great Britain:

Lufthansa German Airlines
23–26 Piccadilly
London W1V 0EJ
Tel. 071-408 0322

Heathrow Airport
Tel. 081-750 3000

Lufthansa in Germany:

Head Office
Deutsche Lufthansa AG
Von-Gablenz-Straße 2
D-5000 Köln 21
Tel. 0221/8261

Inexpensive flights:

Travel agencies will provide information on ABC (Advance Booking Charter) and APEX (Advance Purchase Excursion) flights, which cost considerably less than normal flights. Tickets must be bought three to four weeks before you begin your journey. However, you cannot change your reservation on such flights.

3.2 Trains

Where's Hamburg's main station?

Wo ist der Hamburger Hauptbahnhof?

Which bus goes to the station?	**Welcher Bus fährt zum Bahnhof?**
Take me to the station, please	**Fahren Sie mich bitte zum Bahnhof**
At which counter can I get international tickets, please?	**An welchem Schalter kann ich internationale Fahrkarten kaufen?**
What's the fare to . . .?	**Was kostet die Fahrt nach . . .?**
Are there any reductions?	**Gibt es Ermäßigungen?**
I'd like a ticket to . . .	**Ich möchte eine Fahrkarte nach . . .**
Two singles to Frankfurt, please	**Zweimal einfach nach Frankfurt, bitte**
Do I need a reservation?	**Brauche ich eine Reservierung?**
Do I have to pay a supplement?	**Muß ich einen Zuschlag bezahlen?**
. . . pay the excess fare	**. . . nachlösen**
How long is the return ticket valid?	**Wie lange gilt die Rückfahrkarte?**
When's the next train to . . .?	**Wann fährt der nächste Zug nach . . .?**
When does the train arrive at . . .?	**Wann kommt der Zug in . . . an?**
When does the last train leave?	**Wann fährt der letzte Zug ab?**
Which platform does the train leave from?	**Von welchem Bahnsteig fährt der Zug ab?**
Where do I have to change?	**Wo muß ich umsteigen?**
Is this the train for . . .?	**Ist dies der Zug nach . . .?**
Does the train stop at . . .?	**Hält der Zug in . . .?**
I've just missed my train, will there be another one?	**Ich habe gerade meinen Zug verpaßt, gibt es einen anderen?**

Where will I find a porter?	**Wo finde ich einen Gepäckträger?**
Can you help me with my luggage, please?	**Können Sie mir mit dem Gepäck helfen?**
Where can I check-in my luggage?	**Wo kann ich das Gepäck aufgeben?**
Excuse me, please	**Darf ich mal durch?**
Is this seat free/taken?	**Ist dieser Platz frei/besetzt?**
Is anybody sitting here?	**Sitz hier schon jemand?**
I'm afraid this is my seat	**Dies ist mein Platz**
Are there any free compartments in the sleeping car?	**Gibt es freie Schlafwagenabteile?**
Is this a non-smoking compartment?	**Ist dies ein Nichtraucher-Abteil?**
Whose suitcase is this?	**Wessen Koffer ist das?**
▶ It's mine	**▶ Meiner**
Do you mind if I open the window/shut the window?	**Darf ich das Fenster öffnen/schließen?**
Would you mind keeping an eye on that, please?	**Können Sie darauf aufpassen?**
Where do I have to get off?	**Wo muß ich aussteigen?**
Could you tell me when we're there please?	**Sagen Sie mir bitte, wenn wir da sind**
Where can I get a taxi, please?	**Wo kann ich ein Taxi bekommen?**

At railway stations and on trains you may hear or read the following:

Einfache Fahrt oder Rückfahrt?	Single or return?
Erster oder zweiter Klasse?	First or second class?
Wann reisen Sie?	When do you wish to travel?

Sie müssen in . . . umsteigen	You have to change at . . .
Der Zug fährt von Bahnsteig eins	The trains leaves from platform one
Jede Stunde fährt ein Zug	There's a train every hour
Der Zug hat eine Verspätung von zehn Minuten	The train will be delayed by ten minutes
Der nächste Zug nach . . . hat Verspätung	The next train for . . . is late
Die Fahrkarten bitte	Tickets please
Noch zugestiegen?	Any more tickets, please?
Einsteigen bitte!	All aboard!
In Hannover umsteigen	Change at Hannover
Reisende nach Hannover steigen hier um	Change here for Hannover
Alle umsteigen bitte	All change please
Hier/da drüben	Here/over there
Dafür müssen Sie Zuschlag zahlen	You'll have to pay a supplement
Achtung, auf Gleis 11 fährt ein: EuroCity MERKUR von Kopenhagen nach Frankfurt	Attention, please. The train now arriving at platform 11 is the EuroCity Merkur from Copenhagen to Frankfurt
Planmäßige Abfahrt 17 Uhr 34	Scheduled time of departure 17.34
Die Wagen der 1. Klasse halten in den Abschnitten A und B, die Wagen der 2. Klasse in den Abschnitten C bis E. Den Stand der einzelnen Wagen entnehmen Sie bitte den Wagenstandanzeigern. Nächster Halt ist Bochum.	First-class carriages stop in sections A and B, second-class carriages in sections C–E. Please refer to the plan of the order of the carriages for the exact position of the carriages. The next stop is Bochum.

Achtung, Dortmund Hauptbahnhof, Gleis 11. Der eingefahrene Euro-City fährt um 17 Uhr 34 weiter nach Frankfurt über Bochum, Essen, Düsseldorf, Köln, Bonn, Koblenz	Attention, please. Dortmund Central. The train which has now arrived at platform 11 is the 17.34 to Frankfurt, calling at Bochum, Essen, Düsseldorf, Köln, Bonn, Koblenz
Für diesen Zug ist ein Euro-City Zuschlag erforderlich	For this train a supplement is required
Fahrausweise des Verkehrsverbundes gelten nicht	Local network tickets are not valid
Sie haben Anschluß an den InterCity 'Rheinblitz'. Planmäßige Abfahrt 17 Uhr 45 am selbem Bahnsteig gegenüber	There is a connection to Munich on the InterCity 'Rheinblitz'. Time of departure: 17.45 from the same platform, on the opposite side
An Gleis 11 bitte einsteigen. Die Türen schließen selbsttätig. Vorsicht bei der Abfahrt des Zuges	All aboard on platform 11. Doors close automatically. Please be careful as the train is pulling out of the station.

If you do not understand announcements over a public address system such as those given above, you can ask: **'Können Sie mir bitte sagen, was eben durchgesagt worden ist?'** (Can you tell me what was announced over the PA?)

Ankunft/Abfahrt	Arrivals/Departures
Ausgang	Exit
Bahnsteig	Platform
Besetzt	Engaged
Damen	Ladies
Deutsche Bundesbahn	German Railways
Die Hinteren Wagen	Rear Coaches
Die Vorderen Wagen	Front Coaches
Eingang	Entrance
Erfrischungen	Light Refreshments
Fahrkartenschalter	Ticket Office
Fahrplan	Timetable
Frei	Vacant
Gepäckaufbewahrung	Left Luggage Office

Gleisanzeige	Platform Indicator
Herren	Gentlemen
Informationsschalter	Information Desk
Kofferkuli	Self-help Trolley for Luggage
Liegewagen	Couchette
Raucher/Nichtraucher	Smoker/Non-smoker
Reisebüro	Travel Agency
Schaffner	Guard/Ticket Collector
Schlafwagen	Sleeping Car
Schließfächer	Left Luggage Lockers
Speisewagen	Restaurant Car
Stationsvorsteher	Station Master
Toiletten	Lavatories
Wartesaal	Waiting Room
Zu den Zügen	To the Trains

■ Please note:

There are various kinds of trains, abbreviated as follows:

EC	EuroCity – fast, quality train, connecting European cities. Subject to payment of supplement (DM 6.00). The supplement includes seat reservation if requested.
IC	InterCity – fast, quality train, connecting major German cities, hourly, supplement (DM 6.00) required. All InterCity trains have telephones and a conference compartment.
IR	InterRegio – quality train, connecting medium-sized centres, two-hourly, payment of surcharge (DM 3.00) required for journeys of 50 km or less.
FD	Fern-Express – long-distance express train, supplement required for journeys of 50 km or less.
D	D-Zug – express trains, supplement required for journeys of 50 km or less.
E	Eilzug – semi-fast train, stopping at smaller stations.
N	Nahverkehrszug – local train, stopping at all stations.
S-Bahn	fast local commuter trains.

Park and rail:

There are forty-one railway stations where it is possible to reserve a parking space for your car by buying a train ticket.

Rail and fly:

'With the train to the plane'. Frankfurt/Main and Düsseldorf airports have their own railway stations from where it is possible to travel to major cities.

Motorail services:

Eighteen stations have loading platforms for motorail trains.

Taxi service and baggage service:

Available at many stations.

Timetable information:

Timetables showing times of departures are yellow, those with times of arrival are white.

Larger railway stations also have a plan of the order of the carriages ('Wagenstandanzeiger') which will help you find the right carriage quickly.

Train information and advice in all (2,200) DB stations, (1,500) DER Travel Agencies and other DB agencies.

Leaflets may be obtained, free of charge, at the ticket office of any railway station.

It may be useful to know the following abbreviations found in timetables:

MEZ   Central European Time
WEZ   Greenwich Mean Time (one hour behind MEZ)
Hbf.   Central Station
DB   Federal Railway
DER   Deutsches Reisebüro GmbH
. . .   daily except on Sundays and public holidays
. . .   runs on Sundays and public holidays only

Wagenstandsanzeiger   order of cars
verkehrt nicht an . . .   doesn't run on . . .

Generally trains have first- and second-class coaches. Exceptions are printed under the train number.

Don't forget to ask about reductions, such as 'Sparpreis'.

It is helpful to know that railway stations in Germany resemble miniature shopping centres, with bookshops, 'Drogerien' (where you can buy toiletries), hairdressers, bureaux de change, etc. Shops at stations are usually open till late in the evening and also on Sundays.

Details of German public holidays are given on p. 207.

Some useful addresses:

**Generalvertretung der Deutschen
  Bundesbahn in Großbritannien
(Sole Agency of the German Federal
  Railways in the UK)
10 Old Bond Street
London W1K 4EN
Tel. 071-499 0578
Telex 25671 Germanrail London**

**DER Travel Service
(German Railways' associated tour
  operator)
18 Conduit Street
London W1R 9DT
Tel. 071-408 0111**

**Zentrale der Deutschen Bundesbahn
  Hauptverwaltung
(Head Office of the German Federal
  Railways)
Friedrich Ebert-Anlage 43–45
D-6000 Frankfurt/Main
Tel. 0611/265 6108**

**Britische Eisenbahnen in Deutschland
(British Rail in Germany)**

Neue Mainzer Straße 22
D-6000 Frankfurt/Main
Tel. 069/232 381 (information, bookings,
    tickets)
069/252 033 (freight)

3.4 Ships, boats, ferries

When does the boat for Ostend leave?	Wann fährt die Fähre nach Oostende ab?
Where can I get tickets?	Wo kann ich Fahrkarten kaufen?
I'd like a single cabin/double cabin	Ich möchte eine Einzelkabine/ Doppelkabine
How long does the crossing take?	Wie lange dauert die Überfahrt?
When do we land at Dover?	Wann kommen wir in Dover an?
Is the sea rough?	Ist hoher Seegang?
Where's the purser's office?	Wo ist das Zahlmeisterbüro?
I feel sick, have you got anything for seasickness?	Mir ist übel, haben Sie etwas gegen Seekrankheit?

■ Please note:

There are various routes from the UK to the Continent, e.g.:

Dover:

to Oostende by ferry	3¾ hours
by jetfoil (no cars!)	100 minutes
to Zeebrugge by ferry	4½ hours
to Calais by ferry	1½ hours
by hovercraft (no lorries!)	35 minutes

Harwich:

to Hoek van Holland by boat	6½ hours
to Hamburg by boat	20 hours

Useful phone numbers for information and bookings:

Sealink UK Limited	**P&O European Ferries**
Southern House	**Natienkaai 5**
Dover	**Oostende**
Kent CT17 9DH	**Tel: 00-32-59/707601**
Tel. 0304-203203	**Dover:**
Telex 96139	**Tel. 0304-203 388**
Sealink in Ashford	**P&O in Germany**
Tel. 0233-47047 (reservations)	**Graf Adolf Straße 41**
	D-4000 Düsseldorf
	Tel. 0211/38706-971

Information on further ferry services (e.g. Sally Line, Olau Line, North Sea Ferries) can be obtained at German and British travel agencies.

Should you only be going on a short business trip, ask for reduced rates valid for 60 or 120 hours when buying your ferry tickets.

Otherwise car tariffs depend on the season and time of the day (Tariffs A–E).

3.5 Cars

Which is the best road to . . .?	**Was ist die beste Straße nach . . .?**
How many kilometres is it to . . .?	**Wieviele Kilometer sind es bis . . .?**
Have you got a road map?	**Haben Sie eine Straßenkarte?**
Where does this road go to?	**Wohin führt diese Straße?**
Where's the nearest garage, please?	**Wo ist die nächste Tankstelle/ Werkstatt?**
Fill it up, please	**Bitte voll tanken**
50 marks' worth please	**Für fünfzig Mark**
Please check the oil/tyres/ battery/water	**Prüfen Sie bitte Öl/Reifen/ Batterie/Wasser**

Wash and wax, please	**Bitte waschen und schmieren**
I've had an accident	**Ich habe einen Unfall gehabt**
My car has broken down	**Ich habe eine Panne**

(Refer to 7.5 on the subject of 'Accidents and breakdowns')

Where can I park here?	**Wo kann ich hier parken?**

You may hear or read the following words in German:

die Abkürzung	short cut
das Autokennzeichen	registration number
die Autovermietung	car hire service
bleifrei	lead-free, unleaded
der Diesel	diesel
der Führerschein	driving licence
der Gebrauchtwagen	secondhand car
die Geschwindigkeitsber-	speed limit
grenzung	
der LKW	lorry/truck
das Parkhochhaus	multi-storey car park
der Parkplatz	car park
SB (die Selbstbedienung)	self-service
die Tankstelle	petrol station/garage
die Tiefgarage	underground car park
die Versicherungsnummer	insurance number

▣ Please note:

In Germany parking is permitted in specifically designated areas for a limited time:

- beside a parking meter (subject to a charge)
- with a car park ticket (subject to a charge)
- with a parking disc (free of charge)

Parking discs must be fixed behind the windscreen with the time of arrival visible. They are obtainable at all filling stations and motoring organizations.

In Germany you drive on the right and overtake on the left. As a rule, vehicles coming from the right have the right of way. On a roundabout (of which there are not many in Germany) the vehicle already in the circle has the right of way.

Information on the highway code can be obtained from automobile associations; for example:

ADAC (Allgemeiner Deutscher
**   Automobilclub)**
Am Westpark 8
D-8000 München
Tel. 089/7676-1
(The ADAC is affiliated to the
**   AA and RAC)**

AVD Automobilclub von Deutschland
Lyoner Straße 16
D-6000 Frankfurt/Main
Tel. 0611/66060

British automobile associations will be able to give you further advice.

AA: Automobile Association
Tel. 081-954 7373

RAC: Royal Automobile Club
Tel. 081-686 2525

If you are travelling from the UK to Germany by car, in addition to your national identity card or passport, you will need a national driving licence or an international driving permit, plus the vehicle registration document and a green card.

You will also need a warning triangle and a first-aid box.

It is compulsory to wear a safety belt on both front and back seats, even for short journeys in built-up areas and for passengers in taxis.

In cases of emergency on the Autobahn you can make a phone call from an emergency telephone, which is never any further than 1 km away. Ask for the 'Straßenwacht' (Autobahn control).

Speed limits

	FRG	former GDR
in built-up areas	50 km/h	50 km/h
on B-roads	100 km/h	80 km/h
on A-roads	100 km/h	80 km/h
on motorways	130 km/h	100 km/h

Motorways in the FRG are indicated by a blue sign. The recommended speed limit is 130 km/h.

Yellow signs indicate A- and B-roads.

Reports on traffic conditions and road congestion are broadcast on the radio. Road signs erected at regular intervals inform motorists about the regional radio frequencies.

With regard to traffic reports, you should be able to understand the following words and phrases:

der Verkehrsbericht	traffic report on the radio
fünf Kilometer Stau	5 km hold-up/tailback
nach einem Unfall	after an accident
der Falschfahrer	person driving on the wrong side on a motorway
fahren Sie äußerst rechts und überholen Sie nicht	drive on the far right and do not overtake
die Autobahn	the motorway
die Bundesstraße	the A-road
die Landesstraße	the B-road

Litres and gallons:

Gallons	1.1	2.2	4.4
Litres	5	10	20

Petrol

The types of petrol are:

Normal (bleifrei)	Standard (unleaded, 91 octane)
Super (verbleit)	Four-star (leaded, 95 octane)
Super (bleifrei)	Four-star (unleaded, 95 octane)
Super plus (bleifrei)	Four-star plus (unleaded, 98 octane)
Diesel	Diesel

Petrol is sold in litres.

Both the German word 'Garage' and the English word 'garage' mean a building in which your car is kept. However, the English word carries two other meanings: you need to distinguish between 'die Tankstelle', where you buy petrol, and 'die Werkstatt', where repair work is done.

Distances are expressed in kilometres:

1 km is 0.622 mile
1 mile is 1.609 km

Distance table:

Distances in km

	AAC	BER	BON	BRE	DUS	FRA	HAM	HAN	HEI	KÖL	MÜN	STU
Aachen	—	644	94	382	79	256	486	363	316	72	628	480
Berlin	644	—	633	402	571	554	285	284	636	570	592	624
Bonn	94	633	—	374	70	171	454	349	240	27	558	362
Bremen	382	402	374	—	302	426	120	110	509	330	729	608
Düsseldorf	79	571	70	302	—	218	407	284	301	43	628	403
Frankfurt	256	554	171	426	218	—	494	340	83	191	372	182
Hamburg	486	285	454	120	407	494	—	156	583	427	757	690
Hannover	363	284	349	110	284	340	156	—	423	322	619	530
Heidelberg	316	636	240	509	301	83	583	423	—	258	333	103
Köln	72	570	27	330	43	191	427	322	258	—	567	360
München	628	592	558	729	628	372	757	619	333	567	—	218
Stüttgart	480	624	362	608	403	182	690	530	103	360	218	—

3.6 Car hire

Is there a car hire service nearby?	**Gibt es in der Nähe eine Autovermietung?**
I'd like to hire a car	**Ich möchte ein Auto mieten**
I need a big/small car for one week	**Ich brauche ein großes/kleines Auto für eine Woche**
How much does it cost per week/per day/per weekend?	**Was kostet es pro Woche/ pro Tag/pro Wochenende?**
What do you charge per kilometre?	**Was nehmen Sie pro Kilometer?**
What type of petrol does it run on?	**Welches Benzin braucht es?**
Is the mileage unlimited?	**Ist die Kilometerzahl unbegrenzt?**
How much is the insurance?	**Was kostet die Versicherung?**
Do I have to pay a deposit?	**Muß ich eine Kaution hinterlegen?**
Here's my driving licence/my identity card	**Hier ist mein Führerschein/ mein Ausweis**
Do you accept credit cards?	**Nehmen Sie Kreditkarten an?**
What documents do I need?	**Welche Papiere benötige ich?**
exclusion of liability	**Haftungsausschluß**
passenger insurance	**Insassenversicherung**
exclusion of the deductible	**Selbstkostenbeteiligungs- ausschluß**

If you hire a car you may read or hear the following sentences in German:

Darf ich Ihren Führerschein sehen?	May I see your driving licence?
Füllen Sie dies bitte aus	Fill in this form, please

Eine Versicherung ist Pflicht	Insurance is required
Haben Sie im Augenblick eine Kraftfahrzeugversicherung?	Do you currently have car insurance?
Möchten Sie die Zusatzversicherung?	Would you like the extra insurance?
Wo möchten Sie das Auto abgeben?	Where would you like to leave the car?
Möchten Sie es wieder hierher zurückbringen?	Would you like to return it here?
Bitte Bedingungen auf der Rückseite lesen	Please read other side for conditions
Hiermit erkläre ich, daß die obigen Angaben wahr sind	I hereby declare that the above statements are true
Zeichnen Sie bitte mit Ihren Initialen	Your initials, please

When hiring a car in Germany you will be required to produce a valid driving licence and a passport. You must be at least 21 years of age and have held a full driving licence for at least one year. A deposit will not be necessary if you have a credit card. Always enquire whether insurance is included in the stated price or whether it is extra:

eine Versicherung für Insassen	passenger accident insurance
für Ausschluß der Selbstbeteiligung	collision damage waiver

There are several car-hire companies in Germany, e.g.:

Autohansa
Tel. 0130/5001
Fax 069/749349
Telex 414 101

Avis
Tel. 0130/7733

Eurorent
Tel. 0211/4180881

115

Globus/Sixt Budget
Tel. 0130/3366

Hertz
Tel. 0130/2121

Interrent/Europcar
Tel. 0130/2211
Fax 040/52018483

More often than not, it is wise to hire a car for Germany before leaving the UK. The following companies offer such a service:

Avis Rent-a-Car
35 Headfort Place
London SW1
For reservations, Tel. 081-848 8733

Hertz Rent-a-Car
Radnor House
1272 London Road
London SW16 4XW
For reservations, Tel. 081-679 1799

You will also find offices at airports and at major railway stations. Travel agencies and tourist information centres will be able to give you further addresses.

There follows a selection of the road signs you are likely to encounter.

Gefahr unerwarteter
Glatteisbildung!
Danger! Black ice

Verlauf der Vorfahrtsstraße
Priority to main road

**Beginn eines
verkehrsberuhigten
Bereichs**
Start of pedestrian zone

Einbahnstraße
One-way street

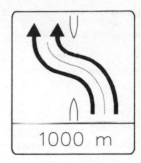

Stau
Traffic jams likely

Überleitungstafel
Contraflow

4

Hotels and Restaurants

4.1 Hotels

Have you got a room free?

Haben Sie ein Zimmer frei?

Can I have a quiet room, please?
. . . not facing the street
. . . a single room
. . . a double room

Kann ich ein ruhiges Zimmer bekommen?
. . . nicht zur Straße
. . . ein Einzelzimmer
. . . ein Doppelzimmer

117

. . . a double bed	. . . ein Doppelbett
. . . twin beds	. . . zwei Einzelbetten
. . . with a bath/shower	. . . mit Bad/Dusche
. . . without	. . . ohne
. . . with breakfast	. . . mit Frühstück
. . . with half board	. . . mit Halbpension
. . . with full board	. . . mit Vollpension

I made a reservation by phone	Ich hatte telefonisch reserviert
Can I see the room, please?	Kann ich bitte das Zimmer sehen?
I'll take it	Ich nehme es
I'm sorry, it's too small/too noisy	Es tut mir leid, es ist zu klein/zu laut
Can you show me another room, please?	Können Sie mir bitte ein anderes Zimmer zeigen?

Requests:

Can you wake me at seven o'clock, please?	Können Sie mich um sieben Uhr wecken?
Can you call a taxi, please?	Können Sie ein Taxi bestellen?
Where can I leave my luggage?	Wo kann ich mein Gepäck lassen?
Where can I deposit our valuables?	Wo kann ich unsere Wertsachen hinterlegen?
Where can I post a letter?	Wo kann ich einen Brief einwerfen?
Could you forward my post to . . ., please?	Können Sie meine Post bitte nach . . . nachsenden?
Could you bring me . . ., please?	Könnten Sie mir bitte . . . bringen?
. . . some coathangers	. . . einige Kleiderbügel
. . . a blanket	. . . eine Decke
. . . a pillowcase	. . . ein Kissen
. . . an ash-tray	. . . einen Aschenbecher

What's the voltage here? (in Germany: 220 volts, 50 Hz)	**Wieviel Volt haben Sie hier?**
The lights are not working	**Das Licht funktioniert nicht**
Can you repair this?	**Können Sie das reparieren?**
The TV needs repairing	**Der Fernseher muß repariert werden**
switch/socket/plug	**Schalter/Steckdose/Stecker**

(Plugs normally used in Britain cannot be used in most German hotels. You are therefore advised to take a multiple adapter with you.)

Can I have the bill, please?	**Kann ich bitte die Rechnung haben?**
Are tax and service included?	**Sind Steuern und Bedienung eingeschlossen?**
We're leaving tomorrow	**Wir fahren morgen ab**
Thank you for everything, we enjoyed ourselves very much	**Vielen Dank für alles, wir haben uns sehr wohlgefühlt**

Services:

I'd like to have my shoes cleaned, please	**Ich möchte gerne meine Schuhe putzen lassen**
Can you wash these clothes, please?	**Können Sie diese Kleidungsstücke bitte waschen?**
Can you clean and press my suit, please?	**Können Sie meinen Anzug reinigen und bügeln?**
Can I have it back as soon as possible?	**Kann ich es so schnell wie möglich zurückbekommen?**
Can you repair these shoes, please?	**Können Sie diese Schuhe reparieren?**
How much do I owe you?	**Was bin ich Ihnen schuldig?**
Is there a hairdresser's in the hotel?	**Gibt es einen Friseur im Hotel?**

I'd like a haircut, please	**Ich möchte meine Haare schneiden lassen**
Is service included?	**Ist Bedienung inbegriffen?**

General questions:

Has anyone asked for me?	**Hat jemand nach mir gefragt?**
Are there any messages for me?	**Hat jemand eine Nachricht für mich hinterlassen?**
Can you post these letters for me please?	**Können Sie diese Briefe für mich einwerfen?**
Do any tours leave from this hotel?	**Fahren Besichtigungstouren vom Hotel ab?**
Is there a good restaurant nearby?	**Gibt es hier in der Nähe ein gutes restaurant?**
I need an interpreter who speaks English	**Ich brauche einen Dolmetscher, der Englisch spricht**

What you might hear or read in German in your hotel:

Kann ich Ihnen helfen?	Can I help you?
Haben Sie ein Zimmer reserviert?	Have you booked a room?
mit Bad/Dusche	with a bath/a shower
ohne . . .	without . . .
Wie lange möchten Sie bleiben?	How long do you want to stay?
Nur für eine Nacht?	Just for one night?
Für wieviele Nächte?	For how many nights, please?
Für wann bitte?	For what time, please?
Es tut mir leid, wir sind ausgebucht	I'm sorry, we're fully booked
Wir sind leider ausgebucht	Sorry, we're full

Möchten Sie das Zimmer sehen?	Would you like to see the room?
Das Zimmer kostet . . .	The room costs . . .
Frühstück (nicht) inbegriffen	Breakfast is (not) included
Das Frühstück wird von . . . bis . . . serviert	Breakfast is served from . . . to
Dort drüben ist ein Fahrstuhl	There's a lift over there
Der Gepäckträger wird Ihr Gepäck nach oben tragen	The porter will take your luggage up
Würden Sie sich bitte eintragen?	Will you sign the register, please?
Darf ich bitte Ihren Paß sehen?	May I see your passport, please?
Haben Sie Ausweispapiere?	Do you have some means of identification?
Würden Sie bitte dies Formular ausfüllen?	Could you fill in this form, please?
Bitte unterschreiben Sie hier	Please sign here
Was sind Sie von Beruf?	What's your occupation?
Ihre Initialen bitte	Your initials, please?
Ihre Heimatadresse bitte	Your home address, please?
Wie möchten Sie zahlen, bar oder mit Kreditkarte?	How would you like to pay: in cash or by credit card?
Bitte nicht stören	Please do not disturb
Empfang	Receptionist
Gepäckträger	Porter
Telefonist(in)	Switchboard Operator
Zimmermädchen	Chambermaid
Zimmerservice	Room Service

| Die Gäste sollten Ihre Zimmer bis 12.00 Mittags am Abfahrtstage räumen | Guests are requested to vacate their rooms by 12.00 noon on the day of departure |

On the registration form you will find:

Bitte in Druckbuchstaben ausfüllen	Please Complete in Block Letters
Nachname	Surname
Vornamen	First Names
Staatsangehörigkeit	Nationality
Beruf	Occupation
Geburtsdatum	Date of Birth
Geburtsort	Place of Birth
Heimat Adresse	Home Address
Passnummer	Passport Number
Ausgestellt In	Issued At
Nächstes Ziel	Next Destination
Ankunftsdatum	Date of Arrival
Abfahrtstag	Date of Departure
Unterschrift	Signature

Breakfast:

During breakfast you may hear or read the following sentences in German:

Wie ist Ihre Zimmernummer?	What's your room number, please?
Möchten Sie bestellen?	Are you ready to order?
Was möchten Sie zum Frühstück?	What would you like for breakfast?
das Brot/der Toast	bread/toast
das Brötchen	roll
mit Butter/Marmelade	with butter/jam
die Orangenmarmelade	marmalade
der Kaffee/der Tee	coffee/tea
die heiße Schokolade	hot chocolate
der Orangensaft	orange juice
(Pampelmuse/Tomate)	(grapefruit/tomato)

die Milch	milk
mit Sahne/Zucker/Zitrone	with cream/sugar/lemon

If you want to order an 'English breakfast':

fried eggs	**Spiegeleier**
with sausage and tomato	**mit Würstchen und Tomate**
poached eggs	**verlorene Eier**
scrambled eggs	**das Rührei**
bacon and eggs	**Eier mit Speck**
a soft/hard boiled egg	**ein weich/hart gekochtes Ei**
omelette	**das Omelett**

■ Please note:

Waiters, waitresses and hotel staff should not be addressed as 'Herr' or 'Frau'. It is better to say 'Entschuldigen Sie bitte, könnten Sie mir sagen . . .?'
(Excuse me, could you tell me . . ., please?)

Breakfast at German hotels usually consists of bread, rolls, butter, various jams, sliced cold meats and sausage, cheese and boiled eggs, coffee or tea.

In 'international hotels' you often find 'Frühstückbuffets' (breakfast buffets) with a great variety of jams, sliced cold meats and sausage, cheeses, cereals, juices and bread, etc.

Bread:

There are more than a hundred different kinds of bread in Germany; here are just a few types:

das Weißbrot	white
das Graubrot	a mixture of rye and wheat
das Schwarzbrot	black bread
das Vollkornbrot	wholemeal bread, whole-grain bread
das Brötchen	roll

Germany has a number of international hotel chains, e.g.:

Dorint	Tel. 02166/45880 Fax 02116/420250 Telex 852371 BTX 45888	30 Dorint Hotels
Lufthansa	Tel. 069/6963032	4 Kempinski Hotels 11 Interconti Hotels 5 Penta Hotels
Maritim	Tel. 05222/1810 Fax 05222/15953 Telex 8587964	24 Maritim Hotels
Resinter	Tel. 069/740041 Fax 069/746060 Telex 411053	29 Novotel Hotels 18 Urbis, Ibis and Intercity Hotels
Steigenberger	Tel. 069/663080 Fax 069/66656 Telex 414697	26 Steigenberger Hotels

In addition there are numerous private hotels. You will be able to obtain addresses and reserve a room at airports, railway stations and local tourist information offices. Look for the sign 'Zimmernachweis'.

You ought to know the following types of accommodation:

Das Hotel garni	providing breakfast only, otherwise no meals
Der Rasthof/das Motel	on motorways only
Der Gasthof/das Gasthaus	inn
Die Pension	boarding house, bed and breakfast; not as widespread as in Britain, mainly catering for tourists at holiday resorts

Vacancies are indicated by the sign 'Zimmer frei'.

Unlike hotel rooms in Britain, rooms in Germany do not have tea or coffee making facilities.

The price for an overnight stay is often given per person.

Hotel booking services in Great Britain and Germany:

Hotel Booking Service
Cashmere House
13–14 Golden Square
London W1R 3AG
Tel. 071-437 50502

Hotel Reservation Service
HRS, Tel. 0221/20770
Heumarkt 14
D-5000 Köln
Online: BTX *20 770

Hotel guides:

Hotels und Restaurants (Varta)
Hotel- und Restaurantführer Deutschland (Michelin)
Gut und preiswert Übernachten (Kartographischer Verlag Busche)
Hotels und Pensionen (Hoffmann Verlagsgesellschaft)
Hotels and Restaurants in Europe 1990 (AA)

If you want to know whether a hotel has rooms suitable for conferences and business meetings, you can ask:
'Haben Sie Konferenzräume?' or:
'Haben Sie geeignete Räume für Konferenzen und Geschäftsbesprechungen?'

4.2 Food and drink

Can you reserve a table for two, please, we'll come at eight	**Können Sie einen Tisch für zwei Personen reservieren, wir werden um acht Uhr kommen**
Could we have a table by the window, please?	**Könnten wir einen Tisch am Fenster bekommen?**
Is this seat taken?	**Ist dieser Platz besetzt?**

125

Waiter/waitress, please	**Herr Ober/Fräulein**
We'd like something to drink, please	**Wir möchten etwas zu trinken**
May I have the menu, please?	**Kann ich bitte die Speisekarte haben?**
May I have the wine list, please?	**Geben Sie mir die Weinkarte bitte**
What would you recommend?	**Was würden Sie empfehlen?**
hors d'oeuvres/starters	**die Vorspeise**
main course	**das Hauptgericht**
dessert	**der Nachtisch**
a set meal	**das Gedeck**
soup	**die Suppe**
meat	**das Fleisch**
poultry	**das Geflügel**
fish	**der Fisch**
vegetables	**das Gemüse**
salad	**der Salat**
fruit	**das Obst**
pie	**der Auflauf**
baked/grilled	**gebacken/gegrillt**
boiled/stewed	**gekocht/gedünstet**
roasted	**gebraten**
What's today's special?	**Was ist das Tagesgericht?**
I'm hungry/thirsty	**Ich habe Hunger/Durst**
I only want a snack, please	**Ich möchte nur eine Kleinigkeit**
For starters I'll have . . .	**Ich nehme als Vorspeise . . .**
I'm in a hurry – can I have the bill, please?/can I pay, please?	**Ich habe es eilig – die Rechnung bitte**
We'd like to pay separately	**Wir möchten getrennt bezahlen**
All together, please	**Alles zusammen, bitte**
Is everything included?	**Ist alles inklusive?**

Is service included?	**Ist die Bedienung eingeschlossen?**
How much is it?	**Was kostet es?**
I'm afraid you've made a mistake	**Ich fürchte, Sie haben sich verrechnet**
Do you accept traveller's cheques/credit cards?	**Nehmen Sie Reiseschecks/ Kreditkarten?**
Thank you, that's for you	**Danke, das ist für Sie**
Keep the change	**Stimmt so**
Where are the toilets?/Where can I wash my hands, please?	**Wo sind die Toiletten?**
It tastes very good/nice	**Es schmeckt sehr gut**
I enjoyed the meal	**Das Essen hat mir gut geschmeckt**
I'm afraid that's not what I ordered	**Das hatte ich nicht bestellt**
It's too cold/tough/salty	**Es ist zu kalt/zäh/salzig**

At a restaurant you can hear or read:

Bitte hier entlang	Come this way, please
Was möchten Sie trinken?	What would you like to drink?
Ich kann . . . empfehlen	I can recommend . . .
Was möchten Sie als Vorspeise?	What would you like to start with?
Was möchten Sie? ... als Hauptgericht ... als Nachtisch	What would you like? ... as a main course ... as a dessert?
Wie möchten Sie Ihr Steak?	How would you like your steak done?
durchgebraten/mittel/rot	well-done/medium/rare
Wir haben leider keine . . .	Sorry, we don't have any . . .

127

Wir haben montags leider nicht geöffnet	I'm sorry, we don't open on Mondays
Tagesgericht	dish of the day
Tagesmenu	set menu
Spezialität des Hauses	speciality of the house
'Hausgemacht'	home-made
'Der Küchenchef empfiehlt'	'Recommended by the chef'
Kaltes Buffet	cold buffet
Eintopfgericht	stew

If you want to eat out in Germany there are a variety of places to go:

das Restaurant	restaurant
die Gaststätte, das Gasthaus	restaurant/inn. Here you can have a meal or just something to drink.
die Raststätte	motorway service area. Have your tank filled up, have a meal or go shopping.
das Cafe/die Konditorei	cafe/coffee house. Coffee, tea and cakes are served.
die Besenwirtschaft	in south Germany, with local wines and plain food.
der Weinkeller	wine bar
der Biergarten	beer garden
die Kneipe, die Schänke	similar to a pub
der Würstchenstand	sausage stand. Here you can buy frankfurters and 'Bratwurst' (a type of fried sausage) with mustard or curry.
der Schnellimbiß	snack-bar

Meals:

Frühstück	breakfast, often larger than a 'continental breakfast' and consisting of various types of bread, rolls, jam, honey, cold meats, cheese, cottage cheese.
Mittagessen	lunch, usually the main (hot) meal of the day.
Abendessen	supper, often only a light meal, usually at home, consisting of bread, cold meats and cheese.
Nachmittags-Kaffee	coffee, tea and cakes, especially at the weekend.

■ Please note:

Before starting to eat it is the custom to wish those sharing your table 'Guten Appetit'. The answer is 'Danke gleichfalls'. (Thank you, the same to you.)

Tipping:

A service charge ('die Bedienung') of 10–15% is usually included in the bill. However, most people do round the bill up. It is not usual to leave the tip on the table; you should give it to the waiter/waitress directly when he/she brings you the bill.

Outside a 'Gaststätte' you may see a sign which says:

Heute Ruhetag	closed today
Durchgehend warme Küche	hot meals served all day
Zum Mitnehmen	take-away
Gutbürgerliche Küche	good home cooking

Typical dishes:

Das Schnitzel (breaded veal or pork cutlet), das Sauerkraut, die Klopse (meat balls), die Spätzle (a form of pasta), der Eintopf (stew), die Erbsensuppe (pea soup), der Pichelsteiner (meat and vegetable stew), die Leber mit Zwiebeln und Apfelmus (liver with onion rings and apple sauce).

Potatoes are popular in Germany and are served in a variety of ways: Salzkartoffeln (boiled potatoes), Bratkartoffeln (fried potatoes), Pellkartoffeln (jacket potatoes), Pommes frites (chips, French fried potatoes), Reibekuchen (potato-pancakes). Pasta and 'Spätzle' (a form of pasta) are also very popular.

'Pudding' is always a dessert in Germany, unlike many English dishes which carry this name.

Book tips:

Kartographischer Verlag Busche (Schlemmeratlas)

Hotel- und Restaurantführer Deutschland (Michelin)

Hotel- und Restaurantführer (Varta)

Drinks:

I'd like . . .	Ich möchte . . .
a black coffee	einen schwarzen Kaffee
with cream	mit Sahne
without sugar	ohne Zucker
a tea	einen Tee
with lemon/milk	mit Zitrone/Milch
a glass of milk	ein Glas Milch
a hot chocolate	eine heiße Schokolade
a glass of mineral water	ein Glas Mineralwasser
lemonade	die Limonade
orange juice	der Orangensaft
a beer/a lager	ein Bier/ein Pils
a pint	einen halben Liter
a cognac/a brandy	ein Cognac
a gin and tonic	ein Gin Tonic
a red wine/white wine	einen Rotwein/Weißwein
dry/sweet	trocken/süß
champagne	der Sekt
sherry	der Sherry
dry/medium/sweet	trocken/mittel/süß

a whisky with/without ice	**ein Whisky mit/ohne Eis**
a glass of tap water	**ein Glas Leitungswasser**
waiter/waitress	**Herr Ober/Fräulein**
The bill, please	**Die Rechnung, bitte**
Is service included?	**Ist Bedienung eingeschlossen?**

German wines:

der Tafelwein	ordinary table wine, light and digestible, does not carry a test number (Amtliche Prüfungsnummer)
der Qualitätswein	full bodied wine, typical of its region, of tested quality, with added sugar
der Qualitätswein mit Prädikat	quality wine with a title without added sugar
Kabinett	fully matured wine
die Spätlese	made from mature grapes
die Auslese	separate pressing of mature grapes
die Beerenauslese	made from overripe grapes only
der Eiswein	from grapes frozen to ice during gathering and pressing
der Schillerwein	pink wine made from red and white grapes
der Gespritzte	wine with soda water

Famous sites of German vineyards:
Ahr, Nahe, Pfalz, Rheingau, Rheinhessen, Mosel-Saar-Ruwer, Baden, Württemberg, Franken.

Taste:

vollmundig	full-bodied
fruchtig	fruity
trocken	dry
süß	sweet
leicht	light

If you are not sure which wine to drink, simply ask: **'Welchen Wein können Sie mir empfehlen?'**

The toast is: **'Zum Wohle'** or **'Prost'** (**'Prosit'**).

Book tips:

Everybody's Wine Guide
Anthony Hogg (Quiller Press, London, 1985)

Pocket Wine Book 1990
Hugh Johnson (Mitchell Beazley)

The World Atlas of Wine
(Mitchell Beazley, London)

Deutschlands Weine
Horst Scharfenberg (Verlag Hallwag AG, Bern)

Pubs:

Germany has no pubs, but there are 'Kneipen' ('die Kneipe', similar to a combination of pub and inn), 'Schänken' (bars), and 'Biergärten' (beer gardens). In southern Germany you will find, in addition, many 'Weinstuben' (wine bars) and 'Besenwirtschaften'.

Beer, by far the most popular drink served in Kneipen, can vary considerably from region to region. For example, 'Kölsch', which is a light-coloured, top-fermented beer, is drunk in Cologne, and 'Alt', a dark-coloured beer, also top-fermented, is drunk in Düsseldorf.

Several other drinks:

das Alsterwasser	beer and lemonade
das Altbier	a dark beer
das Malzbier	dark, sweet beer, contains no alcohol
das Export	a light bottom-fermented beer
das Pils, Pilsener	a light beer, similar to lager, the most popular beer
das Weißbier	a pale fizzy wheaten beer
das Bockbier	a strong beer
vom Faß	draught
die Berliner Weiße	wheaten beer with raspberry or woodruff juice
der Gespritzte	wine and soda water
der Schnaps	a strong clear spirit

In a German pub you might read or hear the following:

Wein- und Spirituosen-Verkauf	Off-Licence
Noch ein Bier?	Another beer?
Groß oder klein?	Large or small?
Das gleiche noch einmal?	The same again?
Was möchten Sie trinken, diese Runde bezahle ich	What are you drinking, it's my round

Was möchten Sie trinken?
▶ ich hätte gern ein Pils
▶ ein kleines Pils, bitte
▶ Etwas Nicht-Alkoholisches bitte

What will you have?
▶ I'll have a Pils, please
▶ A small Pils, please
▶ A soft drink, please/ a non-alcoholic drink, please

Darf es sonst noch etwas sein?
▶ Nein danke, im Augenblick nicht

Anything else?
▶ No, thank you, not at the moment

133

Zum Wohle!	Cheers!
Ich lade Sie ein	Let me pay, please
▶ **Das ist sehr nett von Ihnen, danke**	▶ That's very nice of you, thank you

■ Please note:

Bear in mind that you are always served in a German 'Kneipe'; you do not fetch your drink yourself. Beer is served relatively cool and with a lot of froth (die Blume). Otherwise a 'Kneipe' is very similar to a pub. As in a pub, you can either sit down, or stand at the bar (die Theke, der Tresen).

'Der Stammtisch' is a table reserved for local regular customers, and you should not sit down there.

By the way, you do not pay each time you buy a drink. Instead you pay for all your drinks just before you leave.

Occasionally, restaurants and 'Kneipen' have areas reserved for non-smokers ('Nichtraucher'). Cigarettes can be bought from slot machines.

4.3 Cafés

Cafés (pronounced: ka'fes) are establishments which can probably be best compared with 'tea-rooms' in England. They tend to be considerably larger, however, and offer a wide selection of cakes and pastries and often a limited selection of light meals.

Whereas drinks and small meals 'a la carte' are ordered at tables you choose your cake from a cake-counter yourself. There you receive an order token which you give to the waiter/waitress at your table. Drinks, meals and cakes are brought to your table.

It is customary to round up the amount of a bill or give a tip of approximately 10%.

Cake:

There is a wide variety of cakes and gateaux. Some have fanciful names known only regionally. If you want ask about a particular

Speisekarte:

Vorspeisen:	Rinderkraftbrühe
	Ochsenschwanzsuppe
	Hühnersuppe mit Einlage
	Matjes mit Zwiebelringen
Hauptgerichte:	Wiener Schnitzel mit Röstkartoffeln und Gemüse
	Gebratene Rindsleber mit Apfelmus
	Linseneintopf nach Hausmacher Art
	Forelle 'Müllerin'
	Rumpsteak mit Kräuterbutter
Nachtisch:	Gemischtes Eis mit Sahne
	Obstsalat
	Rote Grütze mit Sahne

cake, say: 'Was für ein Kuchen ist das?' and you will be given some information on the ingredients.

der Apfelstrudel	pastry filled with apples and raisins
der Berliner	a jam-filled doughnut
der Bienenstich	cream or custard cake coated with almonds and honey
der Florentiner	florentine slice
der Gugelhupf	round poundcake with a hole in the middle (common in Bavaria)
der Käsekuchen	cheesecake
der Marmorkuchen	marble cake
die Mokka-Krokanttorte	mocca-cracknel gateau
der Napfkuchen	ring-shaped poundcake
der Obstkuchen	fruit flan/tart
der Pfannkuchen	pancake
der Sandkuchen	a Madeira cake
die Sahnetorte	cream gateau
die Schwarzwälder Kirschtorte	Black Forest gateau with cherry liqueur
der Streußelkuchen	thin sponge cake with crumble topping
die Waffel	waffle

The easiest way to order cake is simply to point to a piece of cake and say 'Bitte ein Stück davon'. You are usually asked 'Mit Sahne'? (with cream?).

If you like drinking tea, you should bear in mind that in Germany tea is drunk without milk, although sometimes with lemon-juice or condensed milk. If you prefer fresh milk you can ask: 'Kann ich normale Milch bekommen?'

5

In Town

5.1 Asking the way

Can you help me, please?
Können Sie mir helfen?

I've lost my way
Ich habe mich verlaufen

How do I get to . . .?
Wie komme ich nach . . .?

I'm looking for . . .
Ich suche . . .

I wonder if you can tell me the way to . . .?
Können Sie mir zufällig sagen, wo . . . ist?

Where's the nearest bank?
Wo ist die nächste Bank?
- ▶ straight on at the traffic lights
- ▶ bei der Ampel geradeaus
- ▶ (to the) right
- ▶ nach rechts
- ▶ (to the) left
- ▶ nach links
- ▶ straight ahead
- ▶ gerade aus
- ▶ first left
- ▶ erste links
- ▶ second right
- ▶ zweite rechts
- ▶ at the roundabout
- ▶ beim Kreisverkehr
- ▶ you'll see it opposite
- ▶ es liegt gegenüber
- ▶ you'll see it on your right
- ▶ Sie sehen es rechts
- ▶ I'm afraid you're going in the wrong direction
- ▶ Ich fürchte, Sie gehen in die falsche Richtung
- ▶ I'm afraid I don't know
- ▶ Es tut mir leid, ich weiß es nicht
- ▶ I couldn't tell you, you'd better ask again
- ▶ Das kann ich Ihnen nicht sagen, fragen Sie nochmal

Is it far?/Is it nearby?
Ist es weit?/Ist es nahe?
- ▶ it's five minutes' walk
- ▶ fünf Minuten zu Fuß
- ▶ ten minutes by car
- ▶ zehn Minuten mit dem Auto
- ▶ take the bus/train/tram
- ▶ nehmen Sie den Bus/Zug/Bahn
- ▶ You can't miss it
- ▶ Sie können es nicht verfehlen

137

5.2 Public transport: buses, trams, Underground, S-Bahn

Buses, trams:

How often do the buses run?	**Wie oft fahren die Busse?**
Do you go near . . .?	**Fahren Sie in die Nähe von . . .?**
Do you go to Hauptstraße?	**Fahren Sie zur Hauptstraße?**
Whereabouts in Kortumstraße?	**Wo genau in der Kortumstraße?**
Please let me know when we arrive at the station	**Sagen Sie mir bitte Bescheid, wenn wir beim Bahnhof ankommen**
Would you let me off, please?	**Lassen Sie mich bitte aussteigen**
Are you getting off at the next stop?	**Steigen Sie an der nächsten Station aus?**
Does this bus go to . . .?	**Fährt dieser Bus nach . . .?**

Underground, S-Bahn:

Where's the nearest Underground station, please?	**Wo ist die nächste U-Bahn Station?**
Where can I buy tickets?	**Wo kann ich Fahrkarten kaufen?**
▶ at the counter	**▶ am Schalter**
▶ at the automatic ticket machine	**▶ beim Fahrkartenautomaten**
How much is it to Neuer Park?	**Was kostet es bis Neuer Park?**
Do I have to change?	**Muß ich umsteigen?**
Where do I change for Marienplatz?	**Wo steige ich zum Marienplatz um?**
Is the next station Hauptwache?	**Ist die nächste Station Hauptwache?**

Where do I have to get off?	**Wo muß ich aussteigen?**
Are you getting off at the next station?	**Steigen Sie an der nächsten Haltestelle aus?**
Could you tell me when we get there, please?	**Sagen Sie mir bitte, wenn wir dort ankommen?**

In this connection you might hear or read the following:

Fahrkartenautomat	ticket machine
Notausgang	emergency exit
Notbremse	emergency brake
Einstieg vorne	entry at the front
Einstieg hinten	entry at the rear
abgezähltes Fahrgeld bitte	exact fare, please
Sie nehmen einen 25-er Bus	you want a number 25 bus
Ich sage Ihnen Bescheid, wenn wir dort ankommen	I'll tell you when we get there
der Schwarzfahrer	fare-dodger

What you can read in German on ticket machines at underground and suburban railway stations:

Fahrtziele	destinations
Städte/Stadtteile	cities/towns/parts of towns
Einzelausweis/Einzelfahrkarte	single ticket
Mehrfachausweis/ Mehrfachfahrkarte	book of tickets
Bei Fahrtantritt entwerten	Stamp your ticket before getting on a train
1 Fahrtziel ermitteln und Taste drücken	1 Select your destination and press the button.
2 Angezeigten Bertrag zahlen	2 Pay the amount displayed.
Auch 10 DM und 20 DM-Scheine möglich	Machine accepts DM 10 and DM 20 notes
Restgeld wird zurückgegeben Rückgabe: unterer Schlitz	Change can be given: lower slot

139

3 Bei Irrtum oder Störung bitte Korrekturtaste C drücken	3 Press button C in case of a mistake or fault
4 Reklamationen melden Sie bitte unter der Angabe der Automatennummer . . . sowie der Uhrzeit bei der Fahrkartenausgabe	4 Complaints are to be made to the ticket office, stating the number of the machine . . . and the time

■ Please note:

On buses and trams tickets can usually be bought from the driver. Otherwise you will find ticket machines at some bus and tram stops and at all S-Bahn and Underground stations. It is best to buy a book of tickets; also ask for a 24-hour ticket.

Remember that you may have to stamp your ticket yourself. There are cancelling machines (Entwerter) at stops or stations or on buses and trams. The stamp shows the date and time. If you are not sure whether you have to cancel your ticket, ask the driver: **'Muß ich den Fahrschein entwerten?'**

There are often no cancellers on S-Bahn and Underground trains; instead they are usually to be found at the entrance to the platforms, but unfortunately you may fail to see them as there are no barriers or gates.

Fines for 'fare dodging' are often high in Germany.

S-Bahn: S on a green sign, fast local system, e.g. in the Ruhr area, Frankfurt, Hamburg, Stuttgart, Köln, München, Berlin.
U-Bahn: Underground, abbreviated to U, in many cities, e.g. Frankfurt, Hamburg, München, Köln, Ruhr area, Berlin, Hannover, etc.
Buses: Buses are run by public transport authorities, in rural areas often by the Federal Post (Bundespost), or the Federal railways and by local government.

For further information on bus journeys you can write to:

> **Deutsche Touring GmbH**
> **Am Römerhof 17**
> **D-6000 Frankfurt/Main**

In conurbations there are regional networks enabling you to use one single ticket on all means of transport, e.g. in the Ruhr area, in Frankfurt, Hamburg, München, etc.

People do not queue at bus stops in such an orderly fashion as they do in Britain.

5.3 Taxis

Where can I find a taxi?	**Wo finde ich ein Taxi?**
Can you call me a taxi, please?	**Bitte rufen Sie mir ein Taxi**
Is there a taxi rank nearby?	**Gibt es hier in der Nähe einen Taxistand?**
Is there any chance of hailing a taxi at this time of day?	**Hat man hier um diese Zeit eine Chance, ein Taxi heranzuwinken?**
To the . . . Hotel, please	**Zum . . . Hotel, bitte**
Can you take me to . . .?	**Können Sie mich zu . . . fahren?**
What's the fare to . . .?	**Was kostet die Fahrt nach . . .?**
I'm in a hurry, can you take the shortest route, please?	**Ich habe es eilig, nehmen Sie bitte den kürzesten Weg**
Can you stop on the corner, please?	**Halten Sie bitte an der Ecke**
Can you wait, please?	**Können Sie bitte warten?**
Could you put my bags into the taxi, please?	**Bitte tragen Sie meine Taschen in das Taxi**
Can you give me change, please?	**Können Sie mir herausgeben?**
Keep the change, please	**Es stimmt so**

■ Please note:

In Germany taxis (generally Mercedes cars) are beige with a black sign saying 'Taxi' on the top.

It is best to get a taxi at a taxi rank. It is not customary to hail a taxi in the street as in the UK, but you can telephone for one. You will find telephone numbers in phone boxes or in the phone book.

The fare is displayed on a meter inside the taxi.

It is compulsory to wear a seatbelt in a taxi and smoking is usually forbidden. Although not expected, it is common to give a small tip of up to a maximum of 10%. There is generally an extra charge for luggage and for long-distance journeys.

5.4 Shopping

antique shop	**das Antiquitätengeschäft**
baker's	**die Bäckerei**
bookshop	**die Buchhandlung**
boutique, fashion shop	**das Modegeschäft**
chemist's	**die Apotheke/die Drogerie**
china shop	**das Porzellangeschäft**
confectioner's	**die Konditorei**
(currency) exchange office	**die Wechselstube**
dairy	**die Milchegeschäft**
department store	**das Kaufhaus**
dry cleaners	**die chemische Reinigung**
electrical supplies shop	**das Elektrogeschäft**
flea market	**der Flohmarkt**
florist's	**das Blumengeschäft**
furniture shop	**das Möbelgeschäft**
furrier's	**das Pelzgeschäft**
greengrocer's	**der Gemüseladen**
grocer's	**das Lebensmittelgeschäft**
haberdasher's	**die Kurzwarenhandlung**
hairdresser's	**der Friseursalon**
health food shop	**das Reformhaus**
ironmonger's	**die Eisenwarenhandlung**
jeweller's	**das Juweliergeschäft**
laundry/laundrette	**die Wäscherei/der Waschsalon**

leather shop	das Lederwarengeschäft
market	der Markt
music shop	die Musikalienhandlung
newsagent	der Zeitungshändler
off-licence	die Spirituosenhandlung
optician	der Optiker
perfumery	die Parfümerie
photographer's	das Fotogeschäft
record shop	das Schallplattengeschäft
self-service	die Selbstbedienung
shoe shop	das Schuhgeschäft
souvenir shop	der Andenkenladen
sports shop	die Sportartikelgeschäft
stationer's	das Schreibwarengeschäft
sweet-shop	das Süßwarengeschäft
supermarket	der Supermarkt
tailor's/dressmaker's	der Schneider/die Schneiderin
toyshop	das Spielwarengeschäft
tourist information centre	das Fremdenverkehrsamt
travel agency	das Reisebüro
watchmaker's	der Uhrmacher
wine merchant's	die Weinhandlung

Where are the biggest department stores?	**Wo sind die größten Kaufhäuser?**
Can you tell me where I can find a good bookshop?	**Wo ist hier eine gute Buchhandlung?**
Where can I buy . . ./get . . .?	**Wo kann ich . . . kaufen?**
Is it far/nearby?	**Ist es weit/nah?**
How do I get there?	**Wie komme ich dahin?**
Which floor is the gift department on, please?	**In welcher Etage ist die Geschenkabteilung?**
Can you help me, please?	**Können Sie mir bitte helfen?**
I'd like an electrical adapter, please	**Ich hätte gern einen elektrischen Adapter**
Can you show me . . ., please?	**Können Sie mir bitte . . . zeigen?**

143

Can you show me some other . . . please?	**Können Sie mir bitte andere . . . zeigen?**
Can I try it on?	**Kann ich es anprobieren?**
How much is this?	**Wieviel kostet das?**
Could you write it down for me, please?	**Schreiben Sie es mir bitte auf**
It's too expensive/small	**Es ist zu teuer/klein**
Have you got anything cheaper?	**Haben Sie etwas Billigeres?**
It's fine, I'll take it	**Es ist gut, ich nehme es**
No, thank you, I don't like it	**Danke, es gefällt mir nicht**
I think I'll leave it, thank you	**Ich glaube, ich nehme es nicht, vielen Dank**
I'll come back later	**Ich komme später wieder**
I'd rather take . . .	**Ich nehme lieber . . .**
I'm just looking	**Ich sehe mich nur um**
I'm being served, thank you	**Danke, ich werde schon bedient**
Can I pay with traveller's cheques?	**Kann ich mit Reiseschecks zahlen?**
Do you accept credit cards?	**Nehmen Sie Kreditkarten an?**
Has the VAT been deducted?	**Wird die Mehrwertsteuer abgezogen?**
Can I have a receipt, please?	**Kann ich eine Quittung bekommen?**
Can I have a carrier-bag, please?	**Kann ich eine Tragetasche bekommen?**
Can you wrap it up for me, please?	**Können Sie es mir einpacken?**
Would you send it to this address, please?	**Sende Sie es bitte an diese Adresse**

Can I change this, please? **Kann ich dies umtauschen?**

(See Chapter 7.6 for phrases to use when returning goods.)

When shopping you might hear the following:

Kann ich Ihnen helfen?	Can I help you?
Was darf es sein?	What would you like?
Welche Größe/welche Farbe wünschen Sie?	What colour/size would you like?
Welche Größe tragen Sie?	What size do you take/ What size are you?
Es ist im Erdgeschoß/im ersten/ zweiten Stock	It's on the ground/first/second floor
Es ist leider ausverkauft	I'm afraid we are out of stock
Wir haben keine . . .	We haven't any . . .
Das ist leider alles, was wir haben	I'm sorry, that's all we have
Die Kasse ist da drüben	The cash desk is over there
Wie bezahlen Sie? Bar?	How are you paying? Cash?
Mit Scheck/mit Kreditkarte?	By cheque/by credit card?
Dies ist Ihre Kopie/Quittung	This is your copy/receipt
Bitte unterschreiben Sie hier	Sign here, please
Es tut mir leid, wir nehmen keine Reiseschecks an	I'm sorry, we don't accept traveller's cheques
Ich kann den Schein nicht wechseln	I can't change that note
Mehrwertsteuer	VAT (Value Added Tax)
Ich kann Ihnen einen Gutschein geben	I can give you a credit note
Sonst noch etwas?	Anything else?
Ladenschluß	Closing time

Verkäufer(in)	Shop assistant
Welche Farbe wünschen Sie?	Which colour would you like?
hell/dunkel	light/dark
weiß/schwarz	white/black
rot	red
blau/dunkelblau	blue/navy blue
gelb/grün	yellow/green
braun/beige	brown/beige
lila	lilac
violett	violet
purpur	purple
rosa	pink
grau	grey
gold/silber	gold/silver

Clothing Sizes:

Women's wear						
Germany		36	38	40	42	44
Great Britain		10	12	14	16	18

Menswear						
Germany	46	48	50	52	54	56
Great Britain	36	38	40	42	44	46

Men's shirts						
Germany	36	37	38	39	40	42
Great Britain	14	14½	15	15½	16	17

Shoes							
Germany	38	39	41	42	43	44	45
Great Britain	5	6	7	8	9	10	11

■ Please note:

In town centres shops are usually open from 9 a.m. to 6.30 p.m., and on Thursdays many shops stay open till 8.30 p.m. ('Dienstleistungsabend'); offices also have longer opening times on Thursdays. On Saturdays shops close at 2 p.m., but department stores are generally open until 4 p.m. on every first Saturday in the month.

Please also remember that it is customary to say 'Guten Tag' when entering a shop and 'Auf Wiedersehen' when you leave.

If you have purchased items costing more than DM 810.00, you can reclaim the VAT in Germany. To do so you must obtain a voucher on which the gross amount is stated. Back in Britain this 'import receipt' is then stamped at the customs and sent back to the German trader, who will reimburse the VAT.

Book tips:

Business and Pleasure. One night in Europe: The International Businessman's Guide
Business and Pleasure Verlag, München (contains a number of tips on shops in various German cities)

5.5 At the bank

Where's the nearest bank, please?	**Wo ist die nächste Bank?**
. . . a bureau de change	**. . . eine Wechselstube**
I'd like to change £100	**Ich möchte hundert Pfund wechseln**
What's the exchange rate, please?	**Wie ist der Wechselkurs?**
Where can I buy German currency?	**Wo kann ich deutsche Währung kaufen?**
I'd like to cash traveller's cheques, please	**Ich möchte Reiseschecks einlösen**
What commission do you charge?	**Wie hoch ist die Gebühr?**
I've got a credit card/letter of credit	**Ich habe eine Kreditkarte/einen Kreditbrief**
I'd like DM 10.00/DM 20.00 notes, please	**Ich möchte zehn Mark/zwanzig Mark Scheine**

147

DM 100.00 in small notes, please	**Hundert Mark in kleinen Scheinen**
Some small change, please	**etwas Kleingeld**
Is it possible for foreigners to open an account here?	**Ist es für Ausländer möglich, hier ein Konto zu eröffnen?**
I'd like to open a current account/a deposit account	**Ich möchte ein Girokonto/ein Sparkonto eröffnen**
business account	**Geschäftskonto**
I'd like to pay money into my account	**Ich möchte Geld auf mein Konto einzahlen**
. . . to draw money from my account	**. . . Geld vom Konto abheben**

You might read or hear the following at a bank:

Darf ich Ihren Paß sehen?	May I see your passport, please?
Bitte hier unterschreiben	Sign here, please
Ihre Scheckkarte bitte	Your banker's card, please
Gehen Sie bitte zur Kasse	Go to the cash desk, please
Wie möchten Sie Ihr Geld?	How would you like your money?
die ausländische Währung	foreign currency
die Bankleitzahl	bank sort code
der Barscheck	cash cheque
die Bearbeitungsgebühr	handling/bank charge
der Dauerauftrag	standing order
die Devisenabteilung	foreign exchange department
die Einzugsermächtigung	direct debit
das Girokonto	current account
die Kreditkarte	credit card
die Kundenberatung	customer advisory service
das Sparkonto	deposit account, savings account
die Überweisung	remittance/transfer
der Verrechnungsscheck	crossed cheque
die Wechselstube	foreign exchange

die Zahlungsanweisung	money order
einen Kredit aufnehmen	to raise a loan/to borrow money from the bank

■ Please note:

If you are looking for a bank, look out for the signs: Bank, Sparkasse, Wechselstube, Geldwechsel. 'Die Wechselstube' is a small currency exchange office.

Banks are normally open from 8.30 a.m. to 4 p.m., and till 5.30 p.m. on Thursdays; they are closed on Saturdays and Sundays (except at major railway stations and at airports).

The Deutschmark is divided into 100 Pfennige.
Coins: 1, 2, 5, 10, 50 Pfennige and DM 1, 2, 5
Banknotes: DM 5, 10, 20, 50, 100, 200, 500, 1000

Paying by credit card is not as widespread as in Britain, but cards are accepted in larger hotels, department stores and at filling stations. In addition, you will be able to use Eurocheques in many restaurants and shops which do not accept credit cards.

Eurocheques can be used in about 40 countries, mainly in Europe. In 29 countries Eurocheques can be made out in the national currency for direct purchases.

Look out for the EC symbol (red and blue). Travellers' cheques can be made out either in DM or in the purchaser's own national currency.

Addresses of some German commercial banks:

Deutsche Bank AG
Zentralen:
Taunusanlage 12
D-6000 Frankfurt/Main

Königsallee 45–47
D-4000 Düsseldorf

Commerzbank AG
Zentrale:
Neue Mainzer Straße 32–36
D-6000 Frankfurt/Main

Dresdner Bank AG
Zentrale:
Jürgen-Ponto-Platz 1
D-6000 Frankfurt/Main

Deutscher Sparkassen und
   Giro-Verband
Simrockstraße 4
D-5300 Bonn 1

149

Inquiries on the subject of banks can be made by writing to the following address:

> **Deutsches Börsenadressbuch DBA**
> **Postfach 650 120**
> **D-2000 Hamburg 65**

By the way, the 'Deutsche Bundesbank' is not a commercial bank.

A tip for British business people:

Please bear in mind that German banks are also tailoring themselves to 1992 and are offering programmes and advice to customers at home and from abroad.

5.6 At the post office

Where's the nearest post office?	**Wo ist hier die nächste Post?**
What time does it close?	**Wann schließt sie?**
At which counter can I get stamps, please?	**An welchem Schalter bekomme ich Briefmarken?**
A stamp for a postcard to England, please	**Eine Briefmarke für eine Postkarte nach England, bitte**
How much is a letter to . . .?	**Was kostet ein Brief nach . . .?**
Two DM 1.00 stamps, please	**Zwei Briefmarken zu einer Mark, bitte**
Do you have any special editions?	**Haben Sie Sondermarken?**
I'd like to send a telegram	**Ich möchte ein Telegramm aufgeben**
How long will this letter take to get to England?	**Wie lange braucht dieser Brief nach England?**
By airmail?	**Mit Luftpost?**
By surface mail?	**Mit normaler Post?**
How much is the postage?	**Was kostet das Porto?**

You might read or hear the following at a German post office:

der Absender	Sender
andere Ziele	Other destinations
ins Ausland	Abroad
bitte nachsenden	To be forwarded
der Briefkasten	Letterbox
die Drucksache	Printed matter
die Eilzustellung	Express delivery
das Einschreiben	Registered letter
der Empfänger	Addressee
die Gebühren	Charges
Gelbe Seiten	Yellow Pages
die Leerung	Collection
Öffnungszeiten	Opening hours
Pakete	Parcels
Persönlich, vertraulich	Private and confidential
das Postamt	Post office
die Postanweisung	Postal orders
Postlagernd	Poste restante, to be called for
die Postleitzahl	Postcode

You might see the following signs at post office counters:

Amtliches Verzeichnis der Ortskennzahlen	Telephone dialling codes
Zollinhaltserklärung	Customs declaration
Wertmarken	Stamps
Sondermarken	Special-issue stamps
Massendrucksachen	Bulk mail
Briefmarken und Postkarten	Stamps and postcards
Einzahlungen Inland	Inland payments
Briefe mit Wertangabe	Letters with declaration of value
Abholung von Briefsendungen nach Aufforderung	Letters to be called for by arrangement
Postlagernde Sendungen	Poste restante
▶ mit Nachnahme	▶ COD
▶ mit Nachgebühr	▶ excess postage

151

Auszahlung von Zahlungs-anweisungen und Post-anweisungen	Payment orders
Einschreiben	Recorded delivery
Postsparkasse	Post Office Savings Bank
Information	Information
Einzahlungen und Rückzah-lungen im Postsparkassen-dienst	Payments and repayments within the post office savings service
Ausstellung und Erneuerung von Postsparbüchern	Issuing and renewal of post office Savings Books
Einrichten von Postgirokonten	Opening of postal current accounts
Gutschrift von Zinsen	Crediting of interests
Mehrfahrtenausweise	Multi-ride tickets
Familienkarten	Reduced tickets for a whole family
Tageskarten	Day tickets

■ Please note:

The Deutsche Bundespost provides several services: Postal Service, Postal Bank and Telekom.

The Postal Service covers letter mail, parcels, small packets, express mail service (EMS), postal orders. Postal giro and postal savings accounts are part of the Postal Bank.

There are 18,000 post offices in western Germany. These offices are open from 8 a.m. to 6 p.m. Monday to Friday, and on Saturdays until 12 p.m. In big cities there are post offices which close later or which may be open all night.

The sign for a post office is a yellow posthorn.

Stamps are sold at every post office as well as from stamp vending machines outside (der Briefmarkenautomat). Books of stamps are also available.

Stamps (Briefmarken) are also referred to as 'Postwertzeichen'. German post-boxes are yellow.

Express delivery:

For an additional fee, letters and parcels can be posted express.
The 'Kurierdienst', a parcel and package express service provided
by the German Federal Railways, is a very fast way to dispatch mail
to and from InterCity stations.

Telegrams:

Telegrams can be sent from the post office during normal opening
hours or phoned in by dialling 01131. There are also letter
telegrams (BT) which convey news very fast and are not as
expensive as telegrams.
It is possible to transfer money by telegram.

Most post offices also provide a fax service. If you do not have
your own machine for sending a telex, there will be one available
at post offices, conference centres and in public buildings.

You can cash Eurocheques and postal cheques at every post office
with the 'EC' symbol. Remember to take your passport with you.

Book tip:

'Postbuch' is a book containing all relevant information on services
provided by the German Federal Post (such as fees, tips, addresses,
ways of delivery). It can be ordered at post offices or by writing
to the following address:

> **Postamt**
> **Postfach 1100**
> **D-3550 Marburg**

5.7 Telephones

Where can I find a public telephone (call) box?	**Wo ist hier eine öffentliche Telefonzelle?**
I'd like to make an international phone call	**Ich möchte ins Ausland telefonieren**
What's the cost of the call?	**Was kostet das Gespräch?**

May I use your telephone, please?	**Kann ich Ihr Telefon benutzen?**
Have you got a phone book?	**Haben Sie ein Telefonbuch?**
Information, please	**Auskunft bitte**
Directory Enquiries	**Telefonauskunft**
I'd like the number . . . please	**Ich möchte die Nummer . . . bitte**
Can I dial direct?	**Kann ich direkt wählen?**
Can you put me through to . . .?	**Können Sie mich mit . . . verbinden?**
I'd like extension 123, please	**Ich möchte Nebenanschluß/ Durchwahl 123**
Can I call abroad from here?	**Kann ich von hier ins Ausland telephonieren?**
I'd like to reverse the charges, please	**Ich möchte ein R-Gespräch anmelden**
Müller speaking	**Hier spricht Müller**
Can I speak to . . ., please?	**Kann ich mit . . . sprechen?**
▶ Speaking	**▶ Am Apparat**
▶ Sorry, he isn't in	**▶ Tut mir leid, er ist nicht da**
When will he be back?	**Wann kommt er zurück?**
Could you take a message, please?	**Könnten Sie ihm etwas ausrichten?**
Please tell him I called	**Sagen Sie ihm bitte, daß ich angerufen habe**
Please ask him to call back	**Bitten Sie ihn zurückzurufen**
I'll give you a ring	**Ich werde Sie anrufen**
I'm ringing about . . .	**Ich rufe wegen . . . an**

■ Please note:

When you answer the phone in Germany it is customary to give your surname or the name of your company – never your phone number.

Phone numbers are often given in pairs, e.g. 72.41.89. 'Zwei' (two) is also 'Zwo'.

The following German words and sentences might be heard on the telephone:

Ein Anruf für Sie	There's a telephone call for you
Ein Orts-/Inlandsgespräch	A local/national call
Ein Auslandsgespräch	An international call
Ein R-Gespräch	A reverse charge call
Wer spricht?	Who's calling, please
Hier ist Schulze	Schulze speaking
Sie ist zur Zeit leider nicht da	Sorry, she's out at the moment/ she's not available
Er ist in einer Sitzung	He's at a meeting
Kann er Sie zurückrufen?	Can he call you back?
Kann ich Ihre Nummer notieren?	Can I take your number?
Was soll ich ihm sagen, wer angerufen hat?	Who shall I say called?
Möchten Sie eine Nachricht hinterlassen?	Would you like to leave a message?
Es meldet sich leider niemand	I'm sorry, there's no answer
Es wird gesprochen, möchten Sie warten?	The line's engaged, will you hold?
Bleiben Sie bitte am Apparat	Hold the line, please
Alle Leitungen sind besetzt	All the lines are busy
Ich verbinde	I'll put you through
Falsch verbunden/ich habe mich verwählt	Sorry, wrong number
Kein Anschluß unter dieser Nummer	Number unobtainable
Solch eine Nummer gibt es nicht	There's no such number
Die Verbindung ist leider nicht sehr deutlich	Sorry, it's a bad line

Das Telefon ist außer Betrieb	The phone is out of order
Wir sind leider unterbrochen worden	I'm afraid we were cut off

■ Please note:

Wherever there is a post office there are also public telephones. You will find pay phones in the yellow telephone boxes located on streets and squares but also in public buildings, such as railway stations, and also in department stores, restaurants, etc. Pay phones for international calls have instructions in several languages.

There are two kinds of pay phones: those taking 10 Pf, DM 1.00 and DM 5.00 coins, and card phones.

Cards for 40 and 200 units can be purchased at post offices for DM 12.00 and DM 50.00 respectively. Recently, phone boxes that take credit cards have been introduced.

Larger post offices have phone booths in which several direct phone calls can be made. The bill is then paid at the counter. You will however, be asked to leave a deposit before phoning.

It is worth remembering that cheap rates for long-distance calls apply from 6 p.m. to 8 a.m. Monday to Friday and on Saturday and Sunday.

International calls can be made from boxes marked 'International' or 'Ausland'.

Codes from western Germany:
UK	0044
Eastern Germany	0037
USA	001

How to phone from Germany to the UK:

1 Lift receiver
2 Insert at least 30 Pf.
3 Listen for dial tone.
4 Dial 0044
5 Dial UK STD code (minus initial 0)
6 Dial local number
7 Insert more coins on signal

Tones:

The most important tones are:
Dialling tone 'tüüüt – continuous tone
Ringing tone 'tüt tüt – the number is being called
Busy tone 'tüt tüt tüt – the line is engaged

Telephone directory (phone book):

You will find all phone books (Telefonbücher) arranged according
to towns and phone-book areas at main post offices. The opening
pages contain information on a number of telephone services, call
charges, phone-book areas and recorded information, e.g.:
Exhibitions and fairs
Entertainment guide (What's on)
Stock Exchange news
Weather forecast
Time check

The first few pages of the 'Yellow Pages' (Die gelben Seiten),
which you will also find at the post office, offer a variety of
information on the town or region, e.g. on local transport
timetables, fares, BTX information, museums.

The remaining pages have names, addresses and phone numbers
of companies arranged according to type of business.

The booklet of trunk codes for Subscriber Trunk Calling (STC)
'Vorwahlnummern, amtliches Verzeichnis der Ortskennzahlen',
known as AVON, also contains a list of trunk codes for the most
important places abroad.

The German Federal Post has also published an official directory
of fax and telex numbers.

Important phone numbers

Police (Polizei)	110
Emergency calls (Notruf)	
Ambulance, fire (Krankenwagen, Feuerwehr)	112
Emergency calls are free of charge!	
Directory Enquiries	
national	1188 or 01188
international	00118
Operator	
national	010
international	0010

130 Service – phoning free of charge:

Phone calls made to numbers beginning with 130 are free of charge; thus in pay phones there is no need to insert 10 Pf coins. In the case of '130' numbers the subscriber called pays all call charges. More and more companies are offering their customers this service.

German Telephone Alphabet

A	Anton	J	Julius	S	Siegfried
Ä	Ärger	K	Kaufmann	Sch	Schule
B	Berta	L	Ludwig	T	Theodor
C	Caesar	M	Martha	U	Ulrich
D	Dora	N	Nordpol	Ü	Übel
E	Emil	O	Otto	V	Viktor
F	Friedrich	Ö	Ökonom	W	Wilhelm
G	Gustav	P	Paula	X	Xanthippe
H	Heinrich	Q	Quelle	Y	Ypsilon
I	Ida	R	Richard	Z	Zacharias

International Telephone Alphabet

A	Amsterdam	J	Jerusalem	S	Santiago
B	Baltimore	K	Kilogram	T	Tripoli
C	Casablanca	L	Liverpool	U	Uppsala
D	Denmark	M	Madagascar	V	Valencia
E	Edison	N	New York	W	Washington
F	Florida	O	Oslo	X	Xanthippe
G	Gallipoli	P	Paris	Y	Yokohama
H	Havana	Q	Quebec	Z	Zürich
I	Italy	R	Roma		

5.8 Telecommunications

The Federal Post runs the following Telecom services:

telephone	
fax	electronic facsimile service
teletex	electronic correspondence service
BTX	interactive videotex service
Datax P/L	data transmission services
telebox	temporary storage of person-to-person messages

Video conferences:

In 13 cities in Germany, booking through a central reservation office in Cologne (Tel. 0130 0180); Service call: 0130 0522.

Telephone conferences:

Conference calls of up to 15 telephone stations to be ordered through the manual exchange office from any ordinary telephone (010).

In addition to the German Federal Post Telekom, private enterprises have been taking preparatory steps for telecommunication services. First trials are scheduled for the beginning of 1992.

British Telecom International:

If your trade transactions require a verbatim translation, the services provided by British Telecom International can be useful. News can be conveyed and transmitted by any combination of telephone, telex, fax, mail or messengers. You can give your text in German: BTI will transmit documents, letters, contracts of sale, quotations, hotel reservations and messages of any kind to your business partners abroad in their native language.

You will receive possible answers again in English. Interpreters will be at your disposal when required. For further information please contact:

> **Bureaufax International Centre**
> **BTI Communications Centre**
> **9 St Botolph Street**
> **London EC3A 7DT**
> **Tel. 071-492 7222**

6

Leisure Time

6.1 Tourist information offices

Where's the tourist information centre, please?	**Wo ist das Fremdenverkehrsbüro?**
When does it open/close?	**Wann öffnet/schließt es?**
Are there any sightseeing tours?	**Bieten Sie Besichtigungsfahrten an?**
Can you make a booking, please?	**Können Sie etwas reservieren?**
When's the sightseeing tour of the town/city?	**Wann ist die Stadtrundfahrt?**
What are the most interesting sights, please?	**Was sind die interessantesten Sehenswürdigkeiten?**
old town	**die Altstadt**

library	die Bücherei
botanical garden	der botanische Garten
monument	das Denkmal
cathedral/church	die Kathedrale/die Kirche
market	der Markt
museum	das Museum
castle	das Schloß
university	die Universität

Have you got a map of the town?	Haben Sie einen Stadtplan?
a list of events	einen Veranstaltungs-kalender
a list of hotels	ein Hotelverzeichnis
a bus timetable	einen Busfahrplan
in English, please	auf Englisch, bitte

| Do you have any information about . . .? | Haben Sie Informationen über . . .? |

| Do you have any brochures in English about . . .? | Haben Sie Broschüren in Englisch über . . .? |

| Can you recommend a good restaurant, please? | Können Sie ein gutes Restaurant empfehlen? |

| Thank you very much for your help | Vielen Dank für Ihre Hilfe |

| Three tickets, please | **Drei Karten bitte** |

| Two full price | **Zwei zum vollen Preis** |

| One half price | **Eine zum halben Preis** |

| Two adults, one child | **Zwei Erwachsene, ein Kind** |

| Where can I book seats for . . .? | **Wo kann ich Karten für . . . reservieren?** |

| When do I have to pick them up? | **Wann muß ich sie abholen?** |

| How much do I owe you? | **Was schulde ich Ihnen?** |

161

Where's the town hall?	Wo ist hier das Rathaus?
▶ Straight on at the traffic lights	▶ Geradeaus bei der Ampel
▶ You can't miss it	▶ Sie können es nicht verfehlen

■ Please note:

Most towns and holiday resorts have tourist information offices, tourist associations or travel agencies, where you will be able to reserve a room (Zimmernachweis = room booking service), obtain information and booklets (street maps, entrance tickets, forthcoming events, programmes, etc.) and book excursions.

**Zentrale für Tourismus
(German Tourist Authority)
Beethovenstraße 69
D-6000 Frankfurt/Main
Tel. 0611/7572-0**

**German National Tourist Office in the UK
Nightingale House
65 Curzon Street
London SW1Y 7PE
Tel. 071-495 3990
Tel. 071-495 3991**

For addresses of tourist associations please refer to Part III, 12.

6.2 Entertainment

Have you got an entertainment guide?	Haben Sie einen Veranstaltungskalender?
What's on at the cinema/at the theatre?	Was gibt es im Kino/im Theater?
Can you recommend a show, please?	Können Sie eine Show empfehlen?

When does the performance begin?	**Wann beginnt die Aufführung?**
Are there any tickets for . . .? the concert the exhibition the dance/the ball the circus the play	**Haben Sie Karten für . . .?** **das Konzert** **die Ausstellung** **den Tanz/den Ball** **den Zirkus** **das Theaterstück**
Can I book in advance?	**Kann ich im voraus buchen?**
Are you doing anything tonight?	**Haben Sie heute abend etwas vor?**
What about a film? ▶ That would be nice ▶ That's a good idea ▶ I'm not sure, I'd prefer a concert ▶ I don't mind	**Wie wär's mit einem Film?** ▶ **Das wäre nett** ▶ **Das ist eine gute Idee** ▶ **Ich bin nicht sicher, ich würde ein Konzert vorziehen** ▶ **Es ist mir gleich**
Is there a good film on tonight?	**Gibt es heute abend einen guten Film?**
Can you tell me when the performance finishes?	**Wann ist die Aufführung zu Ende?**

You might hear or read the following in German:

Kartenverkauf	Booking Office
Vorverkauf	Advance Booking
Garderobe	Cloakroom
Parkett	Stalls
Erster Rang	Dress Circle
Oberer Rang	Upper Circle
Es ist leider ausverkauft	I'm sorry, we're sold out

■ Please note:

A list of plays performed on stages in Germany, Austria and Switzerland and of museum exhibitions – arranged according to towns – is published in the weekly paper *Die Zeit*. You will also find out what's on by looking into local newspapers (Veranstaltungskalender) or by phoning the 'Telefonansage' (recorded telephone announcement/'Guidelines'). The telephone numbers are on the first pages of the telephone directory.

You should bear in mind that in Germany most museums are closed on Mondays.

6.3 Invitations

Are you free tonight?	**Haben Sie heute abend Zeit?**
Are you doing anything tonight?	**Haben Sie heute abend schon etwas vor?**
Could you come for dinner tomorrow?	**Können Sie morgen zum Abendessen kommen?**
▶ I'd like to come	▶ **Ich komme gerne**
▶ I'm sorry, I can't make it	▶ **Ich kann es mir leider nicht einrichten**
Can we meet tomorrow morning?	**Können wir uns morgen früh treffen?**
What about 10 o'clock?	**Wie wär's mit zehn Uhr?**
Where shall we meet?	**Wo sollen wir uns treffen?**
I'll pick you up at the hotel	**Ich hole Sie vom Hotel ab**
Can I give you a lift?	**Kann ich Sie im Auto mitnehmen?**
▶ Thank you, that's really not necessary	▶ **Danke, das ist wirklich nicht nötig**
Thank you very much for a delightful evening	**Vielen Dank für den schönen Abend**
I enjoyed it very much	**Es hat mir sehr gefallen**
Thank you very much for asking me out	**Vielen Dank dafür, daß Sie mit mir ausgegangen sind**
▶ The pleasure was all mine	▶ **Es war mir ein Vergnügen**
Thank you very much for your hospitality	**Vielen Dank für Ihre Gastfreundschaft**

The meal was delicious	**Das Essen war köstlich**
I'm afraid I must go/leave now	**Ich muß jetzt leider gehen**
Nice to have met you	**Es war sehr schön, Sie kennen-gelernt zu haben**
It was very interesting	**Es war sehr interessant**

You might hear the following in German:

Wir geben Freitag ein Fest	We're having a party on Friday
Möchten Sie gerne kommen?	Would you like to come?
▶ **Sehr gerne**	▶ I'd love to
▶ **Wie schade, ich habe Freitag zu tun**	▶ What a pity, I'm busy on Friday
uAwg (um Antwort wird gebeten)	RSVP (Répondez s'il vous plaît) (reply appreciated)
Fühlen Sie sich wie zu Hause	Make yourself at home
Was möchten Sie trinken?	What are you drinking?
Bitte, bedienen Sie sich	Please help yourself
Können Sir mir bitte den Käse reichen?	Could you pass me the cheese, please?
Möchten Sie noch etwas Wein?	Would you like some more wine?
▶ **Ja, bitte**	▶ Yes, please
▶ **Nein, danke**	▶ No, thank you
Nehmen Sie noch etwas mehr	Would you like some more?

If you have had enough to eat you can say:

Danke, ich bin gesättigt	I think I've had enough, thank you
Nette Party, nicht wahr?	Are you enjoying the party?
Es war schön, Sie bei uns zu haben	It was nice of you to have come
Besuchen Sie uns bald wieder	Do come and see us again

■ Please note:

If you have received a private invitation, it is customary in Germany to take along a little gift, usually flowers or chocolates, for the hostess. (Most railway stations have flower shops and confectioners'.)

If you have been invited for dinner in the evening, remember that before beginning to eat you wish one another 'Guten Appetit'. The answer is 'Danke gleichfalls' (Thank you, the same to you).

If you want to send a thank-you letter for an invitation, the specimen letters in Part III will be useful.

 Model Letters 16–19

7

Problems

7.1 At the doctor's

Can you call a doctor, please?	**Rufen Sie bitte einen Arzt**
Is there a doctor in the hotel?	**Gibt es einen Arzt im Hotel?**
When does the doctor have his surgery hours?	**Wann hat der Arzt Sprechstunde?**
Can you call an ambulance, please?	**Rufen Sie bitte einen Krankenwagen**
I feel sick	**Mir ist schlecht**
It hurts here	**Es tut hier weh**
I have a pain in . . .	**Ich habe Schmerzen in . . .**
Can you give me something for . . .	**Können Sie mir ein Mittel für . . . verschreiben?**
I suffer from . . .	**Ich leide an . . .**

attack/fit	der Anfall
asthma	das Asthma
backache	die Rückenschmerzen
blood pressure (too high/too low)	der Blutdruck (zu hoch/zu niedrig)
bronchitis	die Bronchitis
cancer	der Krebs
circulatory trouble	die Kreislaufbeschwerden
a cold	die Erkältung/der Schnupfen
cough	der Husten
concussion	die Gehirnerschütterung
constipation	die Verstopfung
diabetes	die Zuckerkrankheit
diarrhoea	der Durchfall
dizziness	der Schwindel
fever/temperature	das Fieber
flu	die Grippe
fracture	der Knochenbruch
heart trouble	die Herzbeschwerden
hay fever	der Heuschnupfen
headache	der Kopfschmerz
heartburn	das Sodbrennen
infection	die Infektion
insomnia	die Schlaflosigkeit
indigestion	die Verdauungsbeschwerden
an infected wound	eine Wundinfektion
migraine	die Migräne
nausea	die Übelkeit
nephritis	die Nierenentzündung
phlebitis	die Venenentzündung
rheumatism	der Rheumatismus
sciatica	der Ischias
skin disease	die Hautkrankheit
a sore throat	die Halsschmerzen
stomach-ache	die Magenschmerzen
sunburn	der Sonnenbrand
toothache	die Zahnschmerzen
upset stomach	der verdorbene Magen
vomiting	das Erbrechen

At the doctor's you might hear the following:

Welche Beschwerden haben Sie?	What's the trouble?
Wo tut es weh?	Where does it hurt?
Was kann ich für Sie tun?	What can I do for you?
Bitte ziehen Sie sich aus	Get undressed, please
Bitte legen Sie sich hier hin	Lie down here, please
Bitte tief atmen	Breathe deeply, please
Bitte öffnen Sie den Mund	Open your mouth, please
Ich messe Ihren Blutdruck	I'm going to take your blood pressure
Ich gebe Ihnen eine Spritze	I'm going to give you an injection
Ich möchte Sie röntgen lassen	I'd like you to have an X-ray
Est ist nichts Ernstes	It's nothing serious
Ich verschreibe Ihnen etwas	I'll prescribe something for you
Nehmen Sie dreimal pro Tag eine Tablette nach dem Essen	Take one pill three times a day after meals
Dies ist ein Antibiotikum	This is an antibiotic
Ich werde Ihnen eine Rechnung schicken	I'll send you a bill
Sie müssen drei Tage im Bett bleiben	You must stay in bed for three days
Kommen Sie in drei Tagen wieder	Come back in three days
Unfallstation	Emergency ward

■ Please note:

If you need a doctor, ask if there is one available at the hotel. Alternatively, by phoning directory enquiries you will be able to find out names and addresses of doctors nearby. Lists of doctors can also be found in the 'Gelbe Seiten' under the heading 'Ärzte/ Zahnärtze.

In case of emergency you can also go to the casualty department (Unfallaufnahme) at hospitals, or dial 110 for an ambulance or a doctor on emergency call.

Travellers from Britain who fall ill in Germany should go to the local health insurance office AOK (Allgemeine Ortskrankenkassen) and take along the form E111, obtained in Britain, having already completed it. They will then be entitled to medical treatment free of charge.

7.2 At the chemist's

Where is the nearest chemist, please?	**Wo ist die nächste Apotheke?**
Which chemist is open at night?	**Welche Apotheke hat Nachtdienst?**
I'd like some pills for . . .	**Ich möchte Tabletten gegen . . .**
Do I need a prescription?	**Brauche ich ein Rezept?**
adhesive plaster	**das Heftpflaster**
after/before each meal	**nach/vor jeder Mahlzeit**
aspirin	**das Aspirin**
aspirins	**die Kopfschmerztabletten**
burn ointment	**die Brandsalbe**
charcoal tablets	**die Kohletabletten**
cotton wool	**die Watte**
cough mixture	**das Hustenmittel**
indigestion tablets	**die Magentabletten**
for external use	**zum äußeren Gebrauch**
eye drops	**die Augentropfen**
first-aid kit	**die Erst-Hilfe-Kasten**
for internal use	**zum inneren Gebrauch**
laxative	**die Abführtabletten**
pain-killing tablets	**die Schmerztabletten**
pills/tablets	**die Pillen/Tabletten**
sleeping tablets	**die Schlaftabletten**
valerian	**der Baldrian**

■ Please note:

In Germany there is no chain of chemists like Boots in the UK. Each chemist's is privately owned.

Please bear in mind the difference between a chemist's (Apotheke) and a so-called 'Drogerie':

Die Apotheke: If you have been given a prescription you will have to go to an 'Apotheke'. Household remedies are available and the shops are open on Sundays. The names of chemists open 24 hours are displayed at every 'Apotheke'. To identify an 'Apotheke' look out for the red letter A on a white sign.

Die Drogerie: Toiletries, household items and some medicines for which a prescription is not needed can be obtained here.

By the way, 'Reformhaus' is the equivalent of the British 'health food shop.' Toiletries can also be bought at a perfumery (die Parfümerie).

7.3 Lost property office

Where's the lost property office, please? | **Wo ist hier das Fundbüro?**

I've lost my . . . | **Ich habe . . . verloren**
   wallet | **(meine) Brieftasche**
   handbag | **(meine) Handtasche**
   identity card | **(meinen) Personalausweis**
   passport | **(meinen) Paß**
   purse | **(mein) Portemonnaie**
   cheque card/banker's card | **(meine) Scheckkarte**
   watch | **(meine) Uhr**

■ Please note:

If you have lost something, go to the local lost property office, the lost property office at the railway station or the lost property office of the local transport company. The police will also try to help you.

7.4 Police

Please call the police	**Holen Sie bitte die Polizei**
I've been robbed	**Ich bin bestohlen worden**
I'd like to report a theft/a crime	**Ich möchte einen Diebstahl/ein Verbrechen melden**
My car has been broken into	**Mein Auto ist aufgebrochen worden**
My briefcase is missing	**Meine Aktentasche ist verschwunden**
Thank you very much for your help	**Vielen Dank für Ihre Hilfe**
You've been very helpful	**Sie waren sehr hilfsbereit**
I'm very grateful	**Ich bin sehr dankbar**
You are very kind	**Sie sind sehr freundlich**
Thank you very much	**Vielen Dank**
▶ Don't mention it/Not at all	▶ **Nichts zu danken**

Calls for help:

Help	**Hilfe**
Stop	**Halt**
Quick	**Schnell**
Stop, thief!	**Diebe**
Fire	**Feuer**
Watch Out/Careful	**Vorsicht**
Poison	**Gift**
Danger	**Gefahr**

Fire Brigade	**Feuerwehr**
Ambulance	**Krankenwagen**
Police	**Polizei**

At a police station you might hear the following:

Wie sah es aus?	What was it like?/Could you describe it for me?
Wann genau haben Sie es verloren?	When exactly did you lose it?
Kann ich bitte Ihre Papiere sehen?	Can I see your papers, please?
Geben Sie mir bitte Ihren Namen und Adresse	May I have your name and address, please?

■ Please note:

In many cases of emergency the police will be able to help you, e.g.
– if you are looking for a doctor or a chemist's
– if you need garage services
– if you have lost something
– if you have lost your way
– if you are looking for a hotel late at night
– if you have to contact the British Consul-General.

The police wear a green uniform. Police stations are identified by the blue sign 'Polizei'.

Should you have to get in touch with a British consul in Germany, please bear in mind that there are consulates to be found in Berlin, Düsseldorf, Frankfurt, Hamburg, Hannover, München, Stuttgart.

Can anyone here speak English?	**Spricht hier jemand Englisch?**
I need an interpreter	**Ich brauche einen Dolmetscher**
I need a lawyer	**Ich brauche einen Rechtsanwalt**
I'd like to speak to the British consul, please	**Ich möchte mit dem britischen Konsul sprechen**

Where's the British embassy, please?	**Wo ist die britische Botschaft?**

Here is the address of the British embassy:

> **Botschaft des Vereinigten Königreiches**
> **Großbritannien und Nordirland**
> **Friedrich-Ebert-Allee 77**
> **D-5300 Bonn**
> **Tel. 0228/234061**

7.5 Accidents and breakdowns

I've had an accident	**Ich habe einen Unfall gehabt**
My car has broken down	**Ich habe eine Panne**
Could you take me to the nearest garage, please?	**Bitte nehmen Sie mich bis zur nächsten Werkstatt mit**
Could you send someone to repair my car, please?	**Bitte schicken Sie jemanden, der mein Auto repariert**
Can you tow the car into town?	**Können Sie das Auto in die Stadt abschleppen?**
Can you send a mechanic at once, please?	**Können Sie bitte sofort einen Mechaniker schicken?**
How long will it take?	**Wie lange dauert es?**
How much do I owe you?	**Was bin ich Ihnen schuldig?**
This is my insurance document	**Hier sind meine Versicherungspapiere**

See also Part II, 3.5.

I think there's something wrong with the engine	**Ich glaube mit dem Motor ist etwas nicht in Ordnung**
accelerator	**der Gashebel**
battery	**die Batterie**
brake	**die Bremse**
bumper	**die Stoßstange**
clutch	**die Kupplung**

engine	der Motor
exhaust	der Auspuff
headlight	der Scheinwerfer
horn	die Hupe
ignition	die Zündung
spark plugs	die Zündkerzen
starter	der Anlasser
steering wheel	das Steuerrad
windscreen wiper	der Scheibenwischer
wing	der Kotflügel
Have you got . . .?	Haben Sie . . .?
a rope	ein Seil
a spanner	einen Schraubenschlüssel
a screwdriver	einen Schraubenzieher
spare parts	Ersatzteile
The engine is overheating	Der Motor ist heißgelaufen
The keys are locked inside the car	Die Schlüssel sind im Auto eingeschlossen

■ Please note:

In the event of a breakdown or an accident, you can use the emergency telephone on the Autobahn or look up the number of the breakdown service (Abschleppdienst) in the local telephone directory.

The motoring organizations will also be able to provide breakdown services (ADAC/ADV).

In case of an accident you can phone for the police or an ambulance by dialling 110.

**ADAC Luftrettung GmbH
(Automobile Association in the FRG
(Air Rescue) Ltd)
Am Westpark 8
D-8000 München
Tel. 089/7676 2124**

**Deutsche Rettungsflugwacht
(German Air Rescue Service)**

Flughafen
D-7000 Stuttgart 23
Tel: 0711/701070 (Notruf)

7.6 Problems when returning goods

Can you change this, please?	**Können Sie dies umtauschen?**
Can I return this?	**Kann ich es zurückgeben?**
I bought this yesterday	**Ich habe dies gestern gekauft**
Here's the receipt	**Hier ist die Quittung**
This is dirty/torn/damaged	**Das ist schmutzig/zerrissen/ beschädigt**
Can I have the money back?	**Kann ich das Geld zurückbe- kommen?**
Can I see the manager, please?	**Kann ich den Geschäftsführer sprechen?**

7.7 Problems with the tone of voice

If you hear the following expressions and sentences, you are probably being insulted or at least not being treated very politely:

Das ist verdammt ärgerlich	This is a damn nuisance
Es geht mir wirklich auf die Nerven	It really gets on my nerves
Ich habe genug (von . . .)	I'm fed up (with . . .)
Mir reicht's	I've just about had enough
Solch ein Unsinn	It's rubbish
Das ist doch zum Lachen	Don't make me laugh
Das ist der reinste Wucher	It's a rip-off
Na und?	So what?

175

Ist mir doch gleich	I couldn't care less
Also wirklich!	Really!
Wehe!	Don't you dare!
Doofe Ausländer	Stupid foreigners
Hau ab	Get lost
Halten Sie Ihren Mund	Shut up
Lassen Sie mich in Ruhe	Leave me alone
Was bilden Sie sich eigentlich ein	What on earth do you think you're doing!

8

What You Say if You Want . . .

8.1 . . . to make a request

Können/könnten/würden Sie bitte . . .?
Wäre es Ihnen möglich . . .?
Wären Sie bitte so freundlich . . . (+ zu)?
Entschuldigen Sie bitte, aber könnten Sie . . . .?
Würde es Ihnen etwas ausmachen, . . . (+ zu)?

. . . to respond to a request

Gerne
Aber sicher
Ja, natürlich
Mit Vergnügen

Leider nein
Das geht leider nicht
Das kann ich leider nicht

8.2 . . . to say thank you

Danke
Vielen Dank
Tausend Dank
Haben Sie vielen/herzlichen Dank
Ich bin Ihnen sehr dankbar
Ich danke Ihnen für Ihre Hilfe

. . . to respond to thanks

Keine Ursache
Nicht zu danken
Aber nicht doch
Es freut mich, daß ich Ihnen habe helfen können

8.3 . . . to ask for information

Darf ich?
Darf/dürfte/kann ich . . . . .?
Ist es gestattet . . . (+ zu)?
Macht es Ihnen etwas aus, wenn . . . .?
Wenn es Ihnen recht ist, würde ich gerne . . .?

. . . to grant or refuse permission

Ja
Gerne
Ja, sicher

Ja, bitte
Natürlich
Meinetwegen
Einverstanden
Wenn es nach mir geht, gerne

Nein
Ich fürchte, nein
Leider nicht
Bitte nicht
Besser nicht
Eigentlich nicht
Ich glaube nein
Das geht leider nicht

8.4 . . . something to be repeated

Wie bitte?
Was haben Sie gesagt?
Was meinten Sie?
Entschuldigen Sie, ich habe den letzten Satz nicht ganz verstanden
Könnten Sie das bitte nochmal wiederholen?

. . . to show that you are listening

Ach so
Genau
Wirklich?

. . . to sum up

Kurz gesagt, . . .
Das heißt, daß . . .
Das bedeutet also, daß . . .
Wenn ich zusammenfassen darf, . . .
Alles in allem kann man sagen, daß

8.5 . . . to ask for advice/a suggestion

Was meinen Sie dazu?
Was halten Sie von . . . (+ Dativ)
Was schlagen Sie vor?
Was würden Sie mir raten?
Was würden Sie an meiner Stelle tun/sagen?
Dürfte ich Sie um Ihre Meinung/Ihren Rat bitten?

. . . to offer advice/make a suggestion

Ich würde . . .
Warum . . . (verb) Sie nicht
Ich an Ihrer Stelle würde . . .
Ich finde, Sie sollten . . .
Es wäre gut, wenn Sie . . .
Haben Sie schon daran gedacht . . . (+ zu)
Ich würde Ihnen empfehlen zu . . .

. . . to respond to some advice

Gut
Einverstanden
Das ist eine gute Idee
Der Vorschlag gefällt mir

Den Vorschlag finde ich nicht so gut
Ich meine, das wäre nicht sehr klug

8.6 . . . to ask for someone's opinion

Was meinen Sie zu . . . (+ Dativ)
Was halten Sie von . . . (+ Dativ)
Für eine Stellungnahme wäre ich Ihnen sehr dankbar

. . . to give your opinion

Ich meine, daß . . .
Ich glaube, daß . . .
Meiner Meinung/Ansicht nach . . .
Ich gehe davon aus, daß
Ich bin ganz sicher, daß . . .
Es gibt gar keinen Zweifel, daß . . .
Ich persönlich bin davon überzeugt, daß . . .

Vielleicht . . .
Möglich, daß . . .
Es kommt darauf an . . .
Es könnte sein, daß

Wahrscheinlich nicht
Ich glaube nicht, daß . . .
Ich bin (mir) nicht so
Es ist (ganz) unwahrscheinlich, daß . . .
Ich fürchte, das kommt nicht in Frage

8.7 . . . to express delight

Wie schön!
Großartig!
Wie toll!
Ausgezeichnet
Ich freue mich, daß . . .
Ich freue mich zu hören, daß . . .

. . . to show that you are angry

Nein!
So nicht!
Also wirklich!
Das ist sehr ärgerlich
So geht es wirklich nicht
Das ist doch wohl nicht Ihr Ernst?

8.8 . . . to make a complaint

Entschuldigen Sie bitte, aber . . .
Würde es Ihnen etwas ausmachen, nicht zu . . . .
Ich muß Ihnen leider sagen, daß . . .
Leider muß ich mich beschweren
Ich bin sehr unzufrieden mit . . .

. . . to admit that you were wrong

Tut mir leid
Es war mein Fehler
Ich glaube, Sie haben Recht
Das habe ich falsch verstanden
Das muß ein Mißverständnis sein

. . . to apologize

Verzeihung
Entschuldigung
Es war meine Schuld
Es war ein Versehen
Es tut mir sehr leid, daß . . .
Können Sie mir nochmal verzeihen?
Es ist mir sehr peinlich, daß . . .
Dafür muß ich mich wirklich entschuldigen

. . . to respond to an apology

Es macht nichts
Es ist in Ordnung
Das kann vorkommen
Machen Sie sich keine Gedanken
Sie brauchen sich wirklich nicht zu entschuldigen

Das kann vorkommen
Ich hoffe, so etwas kommt nicht wieder vor

8.9 . . . to invite someone

Wollen wir . . .?
Möchten Sie . . .?
Was halten Sie davon, . . . (+ zu)
Ich würde mich sehr freuen, wenn . . .
Ich möchte Sie gerne zum/zur . . . einladen

. . . to accept or decline an invitation

(Sehr) gerne
Einverstanden
Vielen Dank
Vielen Dank für die Einladung
Danke, das ist sehr freundlich

Es tut mir leid, aber . . .
Ich würde gerne, aber . . .
Das ist sehr freundlich, aber . . .
Leider kann ich Ihre Einladung nicht annehmen

PART III

1

Model Letters

 MODEL LETTER 1

(1) Firma **Franz Meyer** **Holzweg 712** **D-4711 Köln 2**	(2) Franz Meyer KG z.H. Frau W. Eckstein (3) Franz Meyer KG z.H. Herrn Dr. G. Eckstein	inside address (three various forms) (1), (2), (3)

Ihr Zeichen	Ihre Nachricht vom	Unsere Zeichen	**Bochum** **5. Mai 1990** **<05.05.1990>**

(1) Sehr geehrte Damen und Herren

        (2) Sehr geehrte Frau Eckstein
        (3) Sehr geehrter Herr Dr. Eckstein

salutation
(three various forms,
corresponding to
the address)
(1), (2), (3)

body of the letter

(1) Mit freundlichen Grüßen
   ILT Verlag

        (2) Hochachtungsvoll

complimentary
close
(two various forms)
(1), (2) = very
formal
signature(s)

Model Letter 2

Hannover Messe 1991

Sehr geehrte Damen und Herren,

Wir sind eine Unternehmensgruppe für Energietechnik und beabsichtigen, unsere Produktpalette auf der Hannover Messe vorzustellen.

Wir wären Ihnen daher sehr dankbar, wenn Sie uns nähere Einzelheiten über die Teilnahmebedingungen mitteilen würden.

Vielen Dank im voraus.

Mit freundlichen Grußen

 # Model Letter 3

Sehr geehrte Damen und Herren,

Wir beziehen uns auf Ihre Anzeige in der . . . . . . Zeitung vom . . . .

Da wir am Import Ihrer Artikel interessiert sind, bitten wir um Zusendung Ihres Kataloges und der gültigen Preisliste.

Für eine kurzfristige Antwort wären wir dankbar.

Mit freundlichen Grüßen

Model Letter 4

Sehr geehrte Damen und Herren,

vielen Dank für Ihr Schreiben vom . . . . . und Ihr Interesse an unseren Erzeugnissen.

Wir freuen uns, Ihnen wie folgt anbieten zu können:

(quantity, name of merchandise, quality, price)

Unsere Allgemeinen Lieferungs- und Zahlungsbedingungen sind beigefügt.

Wir sehen Ihrem Auftrag mit Interesse entgegen und sichern Ihnen sorgfältige Ausführung zu.

Mit freundlichen Grüßen

Anlage

 # Model Letter 5

Sehr geehrte Frau . . . .

wir danken Ihnen für Ihr Angebot vom 27. Januar 1991 und bestellen hiermit zur sofortigen Lieferung frei Haus:

. . . .

Preis:	DM 200,00 pro Stück
Zahlungsbedingungen:	10 Tage, 2% Skonto oder 30 Tage netto

Wir bitten um Auftragsbestätigung.

Mit freundlichem Gruß

Model Letter 6

Unser Auftrag Nr. . . . . . vom 03.01.1991

Sehr geehrte Damen und Herren,

zu unserem Bedauern teilen wir Ihnen mit, daß wir mit der Ausführung unseres obigen Auftrags nicht zufrieden sind.

Die gelieferte Ware entspricht nicht den bestellten Qualitätsmerkmalen. Zu Ihrer Information fügen wir eine Probe bei.

Wir bitten um Ersatzlieferung.

Mit freundlichen Grüßen

Anlage

 # Model Letter 7

Ihr Schreiben vom . . . .

Sehr geehrte Damen und Herren,

vielen Dank für die übersandte Warenprobe.

Leider wurde durch ein Versehen unserer Versandabteilung eine mindere Qualität geliefert.

Heute haben wir eine Ersatzlieferung frei Haus an Sie abgesandt. Bitte senden Sie uns die fehlgelieferte Ware auf unsere Kosten zurück.

Wir bitten Sie, das Versehen zu entschuldigen und hoffen auf weitere gute Zusammenarbeit.

Mit freundlichen Grüßen

Model Letter 8

Sehr geehrte Damen und Herren,

wir bestätigen den Eingang Ihres Schreibens vom . . . . .

Mit großer Sorgfalt haben wir die Qualität der uns zugesandten Probe geprüft und dabei festgestellt, daß es sich um die Qualitätsbezeichnung . . . handelt.

Wie Sie aus der beigefügten Kopie Ihres Auftrages ersehen können, stimmt die gelieferte Qualität mit der Bestellung überein. Wir sind allerdings gerne bereit, die Waren zurückzunehmen und Ihnen eine höherwertige Qualität zu liefern.

Bitte teilen Sie uns Ihre Wünsche mit.

Mit freundlichem Gruß

Anlage

 # Model Letter 9

Sehr geehrte Damen und Herren,

zum Ausgleich Ihrer Rechnung Nr. . . . vom . . . fügen wir einen Verrechnungsscheck über

DM / £ . . . .

bei.

Mit freundlichen Grüßen

Anlage

Model Letter 10

Ihre Rechnung Nr. . . . vom . . . .

Sehr geehrte Damen und Herren,

heute haben wir die XY-Bank gebeten, den Betrag von

DM / £

auf Ihr Konto Nr. . . . bei der XYZ-Bank zu überweisen.

Mit freundlichen Grüßen

 # Model Letter 11

1 Mahnung

Sicher haben Sie übersehen, daß unsere in Fotokopie beigefügte Rechnung noch nicht bis zu unserem Buchungsdatum (31.12.91) beglichen ist.

Wir bitten um kurzfristige Überweisung des Rechnungsbetrages auf unser Konto Nr. . . . . . bei XY Bank.

Mit freundlichen Grüßen

Anlage

Model Letter 12

---

2 Mahnung

Sehr geehrte Damen und Herren,

wir beziehen uns auf unsere Rechnung Nr. . . . vom . . . und auf unsere 1. Mahnung vom . . . .

Leider ist der Betrag bei uns noch nicht eingegangen. Wir bitten Sie deshalb, den offenen Rechnungsbetrag von

DM / £ . . .   bis zum . . .

zu begleichen.

Mit freundlichen Grüßen

 # Model Letter 13

Einschreiben

3 Mahnung

Rechnung Nr. . . . . . .

Sehr geehrte Damen und Herren,

Bei Durchsicht unserer Bücher müssen wir leider feststellen, daß trotz unserer Erinnerungen vom . . . . und vom . . . die obige Rechnung noch nicht von Ihnen beglichen wurde.

Sollte der Betrag von

DM / £ . . . .   bis zum . . . .

nicht bei uns eingegangen sein, sehen wir uns leider gezwungen, rechtliche Schritte einzuleiten.

Hochachtungsvoll

Model Letter 14

> <u>Streng vertraulich</u>
>
> Sehr geehrte Damen und Herren,
>
> mit der auf beigefügtem Blatt genannten Firma stehen wir bisher nicht in Geschäftsverbindung. Wir wären Ihnen daher sehr dankbar, wenn Sie uns Ihre Beurteilung der Bonität mitteilen würden.
>
> Wir versichern Ihnen, daß wir Ihre Auskunft streng vertraulich behandeln werden.
>
> Mit freundlichen Grüßen
>
> Anlage

 # Model Letter 15

> Tabellarischer Lebenslauf
>
> Familienname
>
> Vorname (n)
>
> Anschrift
>
> Tel. Nr.
>
> Geburtsdatum
>
> Geburtsort
>
> Nationalität
>
> Familienstand
>
> Schulausbildung/Abschluss
>
> Berufsausbildung/Berufsabschluss
>
> Zusätzliche Qualifikationen
>
> Referenzen

Model Letter 16

Lieber Herr Johnson,

wir würden uns freuen, Sie und Ihre Gattin auf unserem Empfang anläßlich unseres Firmenjubiläums

am 20. August, 1991, ab 11 Uhr

bei uns begrüßen zu können.

Wir bitten um kurze Antwort.

Mit freundlichen Grüßen

 # Model Letter 17

Lieber Herr Meier,

vielen Dank für Ihre Einladung zum Empfang am . . . . .

Meine Frau und ich haben uns darüber sehr gefreut und werden gerne kommen.

Mit freundlichem Grüß

 # Model Letter 18

Lieber Herr Meier,

meine Frau und ich haben uns über Ihre Einladung zum Empfang am . . . . sehr gefreut.

Leider sind wir an diesem Tage verhindert und können deshalb zu unserem großen Bedauern nicht teilnehmen.

Mit freundlichen Grüßen

Model Letter 18

Lieber Herr Schulte,

nachdem ich meine Geschäftsreise durch Deutschland beendet habe, bedanke ich mich auf diesem Wege noch einmal herzlich für die freundliche Aufnahme bei Ihnen und für Ihre Kooperation.

Der Besuch bei Ihnen war eine wertvolle Ergänzung meines Deutschlandaufenthaltes, und ich erinnere mich gerne an die anregenden Gespräche in Ihrer Firma. Auch meine Frau hat den Einkaufsbummel mit Ihrer Gattin sehr genossen.

Ich bedanke mich vielmals und würde mich über einen Gegenbesuch in Ramsgate sehr freuen.

Ihr

John S Miller

2

Abbreviations

AB	Ausführungsbestim-mungen	implementing regulations
Abb.	Abbildung	illustration
Abf.	Abfahrt	departure
Abk.	Abkürzung	abbreviation
Abs.	Absender	sender
Abt.	Abteilung	department
a.Ch.(n.)	ante Christum	before Christ, B.C.
a.D.	außer Dienst	retired
ADAC	Allg. Dt. Automobilclub	General Automobile Association of Germany

ADB	Allgemeine Deutsche Binnentransport-bedingungen	General Domestic Transport Conditions
Adr.	Adresse	address
ADS	Allgemeine Deutsche Seeversicherungs-bedingungen	General German Ocean Marine Insurance Conditions
ADSp	Allgemeine Deutsche Spediteurbedin-gungen	General German Forwarders' Conditions
AG	Aktiengesellschaft	German Stock Corporation
AGB	Allgemeine Geschäfts-bedingungen	Standard Terms and Conditions
AKA	Ausfuhrkredit-Gesellschaft	German Export Credit Company
allg.	allgemein	general
amtl.	amtlich	official
Anh.	Anhang	appendix
Ank.	Ankunft	arrival
Anl.	Anlage	enclosure
AO	Abgabenordnung	Federal Revenue Code
AR	Aufsichtsrat	Supervisory Board
Aufl.	Auflage	edition
Ausg.	Ausgabe	edition
AZ	Aktenzeichen	file number
b.w.	bitte wenden	please turn over
Bd.	Band	volume
BDI	Bundesverband der deutschen Industrie	Federation of German Industry
beil.	beiliegend	enclosed
Bem.	Bemerkung	note
bes.	besonders	special
betr.	betreff(end)	concerning
Betr.	Betreff	re
bfn	brutto für netto	gross for net
BGB	Bürgerliches Gesetzbuch	Civil Code
BGH	Bundesgerichtshof	Federal Supreme Court
Bhf.	Bahnhoff	station
BLZ	Bankleitzahl	bank sort code

BP	Deutsche Bundespost	Federal Post Office
BRD	Bundesrepublik Deutschland	Federal Republic of Germany
BSP	Bruttosozialprodukt	Gross National Product
bzgl.	bezüglich	with reference to
bzw.	beziehungsweise	respectively
C	Celsius	Celsius
ca	circa	approximately
Co.	Kompagnon/Kompanie	partner/company
CpD	Konto pro Diverse	Collective Suspense Account
d.h.	das heißt	that is, i.e., viz.
d.i.	das ist	that is, i.e.
d.J.	dieses Jahres	of this year
DB	Deutsche Bundesbahn	Federal German Railway
DBP	Deutsche Bundespost	Federal German Post
DDR	Deutsche Demokratische Republik	German Democratic Republic
DGB	Deutscher Gewerkschaftsbund	German Labour Federation
DIN	Deutsche Industrie-Norm	German Industrial Standard
DM	Deutsche Mark	Deutschmark(s)
Dr.	Doktor	Doctor
DRK	Deutsches Rotes Kreuz	German Red Cross
e.V.	eingetragener Verein	Registered Association
E.v.	Eingang vorbehalten	subject to collection
ebd.	ebenda	in the same place
EDV	elektronische Datenverarbeitung	electronic data processing
EG	Europäische Gemeinschaft	European Community
EIB	Europäische Investitionsbank	European Investment Bank
einschl.	einschließlich	including
Erw.	Erwachsene	adults
EST	Einkommensteuer	Income Tax

f	**femininum**	feminine
Fa.	**Firma**	firm
FD	**Fernschnellzug**	long-distance express
Forts.	**Fortsetzung**	continuation
Fr.	**Frau**	Mrs
frdl.	**freundlich**	kind
Frl.	**Fräulein**	Miss
GbR	**Gesellschaft bürgerlichen Rechts**	Civil Law Association
geb.	**geboren**	born
Gebr.	**Gebrüder**	brothers
gegr.	**gegründet**	founded
Ges.	**Gesellschaft**	society
Ges.	**Gesetz**	law
ges.gesch.	**gesetzlich geschützt**	registered
gesch.	**geschieden**	divorced
gez.	**gezeichnet**	signed
ggf.	**gegebenenfalls**	if necessary
GmbH	**Gesellschaft mit beschränkter Haftung**	limited-liability company
GTZ	**Gesellschaft für Technische Zusammenarbeit**	organization for technical assistance and development
HBF	**Hauptbahnhof**	main railway station
Herst.	**Hersteller**	manufacturer
HGB	**Handelsgesetzbuch**	commercial law code
Hr.	**Herr(n)**	Mr
hrsg.	**herausgegeben**	edited
HV	**Hauptversammlung**	shareholders' general meeting
i.A.	**im Auftrag**	by order of
i.J.	**im Jahr**	in the year
i.R.	**im Ruhestand**	retired
i.V.	**in Vertretung**	by proxy
Ing.	**Ingenieur**	engineer
Inh.	**Inhaber**	proprietor
inkl.	**inklusive**	inclusive

jr.	Junior	junior
Kap.	Kapitel	chapter
Kfm.	Kaufmann	merchant
Kfz.	Kraftfahrzeug	motor vehicle
KG	Kommanditgesellschaft	limited partnership
Kl.	Klasse	class
Kto.	Konto	account
KW/KFW	Kreditanstalt für Wiederaufbau	Federal Bank for Reconstruction
lfd.	laufend	current
Lfg.	Lieferung	delivery
LKW	Lastkraftwagen	lorry, truck
lt.	laut	according to
ltd.	leitend	managing
m.E.	meines Erachtens	in my opinion
MdB	Mitglied des Bundestages	member of the Bundestag
MdL	Mitglied des Landtages	member of the Landtag
MEZ	Mitteleuropäische Zeit	Central European Time
Ms.	Manuskript	Manuscript
mtl.	monatlich	monthly
MwSt	Mehrwertsteuer	value added tax, VAT
n	neutrum	neuter
n.Chr.G.	nach Christi Geburt	Anno Domini, A.D.
n.J.	nächsten Jahres	of next year
n.M.	nächsten Monats	of next month
Nachf.	Nachfolger	successor
OFH	Oberster Finanzgerichtshof	Federal Fiscal Court
p.Adr.	per Adresse	care of
p.p.,ppa.	per procura	by proxy
PA	Patentanmeldung	patent application
Pf.	Pfennig	penny
PKW	Personenkraftwagen	car

Abbreviations

Prof.	Professor	professor
PS	postscriptum	postscript
rd.	rund	roughly
Rel.	Religion	religion
resp.	respektive	respectively
s.	Seite	page
s.	siehe	see
s.o.	siehe oben	see above
s.R.	siehe Rückseite	see overleaf
s.u.	siehe unten	see below
SB	Selbstbedienung	self-service
sen.	Senior	senior
sog.	sogenannt	so-called
St.	Stück	piece
StGB	Strafgesetzbuch	penal code
StR	Steuerrecht	tax law
Str.	Straße	street
tägl.	täglich	daily
Tel.	Telefon	telephone
TH	Technische Hochschule	technical college
TU	Technische Universität	technical university
u.	und	and
u.a.	unter anderem	and others
u.A.w.g.	um Antwort wird gebeten	an answer is required (RSVP)
u.E.	unseres Erachtens	in our opinion
u.ff.	und folgende	and the following
u.U.	unter Umständen	circumstances permitting
urspr.	ursprünglich	originally
usf.	und so fort	and so forth
UST	Umsatzsteuer	turnover tax law
usw.	und so weiter	and so on
v.	von	of
v.Chr.	vor Christus	before Christ, B.C.
v.H.	von Hundert	per cent
Verf.	Verfasser	author

Verl.	Verlag	publishing firm
vgl.	vergleiche	compare
Vors.	Vorsitzende (r)	chairman, chairwoman
VP	Vollpension	full board
WEZ	Westeuropäische Zeit	Western European Time
WP	Wirtschaftsprüfer	Certified Public Accountant
Wwe	Witwe	widow
z.B.	zum Beispiel	for example
z.H.	zu Händen	attention of
z.T.	zum Teil	partly
z.Zt.	zur Zeit	for the time being, at present
Ztg.	Zeitung	newspaper
zus.	zusammen	together

3

Signs

Abfahrt	Departures
Abfall abladen verboten	No Tipping/Dumping
Abfälle	Litter
Achtung	Attention
Ampeln	Traffic Lights
Anklopfen	Knock (door)
Ankunft	Arrivals
Ausgang	Exit
Außer Betrieb	Out of Order
Ausverkauf	Sale
Ausverkauft	Sold Out
Bahnsteig	Platform
Besetzt	Engaged
Betreten verboten	No Trespassing

Bitte klingeln	Ring (the bell)
Bitte nicht stören	Do Not Disturb
Briefkasten	Letter-Box
Bürostunden	Office Hours
Damentoilette	Ladies/Ladies' Toilet
Drücken	Push
Durchfahrt verboten	No Through Road
Durchgangsverkehr	Through Traffic
Einbahnstrasse	One-way Street
Eingang	Entrance
Eingang/ausgang	Way In/Way Out
Eingang freihalten	Do Not Block Entrance/ Keep Clear
Eintreten ohne zu klopfen	Walk Straight In
Eintritt	Entry
Eintritt frei	Admission Free
Empfang	Reception
Erdgeschoß	Ground Floor
Erste Hilfe	First Aid
Erster Stock	First Floor
Erwachsene	Adults
Fahrkartenverkauf	Ticket Office
Fahrstuhl	Lift
Feuer	Fire
Frei	Vacant (toilets)
Fremdenführer	Tourist Guide
Frisch gestrichen	Wet Paint
Für Anlieger frei	Residents Only
Fundsachen	Lost Property
Fussgänger	Pedestrians
Garderobe	Cloakroom
Gebrauchsanweisung	Instructions for Use
Gefahr	Danger
Geöffnet von . . . bis . . .	Open from . . . to . . .
Gepäckaufbewahrung	Left Luggage
Gepäckträger	Porter
Gerade aus	Straight On

Geschlossen	Closed
Geschwindigkeitsbegrenzung	Speed Limit
Halt	Stop
Heiß	Hot
Herrentoilette	Men's Toilet
Höchstgeschwindigkeit	Maximum Speed
Im Obergeschoss	On the Top Floor
Informationsbüro	Information Office
Kalt	Cold
Kartenverkauf	Booking Office
Kasse	Cash Desk
Kassierer(in)	Cashier
Kein Eingang	No Entry
Kein Abfall	No Littering
Kein Trinkwasser	Not Drinking Water
Keine Zimmer Frei	No Vacancies
Krankenhaus	Hospital
Krankenwagen	Ambulance
Kreisverkehr	Roundabout
Kreuzung	Crossroads
Kundendienst	Customer Service
Lebensgefahr	Danger of Death
Leerung	Collection
Licht einschalten	Lights On
Liegewagen	Couchette
Lift/Fahrstuhl	Lift (elevator)
Links/rechts gehen (fahren)	Keep Left/Keep Right
Mehrwertsteuer	VAT (Value Added Tax)
Münzen einwerfen	Insert Coins
Münzrückgabe	Returned Coins
Nicht anfassen	Do Not Touch
Nicht Hinauslehnen	Do Not Lean Out
Nicht öffnen	Do Not Open
Notausgang	Emergency Exit
Notbremse	Emergency Brake

Oben	Upstairs
Öffentliche Toiletten	Public Conveniences
Öffentliches Telefon	Public Telephone
Öffnungszeiten	Opening Hours
Parken verboten	No Parking
Parkhochhaus	Multi-storey Car Park
Parkplatz	Car Park
Pension	Bed and Breakfast
Planmäßiger Flug	Scheduled Flight
Polizei	Police
Presse	Press
Privatweg	Private Road
Privatgrundstück	Private Land/Property
Rasen nicht betreten	Keep off the Grass
Rauchen verboten	No Smoking
Räumungsverkauf	Clearance Sale
Rechts abbiegen verboten	No Right Turn
Reisebüro	Travel Agency
Reserviert	Reserved
Rolltreppe	Escalator
Ruhetag	Closed all Day
Sackgasse	Dead End
Schlafwagen	Sleeper
Schliessfächer	Luggage Lockers
Schwimmen verboten	No Swimming
Selbstbedienung	Self-service
Sonderangebot	Special Offer
Speisesaal	Dining Room
Speisewagen	Dining Car
Strassenarbeiten	Roadworks
Taxi frei	For Hire
Tiefgeschoß	Basement
Toiletten	Toilets
Trinkwasser	Drinking Water
U-Bahn	Underground
Überwachter Parkplatz	Supervised Car Park

Umkleidekabine	Changing Room
Umleitung	Diversion
Unbefugten ist der zutritt verboten	No Admission for Unauthorized Persons
Unten	Downstairs
Verboten	Prohibited
Vermittlung	Operator
Volt	Voltage
Vorne einsteigen	Enter at the Front
Vorsicht	Caution
Vorsicht, zerbrechlich	Handle with Care
Vorsicht Hund	Beware of the Dog
Vorsicht Stufe	Mind the Step
Vorsicht vor den Zügen	Beware of Trains
Vorwahl	Dialling Code
Wartesaal	Waiting Room
WC	Toilet
Ziehen	Pull
Zimmer frei	Vacancies
Zoll	Customs
Zollfreie Waren	Nothing to Declare
Zollpflichtige Waren	Goods to Declare
Zutritt verboten	No Admission/Admittance
Zu den Bahnsteigen	To the Platforms
Zu verkaufen	For Sale
Zu vermieten	For Rent, To Let

4

Numbers

0	null	4	vier
1	eins	5	fünf
2	zwei	6	sechs
3	drei	7	sieben

8	acht	22	zweiundzwanzig
9	neun	23	dreiundzwanzig
10	zehn	30	dreißig
11	elf	40	vierzig
12	zwölf	50	fünfzig
13	dreizehn	60	sechzig
14	vierzehn	70	siebzig
15	fünfzehn	80	achtzig
16	sechszehn	90	neunzig
17	siebzehn	100	(ein) hundert
18	achtezehn	1,000	(ein) tausend
19	neunzehn	10,000	zehntausend
20	zwanzig	100,000	hunderttausend
21	einundzwanzig	1,000,000	eine Million

Please note:

137	einhundert(und)siebenunddreißig
9465 or 9.465	neuntausendvierhundert(und)fünfundsechzig ('und') between hundreds and tens may be omitted)

Decimal fractions: a comma is used rather than a point as in Britain. In German, 2.5 becomes 2,5.

Ordinal numbers:

1st	der/die/das erste	10th	zehnte
2nd	zweite	11th	elfte
3rd	dritte	12th	zwölfte
4th	vierte	13th	dreizehnte
5th	fünfte	20th	zwanzigste
6th	sechste	21st	einundzwanzigste
7th	siebte	22nd	zweiundzwanzigste
8th	achte	30th	dreißigste
9th	neunte	31st	einunddreißigste

5

Weights and Measures

Längenmaße/Lengths:

1 Kilometer	km	0.6214 miles
1 Meter	m	1.0936 yards
		3.2808 feet
		39.3701 inches
1 Zentimeter	cm	0.3937 inches
1 Millimeter	mm	0.0394 inches

Flächenmaße/Areas:

1 Quadratkilometer	km^2	0.3861 sq miles
1 Hektar	ha	0.0039 sq miles
1 Quadratmeter	m^2	1.1960 sq yards
		10.7639 sq feet
1 Quadratzentimeter	cm^2	0.1550 sq inches

Hohlmaße/Volumes:

1 Kubikmeter	m^3	1.3079 cu yards
		35.3148 cu feet
		219.9736 gal (imp)
1 Liter	1	0.2200 gal (imp)
		1.7596 pints

Gewichtsmaße/Weights:

1 Tonne 1000 kg	t	0.9843 ton
1 Kilogramm	kg	2.2046 pounds
1 Pfund 0,5 kg		1.1023 pounds
1 Gramm	g	0.0353 ounce
1 cwt		50.8 kg
1 pound		453.59 g
1 ounce		28.25g

Celsius and Fahrenheit:

In Germany temperatures are given in degrees Celsius (centigrade).

Celsius	−10	−5	0	10	21
Fahrenheit	−14	23	32	50	70

To convert Fahrenheit into Celsius, subtract 32, multiply by five and divide by nine.

6

Days of the Week, Months, Bank Holidays

Days of the week:

Monday	Montag
Tuesday	Dienstag
Wednesday	Mittwoch
Thursday	Donnerstag
Friday	Freitag
Saturday	Samstag/Sonnabend
Sunday	Sonntag

Months:

January	Januar
February	Februar
March	März
April	April
May	Mai
June	Juni
July	Juli
August	August
September	September
October	Oktober
November	November
December	Dezember

Seasons

spring	**Frühling**
summer	**Sommer**
autumn	**Herbst**
winter	**Winter**

Public holidays in Germany:

1 January	**Neujahr**	New Year's Day
1 May	**Tag der Arbeit**	May Day
3 October	**Tag der deutschen Einheit**	Unification Day
31 October	**Reformationstag** (northern Germany)	Reformation Day
1 November	**Allerheiligen** (Nordrhein-Westfalen and southern Germany)	All Saints' Day
25 December	**1. Weihnachtstag**	Christmas Day
26 December	**2. Weihnachstag**	Boxing Day

Movable Bank Holidays:

Karfreitag	Good Friday
Ostermontag	Easter Monday
Christi Himmelfahrt	Ascension Day
Pfingstmontag	Whit Monday
Fronleichnam (not in northern Germany)	Corpus Christi
Buß- und Bettag	Repentance Day
Rosenmontag	The day before Shrove Tuesday in regions in which carnival is celebrated, e.g. Aachen, Düsseldorf, Köln.

Of course, a calendar will also tell you the bank holidays.

7

Job Titles

Angestellte(r)	clerk
Anstreicher(in)	decorator
Anwendungs-programmierer(in)	computer applications programmer
Apotheker(in)	pharmacist
Archäologe(-in)	archeologist
Architekt(in)	architect
Archivar(in)	archivist
Arzt/Ärztin	doctor
Auktionator(in)	auctioneer
Ausbildungsleiter(in)	training manager(ess)
Bankangestellte(r)	bank clerk
Baugutachter(in)	surveyor
Bauingenieur(in)	civil engineer
Bausparkassenleiter(in)	building society manager(ess)
Bergbauingenieur(in)	mining engineer
Berufsberater(in)	careers officer
Betriebswirt(in)	business economist
Bibliothekar(in)	librarian
Biochemiker(in)	biochemist
Biologe(-in)	biologist
Börsenmakler(in)	stockbroker
Botaniker(in)	botanist
Brauer(in)	brewer
Buchhalter(in)	book-keeper/accountant
Chemieingenieur(in)	chemical engineer
Chemiker(in)	chemical scientist, chemist
Computer Wartungs-ingenieur(in)	computer maintenance engineer
Dachdecker(in)	roofer/thatcher
Dekorateur(in)	window-dresser
Designer(in)	designer
Direktor(in)	director/general manager(ess)
Dolmetscher(in)	interpreter

Einkäufer(in)	buyer/purchaser
Einkaufsleiter(in)	purchasing manager
Eisenbahner(in)	railwayman (-woman)
Elektriker(in)	electrician
Elektroingenieur(in)	electrical engineer
Elektronikingenieur(in)	electronic engineer
Empfangsdame, Empfangschef	receptionist
Fahrlehrer(in)	driving instructor
Fensterputzer(in)	window cleaner
Fertigungsingenieur(in)	production engineer
Florist(in)	florist
Flugzeugingenieur(in)	aircraft engineer
Forschungsassistent(in)	research assistant
Fotograf(in)	photographer
Friseur(in)	hairdresser
Führungskraft im Exportwesen	export executive
Gärtner(in)	gardener
Gastwirt(in)	publican
Geologe(-in)	geologist
Gepäckträger(in)	porter
Gerüstbauer	scaffolder
Geschäftsstellenleiter(in)	office manager
Glaser(in)	glazier
Grundstücksmakler(in)	property/estate agent
Hausmeister(in)	caretaker/janitor
Herausgeber(in)	editor
Hotelgeschäftsführer(in)	hotel/catering manager
Ingenieur(in)	engineer
Installateur(in)	plumber
Journalist(in)	journalist
Kellner(in)	waiter/waitress
Kfz-Mechaniker(in)	mechanic/mechanical engineer
Klempner(in)	plumber
Konstrukteur	construction engineer
Krankenpfleger	male nurse
Krankenschwester	nurse

Laborant(in)	laboratory technician
Lagerist(in)/	warehouseman (-woman)
Lagerverwalter(in)	
Lehrer(in)	teacher
Leiter(in)	manager(ess)
Markscheider	surveyor
Maschinenbauingenieur(in)	mechanical engineer
Mathematiker(in)	mathematician
Maurer(in)	bricklayer
Metallurge(in)	metallurgist
Meteorologe(-in)	meteorologist
Metzger(in)	slaughterman (-woman)/butcher
Monteur(in)	assembler/fitter
Müller(in)	miller
Nachrichten- und Fernmelde-	telecommunications technician
techniker(in)	
Optiker(in)	optician
Packer(in)	packer
Pflasterer(in)	plasterer
Physiker(in)	physicist
Pilot(in)	(airline) pilot
Politesse	traffic warden
Polizist(in)	policeman(woman)
Polsterer(in)	upholsterer
PR Angestellte(r)	public relations officer
Qualitätskontrolleur(in)	quality controller
Rechtsanwalt (-wältin)	solicitor/barrister/lawyer
Redakteur(in)	editor
Reisebürokaufmann (-frau)	travel agent
Rüstmechaniker(in)	rigger
Schaufenstergestalter(in)	display assistant
Schauspieler(in)	actor/actress
Schleifer(in)	grinder
Schmied(in)	blacksmith

Schneider(in)	tailor
Schweißer(in)	welder
Sozialarbeiter(in)	welfare and social worker
Sportlehrer(in)	sports coach
staatliche Krankenschwester	hospital community nurse
Städteplaner(in)	town planner
Stahlwerker(in)	steel worker
Statistiker(in)	statistician
Systemanalytiker(in)	systems analyst
Tapezierer(in)	decorator
Taxifahrer(in)	taxi driver
Techniker(in)	engineer
technische(r) Zeichner(in)	draughtsman (-woman)
Textiltechniker(in)	textile worker
Tierarzt (-ärztin)	veterinary surgeon
Trainer(in)	sports coach
Übersetzer(in)	translator
Uhrmacher(in)	watch and clock repairer
Verkaufsvertreter(in)	sales representative
Vermessungsingenieur(in)	surveyor
Vermessungstechniker(in)	survey technician
Versicherungsmakler(in)	insurance broker
Vertriebsberater(in)	marketing consultant
Vertriebsleiter(in)	marketing/sales manager(ess)
Verwaltungsleiter(in)	administration manager(ess)
Wartungsingenieur(in)	maintenance/service engineer
Wartungstechniker(in)	maintenance/service engineer
Werbeleiter(in)	advertising media executive
Werkzeugmacher(in)	toolmaker
Wirtschaftsprüfer(in)	chartered accountant
Wirtschaftswissenschaftler(in)	economist
Zahnarzt (-ärztin)	dental surgeon
Zahntechniker(in)	dental technician
Zoologe (-in)	zoologist

8

Information on the Single European Market

Europe
1 Population and GNP of EC States

Country	Population (millions)	GNP (billion ECU)
UK	56.8	565
Belgium	9.9	120
Denmark	5.1	90
France	55.6	740
Germany/West	61.0	970
Germany/East	16.0	100 (estimated)
Greece	10.0	40
Ireland	3.5	25
Italy	57.3	650
Luxembourg	0.4	5
Netherlands	14.7	185
Portugal	10.4	30
Spain	38.8	250
	339.5	3770
Comparison USA:	245.5	3870

Source: EC, Brussels

2 Trade between the UK and the European Community 1989 in million pounds

	Imports	Exports
TOTAL WORLD	120,788	93,249
Germany/West	20,005	11,110
Germany/East	169	106
France	10,785	9,462
Netherlands	9,586	6,515
Belgium and Luxembourg	5,701	4,873
Ireland	4,279	4,715
Italy	6,702	4,631
Spain	2,772	3,138
Denmark	2,229	1,209
Portugal	1,041	916
Greece	395	571
TOTAL EC	63,664	47,246
Comparison North America:	15,349	14,346

Source: DTI

EC countries/currencies/languages

Country	Language	Currency	Parity
			1 ECU corresponds to:
Belgien	Flämisch Französisch	Belg. Franc	43.0 FB
Dänemark	Dänisch	Dän. Krone	7.97 Dkr
Bundesrepublik Deutschland	Deutsch	Deutsche Mark	2.05 DM
England	Englisch	Pfund Sterling	0.706 £
Frankreich	Französisch	Französ. Franc	6.97 FF
Griechenland	Griechisch	Drachme	184 Drch
Holland	Holländisch	Holländ. Gulden	2.31 hfl
Irland	Englisch	Irisches Pfund	0.691 Ir£
Italien	Italienisch	Italien. Lira	1506 Lit
Luxemburg	Französisch	Luxemb. Franc	
Portugal	Portugiesisch	Escudo	176 esc
Spanien	Spanisch	Peseta	131 pst

If you have any questions on the Single European Market you can write to or phone various institutions, e.g. the Chambers of Commerce and Industry and:

Association of British Chambers of Commerce
9 Tufton Street
London SW1P 3QB
Tel. 071-222 1555

Deutscher Industrie- und Handelstag (DIHT)
(Association of German Chambers of Commerce and Industry)
Postfach 1446
Adenauerallee 148
D-5300 Bonn
Tel. 0228/1040

Euro-Chambers
B-1000 Brussels
Tel. 010-322.230 0038

Vertriebsdienst der internationalen
   Handelskammer
(Marketing Service of the International
   Chamber of Commerce)
Postfach 100447
Kolumbastraße 5
D-5000 Köln 1
Tel. 0221/213278

Bundesstelle für Außenhandels-
   Informationen
(Federal Office for Information on Foreign
   Trade)
Postfach 10 80 07
D-5000 Köln 1
Tel. 0221/2057-1
Telex 8 882 735 bfa d

as well as:

Department of Trade and Industry
1 Victoria Street
London SW1H 0ET
Tel. 071-210 3000

DTI HOTLINE
Tel. 071-2000 1992

Further addresses:

SME Task Force
200 rue de la Loi
B-1049 Brussels
Tel. 010-322-236 1676
Telex 61.655 BURAP B
Fax 010-322-236 1241

The SME Task Force was set up by the European Commission to help smaller and medium-sized businesses.

CBI
The Confederation of British Industries
Centre Point
103 New Oxford Street
London WC1A 1DU
Tel. 071-379 7400
Telex 21322

The Confederation of British Industries represents a large number
of branches of industry. It is able to provide a great deal of
material, especially on aspects of the Single European Market.

Commission of the European Communities
Brussels Office
200 rue de la Loi
B-1049 Brussels
Tel. 010-322-235 1111
Telex 21877

European Investment Bank
Head Office
100 bd. Konrad Adenauer
2950 Luxembourg
Tel. 010-352-43791
Telex 3530

Amt für amtliche Veröffentlichungen der
    EG
(Department of Official Publications of the
    European Community)
2 rue Mercier
2985 Luxembourg
Tel. 010-352-499281
Telex 1324 pubog lu

Europäisches Beratungszentrum der
    Deutschen Wirtschaft (EBZ)
(European Advice Centre of the German
    Economy)
Gustav-Heinemann-Ufer 84–88
D-5000 Köln 1

Tel. 0221/3708 621
Fax 0221/3708 730

Bundesverband des Deutschen Gross- und
  Aussenhandels e.V.
(Federal Association of Wholesale and
  Foreign Trade)
Kaiser-Friedrich-Str. 13
Postfach 1349
D-5300 Bonn 1
Tel. 0228/26004 0
Fax 0228/26004 55

Bundesverband der Deutschen Industrie
  e.V. BDI
(Federation of German Industries)
Gustav Heinemann Ufer 84–88
Postfach 51 05 48
D-5000 Köln 51
Tel. 0221/3708 00
Telex 8 882 601
Fax 0221/3708 73

Euro-Info-Centres in Great Britain:

Euro-Info-Centre
Birmingham Chamber of Industry and
  Commerce
75 Harbone Road
PO Box 360
Birmingham B15 3DH
Tel. 021-454 6171

Euro-Info-Centre
Scottish Development Agency
25 Bothwell Street
Glasgow G26 NR
Tel. 041-221 0999

Euro-Info-Centre
Department of Employment
Small Firms Services
Ebury Bridge House
2–18 Ebury Bridge Road
London SW1W 8QD
Tel. 071-730 8451

Ireland:

European Business Information Centre
Irish Export Board/Coras Trachtala
Merrion Hall
PO Box 203
Strand Road
Sandymount
Dublin 4
Tel. 010-353-1-6169 5011

Euro-Info-Centres are still being established. Please write to the following address for corrections and additions:

Jean-Pierre Haber
Commission of the European Community
GD XIII
200 rue de la Loi
B-1049 Brussels
Tel. 010-322-235 0538

There are a number of 'EG-Beratungsstellen' (EC Advice Centres) in Germany called 'Euroschalter' (Euro-Counters). They can be found at many Chambers of Industry and Commerce, at their association (Deutscher Industrie- und Handelstag, DIHI), at the German Trade Corporation Congress (Deutscher Handwerkskammertag) and at ZENIT (Centre for Innovation and Technology in North Rhine-Westfalia, Mülheim/Ruhr).

In view of the Single European Market, Eurocounters offer information and advice with regard to looking for new markets, and also advice on adapting company and marketing strategies.

Addresses of 'Euroschalter' (Euro-advice centres) in Germany:

EG-Beratungsstelle
Deutsches Institut für Normung
(German Institute for Standardization)
Postfach 1107
D-1000 Berlin 30

EG-Beratungsstelle
Deutscher Industrie- und Handelstag
(DIHT)
(Association of German Chambers of
Commerce and Industry)
Adenauerallee 148
D-5300 Bonn 1

EG-Beratungsstelle
Deutscher Handwerkskammertag (DHKT)
(Association of German Chambers of
Crafts/Trades)
Haus des Deutschen Handwerks
Johanniterstraße 1
D-5300 Bonn 1

EG-Beratungsstelle
Deutscher Sparkassen- und Giroverband
(Association of German Savings and
Clearing Banks)
Postfach 1429
D-5300 Bonn 1

EG-Beratungsstelle
Rationalisierungskuratorium der
Deutschen Wirtschaft (RKW)
(Board of Trustees for Rationalization of
the German Economy)
Heilwigstraße 33
D-2000 Hamburg 20

EG-Beratungsstelle
Bundesverband der Deutschen Industrie
(BDI)
(Federation of German Industries)
Gustav Heinemann Ufer 84–88
D-5000 Köln 51

EG-Beratungsstelle
Bundesstelle für
Außenhandelsinformationen (BFAI)
(Federal Office for Information on Foreign
Trade)
Postfach 10 80 07
D-5000 Köln 1

EG-Beratungsstelle
(Euro-Advice Centre)
Zenit
Dohne 54
D-4330 Mülheim/Ruhr
Tel. 0208/30004-21

**Exportleitstellen/Beratungsstellen für
Außenwirtschaft im Handwerk** (Central Offices for
Exports/Advice Centres of Crafts for Foreign Trade and
Investments):

Baden-Württemberg:
Exportberatungsstelle
Heilbronner Straße 43
D-7000 Stuttgart

Bayern:
Exportberatungsstelle
Sulzbacherstraße 11–15
D-8500 Nürnberg 20

Berlin:
Handwerkskammer/Abt.6

Nordrhein-Westfalen:
Landes-Gewerbeförderungs-
stelle

(Chamber of Crafts) Blücher-
straße

(Federal Office for the
Promotion of Trade/
Business)

Mehringdamm 15
D-1000 Berlin 61

Auf'm Tetelberg 7
D-4000 Düsseldorf 1

For further addresses please contact:

Deutscher Handwerkskammertag Referat
Außenwirtschaft
(Association of German Chambers of
Crafts Department of Foreign Trade)
Johanniterstraße 1
D-5300 Bonn 1
Tel. 0228/545-211/-276

Book Tips on the Single European Market:

Wegweiser zum EG-Binnenmarkt: Chancen und Risiken für die deutsche Wirtschaft (Prospects and risks for the German economy)

Guide to the EEC Internal Market

Stabile Währung für Europa
(Stable currency for Europe)

The above-mentioned titles can be obtained from:

Deutscher Industrie und Handelstag
Abteilung Information
(Association of German Chambers of
Industry and Commerce)
Postfach 1446
D-5300 Bonn

Forschungs- und Technologieförderung der EG: Ein Leitfaden für Antragssteller
(Promotion of research and technology by the EC: a manual for applicants)
(Kommission der Europäischen Gemeinschaften,
Generaldirektion XII)

Publications of Statistics
from various fields, e.g. foreign trade and industry, obtainable from:
Statistisches Amt der Europäischen Gemeinschaften:
(Office of Statistics of the European Communities)
Bâtiment Jean Monnet
rue Alcide de Gasperi
L-2920 Luxembourg

221

The Times Guide to 1992: Britain in a Europe without Frontiers
Richard Owen and Michael Dynes
(Times Books, London, 1989)

1992 – The Facts and Challenges
Catherine Taylor and Alison Press
(Industrial Society Press, London, 1989)

Completing the Internal Market of the European Community:
1992 Handbook
Mark Brealey and Conor Quigley
(Graham & Trotman, London, 1989)

Setting up a Company in Europe: A Country by Country Guide
Brebner & Co. International Solicitors
(Kogan Page, London)

1992: Strategies for the Single Market
James W. Dudley
(Kogan Page, London, 1989)

Die EG-Zwölf Wirtschaftslage 1989/90
(The EC-Twelve Economic Situation)
BfAI No. 27.001.90
Telex 8 882 735 bfa d

Free EC publications:

You can obtain EC publications free of charge from the press and
information offices of the EC Commission:

Great Britain:

> **Jean Monnet House**
> **8 Storey's Gate**
> **London SW1P 3AT**
> **Tel. 071-222 8122**

Windsor House
9–15 Bedford Street
Belfast BT2 7EG
Tel. 0232-240 708

4 Cathedral Road
Cardiff CF1 9SG
Tel. 0222-371 631

7 Alva Street
Edinburgh EH2 4PH
Tel. 031-226 4105

Ireland:

39 Molesworth Street
Dublin 2
Tel. 010-353-1-712 244

Germany:

Zitelmannstraße 22
D-5300 Bonn 1
Tel. 0228/53009 0
Telex 8 866 48
Fax 0228/53009 50

EC databanks:

Access to EC databanks is possible through:

Echo Customer Service
European Commission Host Organisation
BP 2373
177 Route d'Esch
L-1023 Luxembourg
Tel. 010-352-48804 1
Telex 2181 euro lu.
Fax 010-352-48804 0

Through ECHO, access to one of the most interesting databanks is possible:

> **TED**
> **(Tenders Electronics Daily)**
> **(Datenbankergänzung des Amtsblattes der EG)**
> **Übersicht über öffentliche Aufträge, Ausschreibungen und Ergänzungsverträge**
> **(Data Bank Supplement of the Official Gazette of the EC)**
> **(Survey of Public Contracts, Invitations to Tender and Supplemental Contracts)**

Access to large numbers of national and international data banks made available by:

> **GENIOS Wirtschaftsdatenbanken**
> **(GENIOS Economic Data Banks)**
> **Verlagsgruppe Handelsblatt**
> **Postfach 11 02**
> **Kasernenstraße 67**
> **D-4000 Düsseldorf 1**
> **Tel. 0211/887 1524**
>
> **BfAI Datenbanken**
> **(Federal Office for Information on Foreign Trade)**
> **Postfach 10 80 07**
> **D-5000 Köln 1**
> **Tel. 0221/2057-253**
> **Telex 8 882 735 bfa d**

9

Reference Libraries

The City Business Library
106 Fenchurch Street
London EC3M 5JB
Tel. 071-638 8215

Department of Trade and Industry
Libraries:
Ashdown House Library
123 Victoria Street
London SW1E 6RE
Tel. 071-212 0614

Headquarters Library
1 Victoria Street
London SW1H 0ET
Tel. 071-215 3124

Reference Library
London Chamber of Commerce and
Industry
69 Cannon Street
London EC4N 5AB
Tel. 071-248 4444

London Business School Library
Sussex Place
Regent's Park
London NW1 4SA
Tel. 071-262 5050

Statistics and Market Intelligence Library
1 Victoria Street
London SW1H 0ET
Tel. 071-215 7877

225

Europe and International Policy Group
Confederation of British Industry
Centre Point
103 New Oxford Street
London WC1A 1DU
Tel. 071–379 7400

(An interesting list of 'ICC Publications' is available.)

German Chamber of Industry and
Commerce in the UK
16 Buckingham Gate
London SW1E 6LB
Tel. 071-233 5656
Fax 071-233 7835
Telex 919442

Bibliothek des Instituts der deutschen
Wirtschaft (IW)
(Library of the Institute of the German
Economy)
Gustav Heinemann Ufer 84–88
D-5000 Köln
Tel. 0221/3708257

Bibliothek des Instituts für Internationale
Politik und Wirtschaft (IPW)
(Library of the Institute for International
Politics and Economy)
Clara Zetkin Straße 112
D-1020 Berlin
Tel. 040/2206215

Gesamtdeutsches Institut
(The All-German Institute)
Referat II 4 Bibliothek
Adenauerallee 10
D-5300 Bonn 1
Tel. 0228/207381
Fax 0228/207322
Telex 88 67 76

You can of course obtain information yourself from the reference libraries of German Chambers of Industry and Commerce in Germany.

10

Newspapers and Magazines

The following German newspapers and magazines are likely to be of interest to business people:

Börsenzeitung
Capital
Die Zeit
Frankfurter Allgemeine Zeitung (FAZ)
Handelsblatt
Manager
Wirtschaftswoche
Wirtschafts-Kurier

You may also find the following BfAI (Federal Office for Information on Foreign Trade) publications useful:

Der Binnenmarkt (NfA)
(The single market)

Nachrichten für Außenhandel
(Information and news for foreign trade)

Auslandsanfragen
(International inquiries)

Presseschau Außenwirtschaft-NfA
(Press reports foreign trade and investment)

Recht, Zoll und Verfahren (RVZ)
(Law, Customs and Procedures)

11

Useful UK Addresses for Part I

→1
**Market Research Society
175 Oxford Street
London W1R 1TA**

**European Marketing and Statistics
Euromonitor Publications
87–88 Turnmill Street
London EC1M 5QU**

→2
**Advertising Association
Abford House
15 Wilton House
London SW1V 1NJ**

**Institute of Practitioners in Advertising
44 Belgrave Square
London SW1**

→3
**British Telecom
Bureaufax International Centre
BTI Communication Centre
9 St Botolph Street
London EC3A 7DT**

The centre provides an extensive German/English and English/German translation service. Interpreters will be available to you when required.

→4
**British Exporters Association
16 Dartmouth Street
London SW1H 9BL**

**SITPRO
Simplification of International Trade
    Procedures
Almack House
26–28 King Street
London SW1Y 6QW**

Department of Trade and Industry
Export Initiative
1 Victoria Street
London SW1H 0ET

→5 Institute of Freight Forwarders Ltd
Redfern House
Browells Lane
Feltham
Middlesex TW13 7ET

Freight Transport Association
Hermes House
St John's Road
Tunbridge Wells
Kent TN4 9UZ

→6 Lloyds of London
51 Lime Street
London EC3M 7DQ

→7 British Institute of International and
Comparative Law
Charles Clore House
17 Russell Square
London WC1B 5DR

The Law Society
113 Chancery Lane
London WC2A 1PL

→8 German Chamber of Industry and
Commerce in the UK
16 Buckingham Gate
London SW1E 6LB

British Chamber of Commerce in Germany
Heumarkt 14
D-5000 Köln 1

12

The Federal States of Former West Germany and Some Useful Telephone Numbers in Major Western Cities

State	Area, km²	Inhabitants (31.12.1986)	Capital
Schleswig-Holstein	15,727	2,612,672	Kiel
Hamburg	755	1,571,267	Hamburg
Niedersachsen	47,439	7,196,127	Hannover
Bremen	404	654,170	Bremen
Nordrhein-Westfalen	34,068	16,676,501	Düsseldorf
Hessen	21,114	5,543,657	Wiesbaden
Rheinland-Pfalz	19,848	3,611,437	Mainz
Baden-Württemberg	35,751	9,326,780	Stuttgart
Bayern	70,552	11,026,135	München
Saarland	2,569	1,042,135	Saarbrücken
Berlin (West)	480	1,879,225	Berlin
Total	248,709	61,140,106	

Please note:

On 14 October 1990 five new federal states were established in the former GDR plus a united Berlin.

See also 'Information on the former GDR', Part III, 13.

Important telephone numbers of some German cities:

Berlin West	Vorwahl (code)	030
	Verkehrsamt (Tourist Information Office)	
	Europa-Center:	2134-4
	Flugauskunft (Airport Information Centre)	
	Tegel:	4101-2306

	Tempelhof:	6909-1
	Deutsche Bundesbahn:	
	(German Federal Railways)	19419
	IHK:	31510 0
	(Chamber of Industry and	
	Commerce)	
	Büroservice:	8015856
	(Office Services)	8827031
Bonn	Vorwahl	0228
	Verkehrsamt	
	Münster Straße 20:	773466
	Flughafenauskunft	
	Köln-Bonn:	02203/40-4001
		40-4002
	Deutsche Bundesbahn:	19419
	IHK:	2284-0
	Büroservice:	256281
		656599
		353107
Bremen	Vorwahl	0421
	Verkehrsverein	
	Hillmann Platz 6:	30800-0
	Flughafenauskunft:	5595-0
	Deutsche Bundesbahn:	19419
	Handelskammer:	3637-0
	Büroservice:	34 7064
		34 7053
		15208
Düsseldorf	Vorwahl	0211
	Verkehrsverein	
	Konrad-Audenauer-Platz:	350505
	Flughafenauskunft:	421-1
	Deutsche Bundesbahn:	19419
	IHK:	3557-0
	Büroservice:	7488139
		396081
		162790
		555790

Frankfurt/Main	Vorwahl	069
	Verkehrsamt	
	Gutleutstraße 7:	212-01
	Flughafenauskunft:	690-3051
	Deutsche Bundesbahn:	19419
	IHK:	2197-0
	Büroservice:	452010
		468485
		172056
Hamburg	Vorwahl	040
	Tourismus-Zentrale	
	Burchardstraße 14:	30051-0
	Flughafenauskunft:	508-0
	Deutsche Bundesbahn:	19419
	IHK:	36138-0
	Büroservice:	333058-88
		78942-222
		457781
		446277
Hannover	Vorwahl	0511
	Verkehrsverein	168-2047
	Friedrichswall 5:	-2319
	Flughafenauskunft:	7305-223
	Deutsche Bundesbahn:	19419
	IHK:	3107-0
	Büroservice:	282140
		669272
Köln	Vorwahl	0221
	Verkehrsamt	
	Am Dom 1:	221-3345
		40400-2
	Flughafenauskunft	
	Köln-Bonn:	02203/40400–1
		40400–2
	Deutsche Bundesbahn:	19419
	IHK:	1640-0
	Büroservice:	120099
		408392

Stuttgart	Vorwahl	0711
	Verkehrsverein	
	Lautenschlager Straße 3:	2228-0
	Flughafenauskunft:	7901-388
	Deutsche Bundesbahn:	19419
	IHK:	2005-0
	Büroservice:	840-548
		840-404
		841-259
München	Vorwahl	089
	Tourist-Information	
	Sendlinger Straße 1:	2391-1
	Flughafenauskunft:	9211-2127
	Deutsche Bundesbahn:	19419
	IHK:	5116-0
	Büroservice:	266078
		403000
		3154711
		391155

13

Information on the Former GDR ('Neue Bundesländer')

Below you will find information on the five new federal states ('die fünf neuen Bundesländer'), which were established on 14 October 1990.

The five new federal states (the former GDR):

State	Area in km²	Inhabitants (1989)	Capital
Mecklenburg–Vorpommern	23,838	1,963,909	Schwerin
Brandenburg	29,059	2,641,152	Potsdam
Sachsen-Anhalt	20,445	2,964,971	Magdeburg
Sachsen	18,337	4,900,675	Dresden
Thüringen	16,251	2,683,877	Erfurt
Berlin incl. Westberlin with 1,879,225 inhabitants	995	3,400,000	Berlin
		18,554,584	

The population of the FRG has thus increased by 16.7 million from 61.1 to 77.8 million.

General situation

It is typical of the present situation that services and information cannot be obtained easily; everything takes longer than one is accustomed to in the West.

Telecommunication

It is best to communicate by telex or telegram; getting through to the former GDR by phone is very difficult, since an efficient telephone network has yet to be set up. If you want to send a fax it is best to do so during the night when the lines are less congested.

Business contacts

For initial contacts it would be best to get in touch with the German Chamber of Industry and Commerce in your country and/or a branch of one of the more important German banks.

The KIS databank (Kammer Informations System) will be able to provide useful services. This Who's Who of German firms has been set up according to regions and products. A fee is charged for its use.

Your first local business contact should in any case be the Chamber of Industry and Commerce and/or the Chamber of Crafts. These Chambers are local/regional service centres providing detailed business information on their region.

The authors of this book consider it very important to point out that much in the former GDR is undergoing major changes. During this period there is likely to be a lot of improvising, and addresses and telephone numbers in particular may be subject to change.

Nevertheless, we think it sensible to name a number of offices and institutions you may wish to contact:

235

Addresses of organizations providing information

General political information:

Gesamtdeutsches Institut
(The All-German Institute)
Adenauer Allee 10
Postfach 1640
D-5300 Bonn 1
Tel: 0228/2070

General information and help for first contacts:

Deutscher Industrie- und Handelstag
  (DIHT)
(Association of German Chambers of
  Commerce and Industry)
Postfach 1446
D-5300 Bonn 1
Tel. 0228/104186
Fax 104158

Verbindungsstelle des DIHT in Berlin
(Liaison Office, Berlin)
Schönbergstraße 10/11
O-1110 Berlin
Tel. 037/2/ 4822117
      0161/ 7208790

Information about Assistance and Development programmes:

Bundesministerium für Wirtschaft
(Federal Ministry of Economic Affairs)
Villemombler Straße 76
D-5300 Bonn 1
Tel: 0228/615-3514/2372
Fax: 615-3822

Kreditanstalt für Wiederaufbau
(Bank for Restructuring)

Palmengartenstraße 5–9
6000 Frankfurt/Main
Tel: 069/74311

Berliner Industriebank
(Berlin Industrial Bank)
Landsbecker Straße 2
1000 Berlin 33
Tel: 030/820030

Deutsche Ausgleichsbank
Wielandstraße 4
D-5300 Bonn
Tel: 0228/8311

Niederlassung Berlin
Sarrazinstraße 11–15
1000 Berlin
Tel: 030/850850

Information on privatization

Treuhandanstalt
(In charge of deconcentration,
    restructuring and privatization of the
    former GDR trusts)
Alexanderplatz 6
O-1026 Berlin
Tel. 030/39071

Trade Fairs in Leipzig:

Leipziger Messeamt
(Leipzig Trade Fair Office)
O-7010 Leipzig
Tel. 037-41-7181 0
Telex 512294
Fax 037-41-7181 575

Chambers of Industry and Commerce in the former GDR (as of January 1991)

Berlin:
IHK Berlin
Hardenbergstraße 16–18
1000 Berlin 12
Tel: 030/315100
Fax 3180278

Chemnitz:
IHK Chemnitz
Straße der Nationen 25
O-9010 Chemnitz
Tel. 037-71-6823801
Fax 643018
Telex 06975465

Cottbus:
IHK Cottbus
Sandower Straße 23
O-7500 Cottbus
Tel. 037-59-24841/43
Telex 06917534

Dresden:
IHK Dresden
August-Bebel-Straße 48
O-8020 Dresden
Tel. 037-51-479547

Erfurt:
IHK Erfurt
Friedrich-List-Straße 36
O-5010 Erfurt
Tel. 037-61-3456/58
Fax 62105

Frankfurt/Oder:
IHK Frankfurt Oder
Humboldtstraße 3
O-1200 Frankfurt/Oder
Tel. 037-30-311412

Halle:
IHK Halle
Georg-Schumann-Platz 5
O-4020 Halle
Tel. 037-46-37991

Leipzig:	IHK Leipzig Friedrich-Engels-Platz 5 O-7022 Leipzig Tel. 037-41-7153438 Fax 037-41-51030 Telex 069512135
Magdeburg:	IHK Magdeburg Alter Markt 8 O-3010 Magdeburg Tel. 037-84-33951 Fax 344491
Neubrandenburg:	IHK Neubrandenburg Katharinenstraße 48 O-2000 Neubrandenburg Tel. 037-90-41101/41148
Potsdam:	IHK Potsdam Große Weinmeister Straße 59 O-1561 Potsdam Tel. 037-33-21591
Rostock:	IHK Rostock Ernst-Barlach-Straße 7 O-2500 Rostock Tel. 037-81-37501 Telex 06931254

Chambers of Crafts in the former GDR

Berlin:	Handwerkskammer der Stadt Berlin Ost (Chamber of Crafts of the Administrative Area of Berlin) Karlplatz 7 O-1040 Berlin Tel. 037-2-2805136
Chemnitz:	Handwerkskammer des Bezirkes Chemnitzes Aue 13 O-9010 Chemnitz Tel. 037-71-34944

239

Cottbus: **Handwerkskammer des Bezirkes Cottbus**
            Altmarkt 17
            O-7500 Cottbus
            Tel. 037-59-22031

Dresden: **Handwerkskammer des Bezirkes Dresden**
            Wiener Straße 43
            O-8020 Dresden
            Tel: 037-51-475981

Erfurt: **Handwerkskammer des Bezirkes Erfurt**
            Fischmarkt 13/16
            O-5010 Erfurt
            Tel. 037-61-51016

Frankfurt/Oder: **Handwerkskammer des Bezirkes**
                 Frankfurt/Oder
                 Bahnhofsstraße 12
                 O-1200 Frankfurt/Oder
                 Tel. 037-30-23665/325490

Halle: **Handwerkskammer des Bezirkes Halle**
            Gräfestraße 24
            O-4010 Halle (Saale)
            Tel. 037-46-37261

Leipzig: **Handwerkskammer des Bezirkes Leipzig**
            Lessingstraße 7
            O-7010 Leipzig
            Tel. 037-41-7691

Neubrandenburg: **Handwerkskammer des Bezirkes**
                 Neubrandenburg
                 Friedrich-Engels-Ring 11
                 O-2000 Neubrandenburg
                 Tel. 037-90-5131

Ostthüringen: **Handwerkskammer des Bezirkes Ostthüringen**
               Puschkinplatz 4
               O-6500 Gera
               Tel. 037-70-51003

Potsdam:	Handwerkskammer des Bezirkes Potsdam Wilhelm-Pieck-Straße 34–36 O-1561 Potsdam Tel. 037-33-4411
Rostock:	Handwerkskammer des Bezirkes Rostock August-Bebel-Straße 104 O-2500 Rostock Tel. 037-81-36191
Sachsen-Anhalt:	Handwerkskammer des Bezirkes Sachsen-Anhalt Humboldtstraße 16 O-3014 Magdeburg Tel. 037-91-31855/42308
Schwerin:	Handwerkskammer des Bezirkes Schwerin Friedensstraße 4a O-2754 Schwerin Tel. 037-84-5521
Südthüringen:	Handwerkskammer des Bezirkes Süthüringen Rosa Luxemburg Straße 9 O-6000 Suhl Tel. 037-66-20113

Book tips:

Wirschaftliche Hilfen für die bisherige DDR
(Economic aid programmes for the former GDR)
Published by
Bundesministerium für Wirtschaft
Villemomblerstraße 76
D-5300 Bonn 1

Innerdeutsche Wirtschaftsbeziehungen: Ansprechpartner für
Auskünfte und Beratungsdienste in der BRD und DDR
(Economic relationships between the two German States. Contacts
for information and advisory services in the FRG and GDR, general
information) obtainable from:
Gesamtdeutsches Institut Bonn, Tel: 0228/207236)

241

Mehr Kontakte mit der DDR: Eine Sammlung wichtiger Adressen von Unternehmen, Kammern, Bezirksräten und sonstigen zentralen Ansprechspartnern
(More contacts with the GDR: a collection of important addresses of companies, chambers, district councils and further offices to contact, as at January 1990), obtainable from:

> Industrie- und Handelskammer Nürnberg
> Hauptmarkt 25–27
> D-8500 Nürnberg
> Tel: 0911/1335396
> Telex 622144

Of course the reference libraries of the Chambers of Commerce and Industry and the reference library of the 'Gesamtdeutsches Institut' are also useful if you have any inquiries to make.

Databanks

DDR-Kooperationsbörse des DIHT
(GDR-cooperation exchange of DIHT)
(German Association of Chambers of Commerce and Industry)
Access through the German Chamber of Commerce in your country, via the DIHT or the new Chambers of Commerce and Industry in the new federal states.

Kammer-Info-System, KIS
presently under preparation in the new federal states. Access through the Chambers of Industry and Commerce in Germany and abroad.

DDR-Firmendatenbank
Informationen zu DDR-Firmen Adressen, Branchen, Eigentumsform
(Information on companies in the former GDR: addresses, lines of business, property)
Handelsblatt GmbH
Genios Wirtschaftsdatenbanken
Postfach 11 02
D-4000 Düsseldorf

DDR Kooperationsbörse:
Originalanfragen aus der DDR
(Direct inquiries from the former GDR)
Handelsblatt GmbH
Postfach 11 02
D-4000 Düsseldorf

BAO-DDR-Datenbank
Informationen über mehr als 3500 DDR Unternehmen, u.a. alle
ehemaligen Kombinate, Volkseigene Betriebe (VEB) und
Außenhandelsbetriebe)
(Information on more than 3500 companies in the GDR,
permanently being updated), obtainable from:
Berliner Absatz Organisation
(Berlin Sales Organization)
Hardenbergstr. 16–18
D-1000 Berlin
Tel. 030/31510 0
Fax 030/31510 316

Deutsche Bank-Datenbank 'DDR'
(Deutsche Bank-Databank 'GDR') is at your disposal at Deutsche
Bank branches.
– Electronic directory of suppliers with approximately 10,000
products
– Information on firms in the GDR: over (hitherto) 131 combines
and 2000 firms
– 'GDR' economic structure, regional data

Die Treuhandanstalt
is preparing a diskette containing information on the firms subject
to privatization and/or for which cooperation partners are being
sought.

Travel

If you are travelling to the former GDR by car, bear in mind that
the speed limit on the open road is 80 km/h, and 100 km/h on the
motorway.

On joining a motorway there will be no slip-road, and you are obliged to give way to vehicles already on the motorway.

At a roundabout the vehicle coming from the right has the right of way.

It is very important to remember that in the former GDR the legal alcohol limit is zero: 0.0 ml of alcohol per ml of blood.

These and other traffic regulations which differ from rules in the western Länder were expected to remain in force until the end of 1991.

The British and German automobile associations will be able to provide information concerning traffic regulations.

AA: Automobile Association
Tel: 081-954 7373

RAC: Royal Automobile Club
Tel: 081-686 2525

ADAC
Am Westpark 8
D-8000 München
Tel: 089/7676-1

AVD
Lyoner Str. 16
D-6000 Frankfurt/Main
Tel: 0611/66060

If you want to travel in the GDR you can book at various travel agencies in the FRG which are contracting partners of travel agencies in the former GDR.

The new Chambers of Industry and Commerce will inform you about regional travel agencies.

Addresses of 'western' travel agencies:

Deutscher Reisebüroverband e.V.
(Association of German Travel Agencies)
Mannheimer Straße 15
D-6000 Frankfurt/Main
Tel: 069/2739070
Fax: 069/236647

Reisebüro Hansa-Tourist GmbH
Hamburger Straße 132
D-2000 Hamburg 76

Olympia-Reisen GmbH
Friedrich Breuer Straße 86
D-5300 Bonn

American Express International
Filiale Frankfurt
Steinweg 5
D-6000 Frankfurt/Main
(also in Düsseldorf, Stuttgart, München)

Airtours International GmbH
in Stuttgart, Düsseldorf, München

They will also be willing to help you reserve a hotel room.

Book tips:

Restaurants und Gaststätten in der DDR
(Restaurants and Pubs/Inns in the GDR)
(Falken-Reise-Verlag)

27.500 Privatquartiere in der DDR
(27,500 possibilities of private accommodation in the GDR)
(Mairs Geographischer Verlag)

Reisen in die DDR: Informationsbroschüre
(Travelling in the GDR: information booklet) obtainable from:
Gesamtdeutsches Institut Bonn, Tel. 0228/207236

Reiseziel heute: DDR
Reiseführer mit Karten, touristischen Informationen und Reisetips
(Destination today: GDR.
Guidebook containing maps, tourist information and tips)
(BLV-Verlag)

Behördenbuch der DDR: Organe, Organisation, Institutionen . . .
(Authorities in the GDR: organs, organizations, institutions . . .)
Verlag R.S. Schulz
D-8130 Starnberg-Percha
Tel. 08151/1490
Fax 08151/14956

DDR 1990 Zahlen und Fakten
(GDR 1990: facts and figures)
Statistisches Bundesamt
Gustav Stresemann Ring 11
D-6200 Wiesbaden 1

DDR-Städte und Kreise Einwohnwerzahlen 1988
(GDR-Cities, Towns and Districts Population 1988)
Deutscher Industrie und Handelstag (DIHT)
Adenauerallee 148
D-5300 Bonn 1
Tel. 0228/1040

IW-Dossier Wo Ist Was?
in Brandenburg, Mecklenburg-Vorpommern, Sachsen,
Sachsen-Anhalt, Thüringen
(Where Is What in . . . .?)
Institut der Deutschen Wirtschaft, 1990
Postfach 510670
D-5000 Köln 51
Tel. 0221/3708/340

MERIAN-Hefte
(Booklets published by MERIAN on the new federal states, mainly
cultural and tourist background information)

14

Reference Books

Taschenbuch des öffentlichen Lebens Bundesrepublik Deutschland 1989/90
(Paperback of Public Life in the Federal Republic of Germany 1989/90)
Festland Verlag Bonn

Statistisches Jahrbuch für die Bundesrepublik
(Statistical Yearbook of the Federal Republic)
Statistisches Bundesamt
(Kohlhammer Verlag)

Handbuch der Großunternehmen
(Handbook of Large-scale Enterprises)
(Verlag Hoppenstedt und Co, Darmstadt–Brüssel–Wien–Zürich)
– alphabetical index of companies
– documentary information

Kompass: Deutschland
(KOMPASS: Germany: Register of selected German industry and commerce)
Kompass Deutschland Verlags- und Vertriebsges. mbH
Wilhelmstraße 1,
D-7800 Freiburg

Duns Europa
(35,000 leading companies in Europe)
Dun & Bradstreet International
High Wycombe
Buckinghamshire HP12 4UL
England

Wer gehört zu wem?
(A guide to capital links in West German companies)
Commerzbank, 1988
Neue Mainzer Straße 32–36
D-6000 Frankfurt/Main

Deutsches Börsenadreßbuch für Banken, Handel, Industrie
(German Exchange Directory for Banks, Trade, Industry)
Verlag Deutsches Börsenadreßbuch
D-2000 Hamburg

How to Approach the German Market
(information for exporters from abroad)
BfAI, 1988

Beim Staat Verkaufen
(information on tenders, granting and execution of contracts)
DIHT, 1981, German

Die Bundesrepublik Deutschland als Wirtschaftspartner
(legal regulations for establishing branch offices/subsidiaries)
BfAI, 1988, German, English

Die deutschen Zollvorschriften
(import and customs regulations, starting 1989)
BfAI, 1989, German

English Translations of German Standards 1988
Beuth Verlag, annually

Stamm, Leitfaden für Presse und Werbung
(addresses and advertising data for German/foreign periodicals)
Stamm Verlag, annually, introduction English

Waren und Märkte – Absatzwege für Konsumgüter in der BRD
(overview of distribution paths in the FRG)
DIHT, 1989, German, English

Meier's Adressbuch der Exporteure und Importeure
Meier-Dudy
Part I: Export/Import Merchants and Shippers in Europe
Part II: Firms Prominently Active in the Export and Overseas Trade
(Bankers, Insurance, Forwarding Contractors, etc.)
Part III: Classified Trade-Index and Display of Trade-marks

The German Export Directory (Germany Supplies)
Volume 1: products/sources of supply/selection terms

Volume 2: company documentation/nomenclature
BDI-Verlag W. Sachon GmbH
D-8948 Mindelheim

Wer liefert was?
(Who supplies what?)
Bezugsquellennachweis für den Einkauf
Postfach 10 05 49
D-2000 Hamburg 1

ABC der deutschen Wirtschaft: Ortslexikon für Wirtschaft und Verkehr
(ABC of the German economy: gazetteer for economy and transport)
Verlagsgesellschaft mbH
D-6100 Darmstadt
(firms are arranged alphabetically by town)

Spediteure-Transporteure: Wer fährt was wohin?
(forwarding agencies – carriers)
Verlag J. E. Hardenack

Hotel-Directory
Hotel Reservation Service (HRS)
Heumarkt 14
D-5000 Köln
Tel. 0221/20770
(14,000 hotels worldwide, 4,000 hotels online: BTX * 20 770 #)

Der große DAS Hotelführer: 12,000 Hotels in 3,000 Orten
(The Big DAS Hotel Guide)
Kartographischer Verlag Busche

Schlummer Atlas:
Hotelführer *(Hotel Guide)*
Kartographischer Verlag Busche

Hotels und Restaurants
Varta

Hotels und Restaurants
Michelin

Jaeger's Inter Travel
(World Guide to Travel Agencies, Tour Operators, Countries, Tours and Selected Hotels)
Jaeger-Verlag
D-6100 Darmstadt

Kursbuch:
Deutsche Bundesbahn (German Federal Railways Timetable)

APPENDIX

1

Pronunciation

a [ɑ]	short 'a' as in:	b<u>u</u>t	hat
a [ɑ:]	long 'a' as in	f<u>a</u>r	Haar
e [e]	short 'e' as in	l<u>e</u>t	fett
e [ə]	at the end of a word	<u>a</u>bove	hatte
e [e:]	long 'e' as in	l<u>a</u>te	steht
ä [ɛ]	short as in	m<u>e</u>t	hätte
ä [ɛ:]	long as in	<u>ai</u>r	. . . . .
i [ɪ]	short 'i' as in	f<u>i</u>t	bitte
i [i:]	long 'i' as in	t<u>ea</u>	viel
o [ɔ]	short 'o' as in	h<u>o</u>t	Topf
o [o:]	long 'o' as in	l<u>ow</u>	Not
o [o]			Phonetik
u [u]	short 'u' as in	p<u>u</u>t	Schutz
u [u:]	long 'u' as in	p<u>oo</u>l	gut
ü	pronounced like German 'i' with rounded lips		
	short: [ʏ]		Hütte
	long: [y:]		Lüge
ö	pronounced like German 'e' with rounded lips		
	short: [œ]		öffnen
	long: [ø]		höflich

Diphthongs:

ei/ai [ɑɪ]	as in	dr<u>y</u>	Wein, Main
au [ɑu]	as in	h<u>ow</u>	Frau
eu/äu [ɔʏ]	as in	b<u>oy</u>	Leute, Läufe
b [b]	as in	<u>b</u>us	Bus
[p]	at the end : pronounced as 'p'		ab
c [k]	as in	<u>c</u>offee	Cafe

[ts]	before e/i/ö/ü		**Circus**
ch [x]	as in	lo<u>ch</u>	**noch**
[ç]	as in	<u>H</u>ugh	**Milch**
	after i/e/r/l/n		
d [d]	as in	<u>d</u>oubt	**das**
[t]	at the end		**Rad**
f [f]	as in	<u>f</u>ive	**fünf**
g [g]	as in	<u>g</u>o	**gehen**
[k]	at the end		**Tag**
[ç]	at the end in syllables ending with -ig		**fleißig**
h [h]	as in	<u>h</u>am	**Heimat**
[:]	before 'h', vowels are long		**Kohlen**
j [j]	as in	<u>y</u>ou	**ja**
k [k]	as in	<u>c</u>offee	**Kaffee**
l [l]	as in	<u>l</u>ong	**lang**
	at the end of a word different from English		**Mehl**
m [m]	as in	<u>m</u>ine	**mein**
n [n]	as in	<u>n</u>o	**nein**
ng [ŋ]	as in	lo<u>ng</u>	**lang**
p [p]	as in	<u>p</u>lan	**Plan**
q [kv]	k plus v (as in veil)		**Quote**
r [r]	different from the English 'r', rolled in the throat		**rund**
s [z̧]	as in	<u>z</u>oo	**sehen**
	before a/e/i/o/u		
[s]	before consonants as in	<u>s</u>ing	**als**
[ʒ]	as in	plea<u>s</u>ure	**Garage**
[ʃp/ʃt]	sp and st		**spät/steht**
ß [s]	as in	<u>s</u>ing	**heiß**

sch [ʃ]	as in	s̲hout	**Schule**
v [f]	as in	f̲ool	**Vertrag**
w [v]	different from English, as in	v̲eal	**wann**
y [j]	as in	y̲et	**Joghurt**
[y:]	as German 'ü'		**Lyrik**
z [ts]	as in	it̲s̲	**Zaun**

2

English–German Listing of Technical Vocabulary with Phonetic Transcriptions

m masculine
f feminine
n neuter
pl plural

to accept an offer	**Angebot** *n* **annehmen**	'angəboːt' anneːmən
accepted in the trade	**handelsüblich**	'handəlsyːplɪç
accordance	**Übereinstimmung** *f*	yːbərˈaɪnʃtɪmuŋ
account	**Konto** *n*	'kɔnto
accountant, bookkeeper	**Buchhalter** *m*	'buːxhaltər
accounting, bookkeeping	**Buchhaltung** *f*	'buːxhaltuŋ
accruals	**Rückstellungen** *pl*	'rʏkʃtɛluŋən
acknowledgement of order	**Auftragsbestätigung** *f*	auftraːksbəˈʃtɛːtɪguŋ
to acquire a licence	**Lizenz** *f* **erwerben**	lɪ'tsɛnts ɛr'vɛrbən
acquisition	**Erwerb** *m*	ɛr'vɛrp
additional period of time	**Nachfrist** *f*	'naːxfrɪst
address	**Adresse** *f*	a'drɛsə
to adjust prices	**Preise** *pl* **ausgleichen**	'praɪzə 'ausglaɪçən
adjustment	**Regulierung** *f* **der Beschwerde** *f*	reguˈliːruŋ deːr bəˈʃveːrdə
administration expenses	**Verwaltungskosten** *pl*	fɛr'valtuŋskɔstən
advance, in . . .	**im voraus**	im 'foraus
advance order	**Vorausbestellung** *f*	fo'rausbəʃtɛluŋ
advance payment	**Vorauszahlung** *f*	fo'raustsaːluŋ
advertisement (printed)	**Zeitungsinserat** *n*	'tsaɪtuŋsɪnzəraːt
advertising	**Werbung** *f*	'vɛrbuŋ
advertising gift, gimmick	**Werbegeschenk** *n*	'vɛrbəgəʃɛŋk
to advise	**anweisen, empfehlen**	'anvaɪzən, ɛm'pfeːlən
affidavit	**eidesstattliche Erklärung** *f*	'aɪdəsʃtatliçə ɛr'klɛːruŋ
after-sales service	**Kundendienst** *m*	'kundəndiːnst

255

after-tax profit	**Gewinn** *m* **nach Steuern** *pl*	gə'vɪn nɑːx 'ʃtɔyərn
agenda	**Tagesordnung** *f*	'tɑːgəsɔrdnuŋ
agent, representative	**Vertreter** *m*	fɛr'treːtər
agreement	**Vereinbarung** *f*	fɛr'aɪnbaːruŋ
air cargo, airfreight	**Luftfracht** *f*	'luftfraxt
air transport	**Lufttransport** *m*	lufttranspɔrt
air waybill	**Luftfrachtbrief** *m*	'luftfraxtbriːf
all-in costs	**Gesamtkosten** *pl*	gə'zamtkɔstən
all-in price	**Preis** *m* **alles inbegriffen**	praɪs 'aləs 'ɪnbəgrɪfən
to allow a claim	**Beschwerde** *f* **anerkennen**	bə'ʃveirdə 'anɛrkɛnən
to amend a contract	**Vertrag** *m* **ändern**	fɛr'traːk 'ɛndərn
amortization instalment	**Tilgungsrate** *f*	'tɪlguŋsraːtə
amount overdue	**überfälliger Betrag** *m*	'yːbərfɛlɪgər bə'traːk
annual financial statement	**Jahresabschluß** *m*	'jaːrəsapʃlus
annual general meeting of the shareholders	**Jahreshauptversammlung** *f*	'jaːrəs'hauptfɛr'zamluŋ
annual report	**Geschäftsbericht** *m*	gə'ʃɛftsbə'rɪçt
application	**Anmeldung** *f*, **Bewerbung** *f*	'anmɛlduŋ, bə'vɛrbuŋ
to apply for	**sich bewerben um**	zɪç bə'vɛrbən um
to apply for space (at a fair)	**anmelden (zu einer Messe** *f***)**	'anmɛldən (tsu: 'aɪnər mɛsə)
to apply for the patent	**Patent** *n* **anmelden**	pa'tent 'anmɛldən
to appreciate	**zu schätzen wissen, dankbar sein für**	tsu: 'ʃɛtsən 'vɪsən, 'daŋkbaːr zaɪn fyːr
apprentice	**Lehrling** *m*, **Azubi** *m/f*	'leːrlɪŋ, 'atsuːbi:
arrears	**rückständige Beträge** *pl*	'rykʃtɛndɪgə bə'trɛgə
as per contract	**laut Vertrag** *m*	laut fɛr'traːk
as per invoice	**laut Rechnung** *f*	laut 'rɛçnuŋ
as per your order, in accordance with your order	**laut Ihrer Bestellung** *f*	laut 'iːrər bə'ʃtɛluŋ
assembly	**Montage** *f*	mɔn'taːʒə,
assembly instruction	**Montageanleitung** *f*	mɔn'taːʒə'anlaɪtuŋ
assembly line	**Fließband** *n*	'fliːsbant
assembly line production	**Fließfertigung** *f*	fliːsfertɪguŋ

asset deal	Kauf *m* der Einzelwirtschafts- güter *pl* der Zielgesellschaft *f*	kauf der 'aıntsəl- 'vırtʃaftsgy:tər der 'tsi:lgəzelʃaft
assets	Aktiva *pl*	ak'ti:va
assignment of a debt	Forderungsabtretung *f*	'fordəruŋs'aptre:tuŋ
at cost	zum Selbstkostenpreis *m*	tsum 'zelpstkɔstən- praıs
at half price	zum halben Preis *m*	tsum 'halbən praıs
at your/our expense	auf Ihre/unsere Kosten *pl*	auf 'i:rə/'unzərə 'kɔstən
attached	beigefügt	'baıgəfy:kt
attachment	Pfändung *f*	'pfɛnduŋ
to attend a conference	an einer Konferenz *f* teilnehmen	an 'aınər kɔnfə'rɛnts 'taılne:mən
auditing	Prüfungswesen *n*	'pryfuŋsve:zən
bad debt	uneinbringliche Forderung *f*	unaın'brıŋlıçə 'fordəruŋ
bag, sack	Sack *m*	zak
balance	Saldo *m*	'zaldo
to balance an account	Konto *n* ausgleichen	'kɔnto 'ausglaıçən
balance sheet	Bilanz *f*	bı'lants
bankruptcy, liquidation	Konkurs *m*	kɔn'kurs
to bargain	handeln, feilschen	'handəln, 'faılʃən
barrel	Faß *n*	fas
to beat prices	Preise *pl* unterbieten	'praızə untər'bi:tən
to become contractual	vertraglich festschreiben	fer'tra:klıç 'festʃraıbən
beneficiary	Begünstigter *m*	bə'gynstiktər
to bill, to invoice	berechnen	bə'rɛçnən
Bill of Exchange (B/E)	Wechsel *m*	'vɛksəl
Bill of Lading (B/L)	Konnossement *n*	kɔnɔsə'mɛnt
bill overdue	überfälliger Wechsel *m*	'y:bərfɛlıgər 'vɛksəl
blank, space	Leerstelle *f*, Füllzeichen *n*	'le:rʃtɛlə, 'fʏltsaıçən
blend (coffee, tea)	Mischung *f* (Kaffee *m*, Tee *m*)	'mıʃuŋ (ka'fe:, te:)
to book, to enter an order	buchen	'bu:xən
to book exhibition space	Ausstellungsfläche *f* mieten	'ausʃtɛluŋsflɛçə 'mi:tən

to book in conformity	gleichlautend buchen	'glaɪçlautənt 'buːxən
book value	Buchwert *m*	'buːxveːrt
bookings	Auftragseingänge *pl*	'auftraːksaɪngeːŋə
bookkeeper, accountant	Buchhalter *m*	'buːxhaltər
bookkeeping, accounting	Buchhaltung *f*	'buːxhaltuŋ
booth	Messestand *m*	'mɛsəʃtant
borrowed capital	Fremdkapital *n*	'frɛmtkapɪtaːl
boss	Chef *m*	tʃɛf
to bounce	platzen (Scheck *m*)	'platsən
branch	Zweigniederlassung *f*, Filiale *f*	'tsvaɪkniːdərlasuŋ, fɪlɪ'aːlə
brand	Marke *f*	'markə
to bring an action against somebody	Klage *f* einreichen gegen	'klaːgə 'aɪnraɪçən geːgən
to bring forward a motion	Antrag *m* stellen	'antraːk 'ʃtɛlən
brochure, leaflet	Broschüre *f*	brɔ:'ʃyːrə
brought forward (b/f)	Übertrag *m*	'yːbərtraːk
budgetary accounting	Finanzplanung *f*	fɪ'nantsplaːnuŋ
bulk goods	Massengüter *pl*	'masəngyːtər
bulk haulage	Massengütertransport *m*	'masəngyːtərtrans'pɔrt
business, company firm	Firma *f*	'fɪrma
business, to do	Geschäfte *pl* tätigen	gə'ʃɛftə 'tɛːtɪgən
business development	Geschäftsentwicklung *f*	gə'ʃɛftsɛnt'vɪkluŋ
business letter	Geschäftsbrief *m*	gə'ʃɛftsbriːf
business partnerships	Geschäftsbeteiligungen *pl*	gə'ʃɛftsbə'taɪlɪguŋən
business reply	Werbeantwort *f*	'vɛrbəantvɔrt
business reputation	geschäftlicher Ruf *m*	gə'ʃɛftlɪçə ruːf
to buy, to purchase	kaufen	'kaufən
buyer	Käufer *m*	'kɔyfər
buying conditions	Einkaufsbedingungen *pl*	'aɪnkaufsbədɪŋuŋən
c/o (care of)	per Adresse *f*	per a'drɛsə
cable connection	Kabelanschluß *m*	kabəl'anʃlus
to calculate	rechnen	'rɛçnən
calculation	Kalkulation *f*	kalkulatsɪ'oːn
calculator (pocket-)	Rechner *m* (Taschen-)	'rɛçnər ('taʃən-)
call-money	Tagesgeld *n*	'taːgəsgɛlt

can, metal container	Kanister *m*	kɑ'nɪstər
to cancel	stornieren	ʃtɔr'ni:rən
to cancel a contract	Vertrag *m* stornieren, kündigen	fɛr'trɑ:k ʃtɔr'ni:rən, 'kʏndɪgən
capacity usage ratio	Ausnutzungsgrad *n*	'ausnutsuŋsgrɑ:t
capital gains tax	Kapitalertragssteuer *f*	kɑpɪ'tɑlɛr'trɑ:ks'ʃtɔyər
capital goods	Investitionsgüter *pl*	ɪnvɛstɪtsɪ'o:nsgy:tər
capital structure	Kapitalverhältnisse *pl*	kɑpɪ'tɑ:lfɛr'hɛltnɪsə
cardboard box, carton	Schachtel *f*	'ʃɑxtəl
cargo, carriage, freight	Fracht *f*	frɑxt
carriage	Gütertransport *m*, Anfuhr *f*, Abfuhr *f*	'gy:tərtrɑnspɔrt, 'ɑnfu:r, 'ɑpfu:r
carrier, forwarder	Spediteur *m*	ʃpedɪ'tø:r
to carry a motion	Antrag *m* durchbringen	'ɑntrɑ:k 'durçbrɪŋən
carry forward (the balance)	vortragen (Saldo *m*)	'fo:rtrɑ:gən
carry over	Übertrag *m*	'y:bərtrɑ:k
case	Kiste *f*	'kɪstə
cash against documents (CAD), documents against payment (D/P)	Kasse *f* gegen Dokumente *pl*	'kɑsə 'ge:gən doku'mɛntə
cash discount	Barzahlungsrabatt *m*	'bɑ:rtsɑ:luŋsrɑ'bɑt
cash flow	Finanzmittelfluß *m*	fɪ'nɑntsmɪtəlflus
cash on delivery (COD)	Nachnahme *f*	nɑxnɑ:mə
cash with order (CWO)	Barzahlung *f* bei Auftragserteilung *f*	'bɑ:rtsɑ:luŋ baɪ auftrɑ:ksɛr'taɪluŋ
catalogue	Katalog *m*	kɑtɑ'lo:k
central processing unit (CPU)	Zentraleinheit *f*	tsɛn'trɑ:laɪnhaɪt
to certify	bescheinigen	bə'ʃaɪnɪgən
to certify a contract	Vertrag *m* beglaubigen	fɛr'trɑ:k bə'glaubɪgən
chairman	Generaldirektor *m*	gene'rɑ:ldɪrɛktor
chairperson	Vorsitzende(r) *f/m*	'fo:rzɪtsəndə(r)
to charge	berechnen, belasten	bə'reçnən, bə'lɑstən
charge, fee	Gebühr *f*	gə'by:r
chartered accountant	Wirtschaftsprüfer *m*	'vɪrtʃaftspry:fər
church tax	Kirchensteuer *f*	'kɪrçənʃtɔyər
circular	Rundschreiben *n*	'runtʃraɪbən
circumstances beyond our control	unvorhersehbare Umstände *pl*	unfo:r'he:rʒe:bɑ:rə 'umʃtɛmdə

claim, debt	Anspruch m,	'anʃprux,
	Schadensfall m,	'ʃɑːdənsfal,
	Forderung f	'fɔrdəruŋ
classifications	Klassifizierungen pl	klɑsɪfɪ'tsiːruŋən
clerk	kaufmännische	'kaufmɛnɪʃə
	Angestellte(r) f/m	'angəʃtɛltə(r)
to close an account	Konto n schließen	'kɔnto 'ʃliːsən
to close the meeting	Sitzung f schließen	'zitsuŋ 'ʃliːsən
co-determination	Mitbestimmung	'mitbəʃtimuŋ
collection agency	Inkassobüro n	ɪn'kɑsobyro
commercial	Werbesendung f	'vɛrbəzɛnduŋ
commercial invoice	Handelsrechnung f	'handəlsrɛçnuŋ
commercial quality	handelsübliche	'handəlsyːplɪçə
	Qualität f	kvalɪ'tɛːt
commercial settlement	Streitfall-	'ʃtraɪtfalrɛːgəluŋ
of a dispute	regelung f	
commission	Provision f	provɪzɪ'oːn
commission agent	Kommissionär m,	kɔmɪsɪo'nɛːr,
	Zwischenhändler m	'tsvɪʃənhɛndlər
commodity, goods,	Güter pl, Ware f,	'gyːtər, 'vaːrə,
merchandise	Handelsware f	'handəlsvaːrə
common market	Gemeinsamer Markt m	gə'maɪnzamər markt
communication line	Datenübertragungs-	'daːtəny:bərtraːguŋs-
	leitung f	laituŋ
Community Transport	Gemeinschaftliches	gə'maɪnʃaftlɪçəs
Procedure (CTP)	Versandverfahren n	fɛr'zantfɛrfaːrən
company, firm,	Firma f	firma
business		
to compel	zwingen, nötigen	'tsvingən, 'nøtɪgən
to compensate	entschädigen	ɛnt'ʃɛːdɪgən
compensation	Schadenersatz m	'ʃaːdənɛrzats
to compete	konkurrieren	kɔnku'riːrən
competition	Konkurrenz f	kɔnku'rɛnts
competitive price	konkurrenzfähiger	kɔnku'rɛntsfɛːɪgər
	Preis m	praɪs
competitor	Konkurrent m	kɔnku'rɛnt
to complain about	sich beschweren über	zɪç bə'ʃvɛːrən yːbər
complaint	Beschwerde f,	bə'ʃvɛːrdə,
	Mängelrüge f	'mɛŋəlryːgə
composition	Vergleich m (Konkurs-)	fɛr'glaɪç (kɔn'kurs-)
compound interest	Zinseszins m	'tsɪnzəstsɪns
compromise	Vergleich m (gütlicher)	fɛr'glaɪç (gyːtlɪçər)
compulsory sale	Zwangsverkauf m	'tsvaŋsfɛr'kauf
concern, group	Konzern m	kɔn'tsɛrn
concerning	betreffend, wegen	bə'trɛfənt, 've:gən

conditions, terms	**Bedingungen** *pl*	bə'dɪŋuŋən
conditions of participation	**Teilnahmebedin- gungen** *pl*	taɪlnɑːməbə'dɪŋuŋən
conference	**Konferenz** *f*	kɔnfə 'rɛnts
consignee	**Empfänger** *m* **einer Sendung** *f*	ɛm'pfɛŋər aɪnər 'zenduŋ
consignment note, waybill	**Frachtbrief** *m*	'fraxtbriːf
consignment, shipment	**Warensendung** *f*	'vɑːrənzenduŋ
consignor, shipper	**Absender** *m* **einer Sendung** *f*	'apzɛndər aɪnər 'zenduŋ
consortium	**Konsortium** *n*	kɔn'zɔrtɪum
to constitute a quorum	**beschlußfähig sein**	bə'ʃlusfɛːɪç zaɪn
consular invoice	**Konsularrechnung** *f*	kɔnsu'lɑːrreçnuŋ
consumer goods	**Verbrauchsgüter** *pl*	fɛr'brauxsgyːtər
consumer price	**Verbraucherpreis** *m*	fɛr'brauxərpraɪs
container	**Container** *m*	kɔn'teːnər
to contract, to enter into a contract	**Vertrag** *m* **abschließen**	fɛr'trɑːk 'apʃliːsən
contract clause	**Vertragsklausel** *f*	fɛr'trɑːksklauzəl
the contract expires	**Vertrag** *m* **läuft ab**	fɛr'trɑːk lɔyft ap
the contract is null and void	**Vertrag** *m* **ist null und nichtig**	fɛr'trɑːk ɪst nul unt nɪçtɪç
contract of employment	**Anstellungsvertrag** *m*	'anʃteluŋsfɛrtrɑːk
contract of sale	**Kaufvertrag** *m*	kauffɛr'trɑːk
contracting parties	**vertragsschließende Parteien** *pl*	fɛr'trɑːkʃliːsəndə par'taɪən
contractors, suppliers	**Lieferfirma** *f*	'liːfərfɪrma
to control	**überwachen**	yːbər'vaxən
convenience, at your convenience	**möglichst bald**	'møːklɪçst balt
co-operation	**Zusammenarbeit** *f*	tsu'zamənɑːrbaɪt
corporation tax	**Körperschaftssteuer** *f*	'kœrpərʃaftsʃtɔyər
cost effective	**kostenwirksam**	'kɔstənvɪrkzɑːm
cost price	**Selbstkostenpreis** *m*	'zɛlpstkɔstənpraɪs
cost-covering	**kostendeckend**	'kɔstəndɛkənt
cost-free, free of charge	**kostenlos**	'kɔstenloːs
costs	**Kosten** *pl*	'kɔstən
country of destination	**Bestimmungsland** *n*	bə'ʃtɪmuŋslant
courtesy	**Gefälligkeit** *f*, **Freundlichkeit** *f*	gə'fɛlɪçkaɪt, 'frɔyntlɪçkaɪt
to cover a risk	**Risiko** *n* **abdecken**	'riːzɪko apdɛkən

261

coverage	**Deckung** f	'dɛkuŋ
crate	**Lattenkiste** f	'latənkɪstə
to credit	**Gutschrift f erstellen**	'gu:tʃrɪft ɛr'ʃtɛlən
credit, short-term/ medium-term/long- term	**kurz-/mittel-/ langfristiger Kredit** m	'kurts-/'mɪtəl-/ 'laŋfrɪstɪgər kre'di:t
credit inquiry	**Auskunftseinholung** f	'auskunftsaɪnho:luŋ
credit insurance	**Kreditversicherung** f	kre'di:tfɛrzɪçəruŋ
credit note	**Gutschriftsanzeige** f	'gu:tʃrɪftsantsaɪgə
credit standing	**Kreditwürdigkeit** f	kre'di:tvʏrdɪçkaɪt
creditor	**Gläubiger** m	'glɔʏbɪgər
current account	**laufendes Konto** n	'laufəndəs 'kɔnto
current assets	**Umlaufvermögen** n	'umlauffɛrmø:gən
curriculum vitae	**Lebenslauf** m	'le:bənslauf
customer	**Kunde** m	'kundə
daisy wheel	**Typenrad** n, **Schreibrad** n	'ty:pənrat, 'ʃraɪpra:t
damage	**Schaden** m	'ʃa:dən
data base	**Datenbank** f	'da:tənbaŋk
data transfer	**Datenaustausch** m	'da:tənaustauʃ
date of invoice	**Rechnungsdatum** n	'rɛçnuŋsda:tum
date of shipment	**Versanddatum** n	fɛr 'zantda:tum
deadline	**Lieferfrist** f, **Endtermin** m	'li:fərfrɪst, 'enttɛrmi:n
deadlines	**Vertragsfristen** pl **für Leistungen** pl	fɛr'tra:ksfrɪstən fy:r 'laɪstuŋən
debit note	**Lastschriftsanzeige** f	'lastʃrɪftsantsaɪgə
debt, claim	**Forderung** f	fɔrdəruŋ
debtor	**Schuldner** m	'ʃultnər
to decide on a motion	**über einen Antrag** m **entscheiden**	y:bər aɪnən 'antra:k ɛnt 'ʃaɪdən
defect	**Mangel** m, **Defekt** m	'maŋəl, de'fɛkt
defective goods	**mangelhafte Ware** f	'maŋəlhaftə 'va:re
delay	**Verzögerung** f	fɛr'tsø:gəruŋ
to deliver	**ausliefern, zustellen**	'ausli:fərn, 'tsu:ʃtɛlən
to deliver within the specified time	**liefern, innerhalb der Lieferzeit** f	'li:fərn, 'ɪnərhalp de:r 'li:fərtsaɪt
delivery	**Lieferung** f	'li:fəruŋ
delivery note	**Lieferschein** m	'li:fərʃaɪn
demand	**Nachfrage** f	'na:xfra:gə
to demand compensation	**Schadenersatz** m **verlangen**	'ʃa:dənɛrzats fɛr'laŋən
to demand payment	**zur Zahlung** f **auffordern**	tsu:r 'tsa:luŋ 'auffɔrdərn

demonstration	**Vorführung**	'foːrfyːruŋ
density	**Speicherdichte** f	'ʃpaɪçərdɪçtə
deposit, savings account	**Sparkonto**	'ʃpaːrkɔnto
depreciations	**Abschreibungen** pl	'apʃraɪbuŋən
detailed information about	**ausführliche Informationen** pl **über**	'ausfyːrlɪçə ɪnfɔrmatsɪ'oːnən yːbər
development of a product	**Entwicklungstätigkeit** f	ɛnt'vɪkluŋstɛːtɪçkaɪt
development (of business), growth	**Geschäftsentwicklung** f	gə'ʃɛftsɛntvɪkluŋ
direct labour	**Fertigungslöhne** pl	'fɛrtɪguŋsløːnə
direct material	**Fertigungsmaterial** n	'fɛrtɪguŋsmateri'aːl
direct memory access	**direkter Zugriff** m	dɪ'rɛktər 'tsuːgrɪf
discount	**Skonto** n, **Rabatt** m	'skɔnto, ra'batt
discount rate	**Diskontsatz** m	dɪs'kɔn't zats
disk	**Diskette** f	dɪs'kɛtə
disk operating system (DOS)	**Plattenbetriebssystem** n	'platənbətriːpszys'teːm
disk storage	**Magnetplattenspeicher** m	ma'gneːtplatənʃpaɪçər
to dismantle a stand	**Stand** m **abbauen**	ʃtant 'apbauən
dismissal	**Entlassung** f	ɛnt'lasuŋ
to dispatch, to send off, to ship, to forward	**senden, abschicken, versenden, befördern**	zɛndən, 'apʃɪkən, fɛrzɛndən, bə'fœrdərn
dispatch department	**Versandabteilung** f	fɛr 'zant'aptaɪluŋ
dispatch note	**Versandanzeige** f	fɛr'zant'antsaɪgə
display material	**Ausstellungsmaterial** n	'ausʃtɛluŋsmateri'aːl
display, screen	**Anzeige** f (**Bildschirm** m)	'antsaɪgə (bɪltʃɪrm)
dispute	**Streitfall** m	'ʃtraɪtfal
distribution network	**Vertriebsnetz** n, **Abzatzorganisation** f	fɛr'triːpsnɛts, apzatsɔrganɪzatsɪ'oːn
dividend	**Dividende** f	dɪvɪ'dɛndə
division	**Konzerngruppe** f	kɔn'tsɛrngrupə
documents against acceptance (D/A)	**Dokumente** pl **gegen Akzept** n	doku'mɛntə 'geːgən ak'tsɛpt
domestic market	**Binnenmarkt** m	'bɪnənmarkt
dot-matrix printer	**Matrixdrucker** m	mat'rɪks'drukər
doubtful debt	**zweifelhafte Forderung** f	'tsvaɪfəlhaftə 'fɔrdəruŋ

263

down payment	**Anzahlung** f	'antsɑːluŋ
draft	**Tratte** f	'tratə
to draw a cheque	**Scheck** m **ausstellen**	ʃɛk 'ausʃtɛlən
to draw money from an account	**abheben (vom Konto** n**)**	'apheːbən (fɔm 'kɔnto)
drive (disk)	**Laufwerk** n	'laufvɛrk
due date	**Fälligkeit** f**, Rückzahlungstermin** m	'fɛlɪçkaɪt, 'rʏktsɑː-luŋstɛr'miːn
dunning letter/ reminder	**Mahnbrief** m	'mɑːnbriːf
duplicate consignment note	**Frachtbriefdoppel** n	'fraxtbriːfdɔpəl
E & OE (errors and omissions excepted)	**Irrtum** m **vorbehalten**	'ɪrtuːm 'foːrbəhaltən
economic position	**wirtschaftliche Lage** f	'vɪrtʃaftlɪçə 'lɑːgə
education, training	**Erziehung** f**, Ausbildung** f	ɛr'tsiːuŋ, 'ausbɪlduŋ
to effect delivery	**Lieferung** f **durchführen**	'liːfəruŋ 'durçfyːrən
to effect payment, to pay, to make payment	**zahlen**	'tsɑːlən
electronic data processing (EDP)	**Datenverarbeitung** f	'dɑːtənfɛrarbaɪtuŋ
electronic mail/E-mail	**elektronische Post** f	elɛk'troːnɪʃə pɔst
electronic mailbox	**elektronischer Briefkasten** m	elɛk'troːnɪʃər 'briːf-kastən
to employ, to engage, to take on	**einstellen**	'aɪnʃtɛlən
employee	**Angestellte (r)** f/m**, Beschäftigte (r)** f/m**, Arbeitnehmer** m	'angəʃtɛltə(r), bə'ʃɛftɪçtə(r), arbaɪt'neːmər(in)
employer	**Arbeitgeber** m**, Arbeitgeberin** f	arbaɪt'geːbər(in)
enclosure	**Anlage** f **(Anl.)**	'anlɑːgə
to engage, to employ, to take on	**einstellen**	'aɪnʃtɛlən
engineering	**technische Planung** f	'tɛçnɪʃə 'plɑːnuŋ
to enter, to book an order	**Bestellung** f **vormerken**	bə'ʃtɛluŋ 'foːrmɛrkən
to enter into a contract, to contract	**Vertrag** m **abschließen**	fɛr'trɑːk 'apʃliːsən

to entrust a firm with the agency	Vertretung f übertragen	fɛr'treːtuŋ yːbər'traːgən
entry	Buchung f	'buːxuŋ
equity capital	Eigenkapital n	'aɪgənkapɪtaːl
to erase	löschen (Datei f)	'lœʃən (daˈtaɪ)
error, oversight	Versehen n	fɛr'zɛːən
to establish, to found	gründen	'grʏndən
estimate	Kostenvoranschlag m	kɔstən'foːr'anʃlaːk
estimated annual turnover	geschätzter Jahresumsatz m	gə'ʃɛtstər 'jaːrəs'umzats
to exchange the goods	Waren f umtauschen	'vaːrən 'umtauʃən
excise tax	Verbrauchssteuer f	fɛr' brauxsʃtɔʏər
to execute an order	Auftrag m ausführen	'auftraːk 'ausfyːrən
executive	Führungskraft f	'fyːruŋskraft
exhibit	Ausstellungsstück n	'ausʃtɛluŋsʃtʏk
to exhibit, to show	ausstellen	'ausʃtɛlən
exhibition	Ausstellung f	'ausʃtɛluŋ
exhibition centre	Messezentrum n	'mɛsətsentrum
exhibition regulations	Messeordnung f	'mɛsəɔrdnuŋ
exhibitor	Aussteller m	'ausʃtɛlər
expected growth	voraussichtliche Entwicklung f	fo'rauszɪçtlɪçə ɛnt'vɪkluŋ
expenditure, expenses	Ausgaben pl	'ausgaːbən
expenses	Spesen pl	'ʃpeːzən
expenses, expenditure	Ausgaben pl	'ausgaːbən
expert	Fachmann m	'faxman
to exploit a patent	Patent n verwerten	pa'tɛnt fɛr'veːrtən
to export	exportieren	ɛkspɔr'tiːrən
export packing	Exportverpackung f	ɛks'pɔrtfɛrpakuŋ
exporter	Exporteur m	ɛkspɔr'toːr
to extend a contract	Vertrag m verlängern	fɛr'traːk fɛr'lɛŋərn
extension	Verlängerung f (Kredit m)	fɛr'lɛŋəruŋ (kre'diːt)
extras	Nebenkosten pl	'neːbənkɔstən
factoring	Darlehnsgewährung f gegen Forderungs- abtretung f	'daːrleːnsgəvɛːruŋ geːgən 'fɔrdəruŋs- aptrɛːtuŋ
fair	Messe f	'mɛsə
fair average quality (f.a.q.)	Durchschnittsware f	'durçʃnɪtsvaːrə
fair management	Messeleitung f	'mɛsəlaɪtuŋ
fair pass	Messeausweis m	'mɛsəausvaɪs
fair price	angemessener Preis m	'angəmɛsənər praɪs

English	German	Phonetic
to fall due	fällig werden	'fɛlɪç 'veːrdən
fault	Fehler m	'feːlər
faulty material	fehlerhaftes Material n	'feːlərhaftəs materɪ'aːl
favourable price	günstiger Preis m	'gʏnstɪgər praɪs
fax	Telefax n	'telefaks
fee	Gebühr f	gə'byːr
file	Datei f	da'taɪ
to file for bankruptcy	Konkurs m anmelden	kɔn'kurs 'anmɛldən
file protection, write lock	Dateienschutz m	'daːtaɪənʃuts
financial standing	Vermögenslage f	fɛr'møgənslaːgə
finished goods	Fertigfabrikate pl	'fɛrtɪçfabrɪ'kaːtə
firm, business, company	Firma f	'fɪrma
first-class quality	erstklassige Qualität f	'eːrstklasɪgə kvalɪtɛːt
fixed assets	Anlagevermögen n	'anlaːgəfɛrmøgən
fixed costs	Fixkosten pl	'fɪkskɔstən
fixed point	Festkomma n	'fɛstkɔma
fixed price	fester Preis m	'fɛstər praɪs
flat rate	Pauschalsatz m	pau'ʃaːlzats
flexible working hours, flexitime	Gleitzeit f	'glaɪttsaɪt
floating point	Gleitkomma n	'glaɪtkɔma
floor plan	Übersichtsplan m	'yːbərzɪçtsplaːn
flowchart	Datenflußplan m	'daːtənflusplaːn
floor space	Ausstellungsfläche f	'ausʃtelunsflɛçə
follow-up letter	Werbebrief m	'vɛrbəbriːf
for the attention of (att: . . .)	zu Händen von (z. Hd . . .) pl	tsu: 'hɛndən fɔn
foreign currency	ausländische Währung f	'auslɛndɪʃə 'vɛːruŋ
foreign exchange department	Devisenabteilung f	de'viːzənapˌtaɪluŋ
foreign language secretary	Fremdsprachen-sekretärin f	frɛmdʃpraːxənˌzɛkrə'tɛrɪn
foreman	Meister m	'maɪstər
to forward, to send off, to ship, to dispatch	senden, versenden	'zɛndən, fɛr'zɛndən
forwarder, carrier	Spediteur m	ʃpedɪ'tøːr
forwarding/freight charges	Frachtkosten pl	'fraxtkɔstən
Forwarding Agent's Certificate of Receipt (FCR)	Spediteurüber-nahmebe-scheinigung f	ʃpedɪ'tøːryːbɜr-naːməbə'ʃaɪnɪguŋ

to found, to establish	gründen	'gryndən
franchise	Konzession f	kɔntsɛsɪ'oːn
franchised dealer	Vertragshändler m	fɛr'traːkshɛndlər
free of charge, cost-free	kostenlos	'kɔstənloːs
free sample	Werbemuster n	'vɛrbəmustər
freight, cargo, carriage	Fracht f	fraxt
freight/forwarding charges	Frachtkosten pl	'fraxtkɔstən
freight collect	Fracht f gegen Nachnahme f	fraxt 'geːgən 'naxnaːmə
freight included	Fracht f inbegriffen	fraxt 'ɪnbəgrɪfən
freight rate	Frachtrate f	'fraxtraːtə
fringe benefits	zusätzliche Vergütung f an Arbeitnehmer pl neben Lohn m und Gehalt n	'tsuːzɛtslɪçə fɛr'gyːtuŋ an 'aːrbaɪtneːmər neːbən 'loːn unt gə'halt
fulfilment of contract	Vertragserfüllung f	fɛr'traːksɛr'fylun
full-time workers	Vollzeitarbeitskräfte pl	'fɔltsaɪtarbaɪtskrɛftə
to furnish a customer with goods, to supply	liefern, beliefern	'liːfərn, bə'liːfərn
general agency	Generalvertretung f	genc'raːlfɛr'treːtuŋ
general meeting of the shareholders	Hauptversammlung f	'hauptfɛrzamluŋ
giro account	Girokonto n	'ʒiːrokɔnto
to give notice	kündigen	'kyndɪgən
to go bankrupt	Konkurs m machen	kɔn'kurs 'maxən
goods, commodity, merchandise	Ware(n) f, (pl), Güter pl, Handelsware f	'vaːrə(n), 'gyːtər, 'handəlsvaːrə
grade	Sorte f, Güteklasse f	'zɔrtə, 'gyːtəklasə
to grant an allowance	Preisnachlaß m gewähren	'praɪsnaːxlas gə've:rən
to grant an extension	Aufschub m gewähren	'aufʃuːp gə've:rən
to grant sole selling rights	Alleinverkaufsrecht n vergeben	a'laɪnfɛrkaufsreçt fɛr'geːbən
gross profit	Bruttoertrag m	'brutoertraːk
gross weight	Bruttogewicht n	'brutogə'viçt
group, concern	Konzern m	kɔn'tsɛrn
guarantee, warrant	Garantievertrag m, Bürgschaft f	garan'tiːfertraːk 'byrkʃaft

hall plan	**Hallenplan** *m*	ˈhalənplɑːn
handbill	**Flugblatt** *n*	ˈfluːçblat
hard disk	**Festspeicherplatte** *f*	ˈfɛstʃpaɪçərplatə
haulage, bulk . . .	**Massengütertransport** *m*	ˈmasəngyːtər-transˈpɔrt
to have in stock	**vorrätig haben**	ˈfoːrrɛːtɪç haːbən
head office, headquarters	**Hauptgeschäftsstelle** *f*, **Zentrale** *f*	hauptgəˈʃɛftsʃtɛlə tsenˈtraːlə
hidden defect	**versteckter Mangel** *m*	fɛrˈʃtɛktər ˈmaŋəl
highly-competitive market	**wettbewerbs-intensiver Markt** *m*	ˈvɛtbevɛrbs-ɪntenˈziːvər markt
hire purchase	**Ratenkauf** *m*, **Abzahlungskauf** *m*	ˈraːtənkauf, ˈaptsaːluŋskauf
holding/parent company	**Dachgesellschaft** *f*	ˈdaxɡəzɛlʃaft
honest	**ehrlich, rechtschaffen**	eːrlɪç, ˈrɛçtʃafən
hostess	**Messehostess** *f*	ˈmɛsəhosˈtes
immediate	**umgehend, unverzüglich**	ˈumgeːənd, unfɛrˈtsyːklɪç
to import	**importieren**	ɪmpɔrˈtiːrən
import licence	**Importlizenz** *f*	ɪmˈpɔrtlitsɛnts
importer	**Importeur** *m*	ɪmpɔrˈtøːr
in advance	**im voraus**	ɪm ˈfoːraus
in transit	**unterwegs, auf dem Transit** *m*	untərˈveːks, auf deːm ˈtranzit
included	**inbegriffen**	ˈɪnbəɡrɪfən
income tax	**Einkommensteuer** *f*	ˈaɪnkɔmənsˈʃtɔyər
indebtedness	**Verschuldung** *f*	fɛrˈʃulduŋ
in-depth knowledge of the trade	**fundierte Branchen-kenntnisse** *pl*	funˈdiːrtə ˈbrɑ̃ːʃən-kɛntnɪsə
industrial fair	**Industriemesse** *f*	ɪndusˈtriːmɛsə
industrial plant	**Industriebetrieb** *m*	ɪndusˈtriːbəˈtriːp
industrial production	**industrielle Produktion** *f*	ɪndustrɪɛlə produktsɪˈoːn
industrial standard	**Industrienorm** *f*	ɪndustriːnɔrm
to inform	**informieren**	ɪnfɔrˈmiːrən
inheritance tax	**Erbschaftssteuer** *f*	ˈɛrpʃaftsʃtɔyər
initial order	**Erstbestellung** *f*	ˈeːrstbəʃtɛluŋ
ink-jet printer	**Tintenstrahldrucker** *m*	tɪntənˈʃtraːlˈdrukər
input	**Dateneingabe** *f*	ˈdaːtənˈaɪngaːbə
inquiry	**Anfrage** *f*	ˈanfraːɡə
insolvency	**Zahlungsunfähigkeit** *f*	ˈtsaːluŋsˈunfɛːɪçkaɪt
to install a stand	**Stand** *m* **aufbauen**	ʃtant ˈaufbauən
instalment	**Rate** *f*	ˈraːtə

to instruct, to train	**beruflich ausbilden**	bə'ru:flıç 'ausbıldən
instructions, leaflet, pamphlet	**Merkblatt** n	'mɛrkblɑt
insurance	**Versicherung** f	fɛr'zıçəruŋ
insurance against loss on the exchange rate	**Kursverlustver- sicherung** f	'kursfɛrlustfɛr- 'zıçəruŋ
insurance certificate	**Versicherungs- zertifikat** n	fɛr'zıçəruŋs- tsɛrtıfı'ka:t
insurance company	**Versicherungs- gesellschaft** f	fɛr'zıçəruŋsgə- 'zɛlʃaft
insurance policy	**Versicherungspolice** f	fɛr'zıçəruŋspo'li:sə
to intend	**beabsichtigen**	bə'apzıçtıgən
interest	**Zinsen** pl	'tsınzən
interest for default	**Verzugszinsen** pl	fɛr'tsu:kstsınzən
interested, to be . . . in	**interessiert sein an**	ıntərɛ'si:rt zaın an
interface	**Schnittstelle** f	'ʃnıtʃtɛlə
interview	**Einstellungs- gespräch** n	'aınʃtɛluŋs- gə'ʃprɛ:ç
inventories	**Vorräte** pl	'fo:rrɛ:tə
inventory	**Inventur** pl	ınvɛn'tu:r
to investigate	**untersuchen**	untər'zu:xən
investment	**Investition** f	ınvɛstıtsı'o:n
invoice	**Rechnung** f	'rɛçnuŋ
invoice amount	**Rechnungsbetrag** m	'rɛçnuŋsbə'tra:k
to invoice, to bill	**berechnen, Rechnung** m **erstellen**	bə'rɛçnən, 'rɛçnuŋ ɛr'ʃtɛlən
invoice number	**Rechnungsnummer** f	'rɛçnuŋsnumər
invoicing	**Rechnungsstellung** f	'rɛçnuŋsʃtɛluŋ
issue (of a magazine)	**Ausgabe** f **(einer Zeitschrift** f)	'ausga:bə (aınər 'tsaıtʃrıft)
to issue, to make out (a cheque)	**ausstellen**	'ausʃtɛlən
item	**Posten** m **(Ware** f), **Rechnungsposten** m	'pɔstən (va:rə) 'rɛçnuŋspɔstən
job, position	**Stellung** f	'ʃtɛluŋ
to join a firm	**in eine Firma** f **eintreten**	ın aınə 'fırma 'aıntre:tən
joint venture	**Beteiligungs- unternehmen** n	bə'taılıguŋs- untər'ne:mən
to keep the minutes	**Protokoll** n **führen**	proto'kɔl 'fu:rən
keyboard	**Tastatur** f	tasta'tu:r
keyword	**kennwort**	'kɛnvɔrt

label	**Etikett** n	etı'kɛt
laser printer	**Laserdrucker** m	'la:zərdrukər
latest catalogue	**neuester Katalog** m	'nɔystər kata'lo:k
lawsuit, litigation	**Prozeß** m, **Rechtsstreit** m	pro'tsɛs, 'rɛçtsʃtraıt
lawyer	**Jurist** m, **Rechtsanwalt** m	ju'rıst, 'rɛçtsanvalt
leaflet, instructions, pamphlet	**Merkblatt** n	mɛrkblat
to lease	**pachten, mieten**	'paxtən, 'mi:tən
ledger	**Hauptbuch** n	'hauptbu:x
legal reserves	**gesetzliche Rücklagen** pl	gə'zɛtslıçe 'rʏkla:gən
legally protected	**gesetzlich geschützt**	gə'zɛtslıç ge'ʃʏtst
letter of credit (L/C)	**Akkreditiv** n	akredı'ti:f
letter of intent	**Absichtserklärung** f	'apzıçtsɛr'klɛ:ruŋ
liabilities	**Passiva** pl	pa'si:va
liability	**Haftung** f	'haftuŋ
liable to tax	**steuerpflichtig**	'ʃtɔyərpflıçtıç
liquid funds	**flüssige Mittel** pl	'flʏsıgə 'mıtəl
liquidation, bankruptcy	**Konkurs** m	kɔn'kurs
liquidity	**Liquidität** f	lıkvıdı'tɛ:t
list of exhibitors	**Ausstellerverzeichnis** n	'ausʃtɛluŋsfɛr-'tsaıçnıs
list of products	**Warenverzeichnis** n	'va:rənfɛr'tsaıçnıs
list price	**Listenpreis** m	'lıstənpraıs
listing	**Listen** pl	lıstən
litigation, lawsuit	**Rechtsstreit** m	'rɛçtsʃtraıt
to load, to unload	**laden, ausladen**	'la:dən, 'ausla:dən
loan	**Darlehn** n	'da:rlɛ:n
long hauls	**Güterfernverkehr** m	'gy:tər'fernferke:r
loss	**Verlust** m	fɛr'lust
lot	**Warenpartie** f	va:rənpar'ti:
lump sum	**Pauschalbetrag** m	pau'ʃa:lbə'tra:k
machine shop	**Werkstatt** f	'vɛrkʃtat
magnetic head	**Magnetkopf** m	ma'gne:tkɔpf
magnetic tape	**Magnetband** n	ma'gne:tbant
mail circular, mailshot	**Postwurfsendung** f	'pɔstvurfzɛnduŋ
maintenance contract	**Wartungsvertrag** m	'vartuŋsfɛr'tra:k
to make, to produce, to manufacture	**herstellen**	'he:rʃtelən
to make out, to issue	**ausstellen (Scheck)**	'ausʃtelən

to make payment, to effect payment, to pay	**zahlen**	tsɑ:lən
to manage	**leiten, führen, verwalten**	'laɪtən, 'fy:rən, fɛr'valtən
management	**Unternehmensleitung** f	untər'ne:mənslaɪtuŋ
manager(ess)	**Leiter(in)** m/f, **Geschäftsführer(in)** m/f	'laɪtər(ɪn), gə'ʃɛftsfy:rər(ɪn)
managing director	**Geschäftsführendes Vorstandsmitglied** n	gə'ʃɛfts'fy:rəndəs 'fo:rʃtantsmɪtgli:t
manual	**Handbuch** n	'hantbu:x
to manufacture, to produce, to make	**herstellen**	'he:rʃtɛlən
to manufacture under licence	**in Lizenz** f **herstellen**	ɪn lɪ'tsɛnts 'he:rʃtɛlən
marginal costs	**Grenzkosten** pl	'grɛntskɔstən
market	**Markt** m	markt
market analysis	**Bedarfsanalyse** f	bə'darfsana'ly:zə
market research	**Marktforschung** f	'marktfɔrʃuŋ
market situation	**Marktlage** f	'marktlɑ:gə
market survey	**Marktumfrage** f	'marktumfrɑ:gə
marketing	**Absatz** m, **Vertrieb** m	'apzats, fɛr'tri:p
marking	**Markierung** f	mar'ki:ruŋ
mask, picture	**Maske** f **(Bildschirm-)**	'maskə ('bɪltʃɪrm-)
mass production	**Serienfertigung** f	'zeriənfɛrtiguŋ
master	**Meister** m	'maɪstər
master file	**Stammdatei** f	'ʃtamdataɪ
maturity date of contract	**Vertragsfällig-keitstag** m	fɛr'trɑ:ksfɛliçkaɪtstɑ:k
meetings	**Sitzungen** pl	'zitsuŋən
memory	**Speicher** m **(Computer-)**	'ʃpaɪçər (kɔm'pu:tər-)
memory protection	**Speicherschutz** m	'ʃpaɪçərʃuts
merchandise, commodity, goods	**Handelsware** f	'handəlsvɑ:rə
merchant, trader	**Händler** m, **Kaufmann** m	'hɛndlər, 'kaufman
to merge	**fusionieren**	fuzio'ni:rən
merger	**Fusion, Zusammenschluß** m	fuzi'o:n, tsu'zamənʃlus
metal container	**Kanister** m	ka'nistər

minutes, to keep the . . .	**Protokoll** *n* **führen**	proto'kɔl 'fy:rən
model, pattern, specimen	**Musterstück** *n*	'mustərʃtʏk
monitor	**Bildschirm** *m*	'bɪltʃɪrm
monopoly	**Monopolstellung** *f*	mono'po:lʃtɛluŋ
mortgage	**Hypothek** *f*	hy:po'te:k
to negotiate the conditions of a contract	**Vertragsbedingungen** *pl* **aushandeln**	fɛr'tra:ksbədɪŋuŋən 'aushandəln
negotiator, intermediary, agent	**Unter-Händler** *m*	'untərhɛntlər
net cash	**netto Kasse** *f*	'nɛto 'kasə
net weight	**Nettogewicht** *n*	'nɛtogə'vɪçt
no hidden extras	**keine versteckten Kosten** *pl*	kaɪnə fɛr'ʃtɛktən 'kɔstən
non-conformity with sample	**Nichtübereinstimmung** *f* **mit Muster** *n*	'nɪçty:bər'aɪnʃtɪmuŋ mɪt 'mustər
notes payable	**Wechselverbindlichkeiten** *pl*	'vɛksəlfɛr'bɪntlɪç- kaɪtən
notification	**Benachrichtigung** *f*, **Mitteilung** *f*	bə'na:xrɪçtɪguŋ, 'mɪttaɪluŋ
notification address	**Avisierungsanschrift** *f*	avi'zi:ruŋs'anʃrift
number, a limited . . . of	**eine begrenzte Auswahl** *f* **von**	aɪnə bə'grɛntstə 'ausva:l fɔn
to object to something	**Widerspruch** *m* **erheben**	'vɪdərʃprux ɛr'he:bən
offer, proposal	**Angebot** *n*	'angəbo:t
to offer (make a firm offer)	**fest anbieten**	fɛst 'anbi:tən
to offer subject to confirmation	**freibleibend anbieten**	'fraɪblaɪbənt 'anbi:tən
office automation	**Büroautomatisierung** *f*	by'ro:automati'zɪ:ruŋ
official catalogue (exhibition)	**Ausstellungskatalog** *m*	'ausʃtɛluŋskata'lo:k
official receiver (OR)	**Konkursverwalter** *m*	kɔn'kursfɛrvaltər
one-off production	**Einzelfertigung** *f*	'aɪntsəlfɛrtiguŋ
on-the-job training	**Ausbildung** *f* **am Arbeitsplatz** *m*	'ausbɪlduŋ am 'arbaɪtsplats
to open a fair	**Messe** *f* **eröffnen**	'mɛsə ɛr'œfnən
to open an account	**Konto** *n* **eröffnen**	'kɔnto ɛr'œfnən
to open the meeting	**Sitzung** *f* **eröffnen**	'zitsuŋ ɛr'œfnən

opening, vacancy	offene Stelle *f*	'ɔfənə 'ʃtɛlə
operating expense and income	betrieblicher Aufwand *f* und Ertrag *m*	bə'tri:plıçər 'aufvant ʊnt ɛr'tra:k
operating instructions	Gebrauchsanweisung *f*	gə'brauxsanvaızuŋ
operating system	Betrlebssystem *n*	bə'tri:pszys'te:m
operations scheduling	Arbeitsvorbereitung *f*	'arbaıtsfo:rbərɑıtuŋ
order	Auftrag *m*	'auftrɑ:k
order book	Auftragsbuch *n*	'auftrɑ·ksbux
order form	Bestellschein *m*	bə'ʃtɛlʃɑın
order number	Auftragsnummer *f*	'auftrɑ:ksnumər
orders on hand	Auftragsbestand *m*	'auftrɑ:ksbə'ʃtant
to organize a fair	Messe *f* veranstalten	'mɛsə fɛr'anʃtaltən
organizer (of a fair)	Messeveranstalter *m*	'mɛsəfɛr'anʃtaltər
to outline	Überblick *m* geben	'y:bərblık 'ge:bən
output	Datenausgabe *f*, Produktions- leistung *f*	'da'tənausgɑ:bə, produktsı'o:ns- laıstuŋ
outstanding accounts	Außenstände *pl*	'ausənʃtɛ̈ndə
outstanding quality	hervorragende Qualität *f*	hɛr'fo:rrɑ:gəndə 'kvalı'tɛ:t
overdraft credit	Überziehungskredit *m*	y:bər'tzı:uŋskre'di:t
to overdraw an account	Konto *n* überziehen	'kɔnto y:bər'tsi:ən
overdue	überfällig	'y:bərfɛlıç
overhead charges	Gemeinkosten- zuschläge *pl*	gə'maınkɔstən- tsu:ʃle:gə
overhead costs	Gemeinkosten pl	gə'maınkɔstən
oversight	Versehen *n*	fɛr'ze:ən
package	Packstück *n*, Kollo *n*	'pakʃtyk, 'kɔlo
packaging	Einzelverpackng *f*	'aıntsel'fɛrpakuŋ
packing	Verpackung *f*	'fɛr'pakuŋ
packing at cost	Verpackung *f* zum Selbstkostenpreis *m*	'fɛr'pakuŋ tsum 'zɛlpstkɔstənpraıs
packing list	Packliste *f*	'paklıstə
pallet	Palette *f*	pa'lɛtə
pamphlet, instructions, leaflet	Merkblatt *n*	'mɛrkblat
paper feed	Papiervorschub *m*	pa'pi:rfo:rʃup
parent/holding company	Muttergesellschaft *f*	'mutərgə'zɛlʃaft
part payment	Teilzahlung *f*	'taıltsa:luŋ
to participate in a fair	sich an einer Messe *f* beteiligen	zıç an aınər 'mɛsə bə'taılıgən

273

part-time workers	**Teilzeitkräfte** *pl*	'taɪltsaɪtkrɛftə
password	**Kennwort** *n*	'kɛnvɔrt
patented	**patentiert**	patɛn'tiːrt
pattern, model, specimen	**Muster** *n*, **Vorlage** *f*, **Modell** *n*	'mustər, 'foːrlɑːgə, mo'dɛl
to pay, to make payment, to effect payment	**zahlen**	'tsɑːlən
to pay into an account	**einzahlen (auf Konto** *n***)**	'aɪntsɑːlən (auf 'kɔnto)
payee	**Zahlungsempfänger** *m*	'tsɑːluŋsɛm'pfɛŋər
payment, settlement	**Zahlung** *f*	'tsɑːluŋ
payment against bank guarantee	**Zahlung** *f* **gegen Bankgarantie** *f*	'tsɑːluŋ 'geːgən 'bankgaran'tiː
payment by acceptance	**Zahlung** *f* **durch Akzept** *n*	'tsɑːluŋ durç ak'tsɛpt
payment by cheque	**Zahlung** *f* **durch Scheck** *m*	'tsɑːluŋ durç ʃɛk
payment by irrevocable confirmed documentary letter of credit (L/C)	**Zahlung** *f* **durch unwiderrufliches bestätigtes Dokumenten-akkreditiv** *n*	'tsɑːluŋ durç unvɪdər'rufliçəs bə'ʃtɛːtiçtəs doku'mɛntən-akredɪ'tiːf
payment by sight draft	**Zahlung** *f* **durch Sichttratte** *f*	'tsɑːluŋ durç 'ziçttratə
payment of the balance	**Restzahlung** *f*	'rɛsttsaluŋ
payment on account	**Abschlagszahlung** *f*	'apʃlaːkstsɑːluŋ
payment on receipt of goods (ROG)	**Zahlung** *f* **bei Erhalt** *m* **der Ware** *f*	'tsaluŋ baɪ ɛr'halt deːr 'vɑːrə
payroll	**Lohnabrechnung** *f*, **Personalliste** *f*	'loːnapreçnuŋ, pɛrzo'nɑːllɪstə
penalties	**Vertragsstrafen** *pl*	fɛr'trɑːksʃtrɑːfən
pension fund, superannuation fund	**Pensionskasse** *f*	pã'sjoːns-kasə
percentage	**Prozentsatz** *m*	pro'tsɛntzats
period of contract	**Vertragsdauer** *f*	fɛr'trɑːksdauər
period of limitation	**Verjährung** *f*	fɛr'jɛːruŋ
personal data sheet	**Kurz-Lebenslauf** *m*	kurts'leːbənslauf
personal secretary	**Chefsekretär(in)** *m/f*	'ʃɛfzekre'tɛːr/in
personnel, workforce, staff	**Belegsschaft** *f*	bə'leːgʃaft
personnel manager	**Personalleiter** *m*	pɛrzo'nɑːllaɪtər
personnel matters	**Personalangelegen-heiten** *pl*	pɛrzo'nɑːlangəleːgən-haɪtən

piggyback (combined road and rail) service	Huckepackverkehr *m*	'hukəpakfɛr'keːr
to place an order	Auftrag *m* erteilen	'auftraːk ɛr'taɪlən
place of destination	Bestimmungsort *m*	bə'ʃtɪmuŋsɔrt
place of dispatch	Versandort *m*	fɛr'zantɔrt
plant manager	Werksleiter *m*	'vɛrkslaɪtər
plotter	elektronisches Zeichengerät *n*	ɛlɛk'troːniʃes 'tsaɪçəngə'rɛːt
plug compatible	steckerkompatibel	ʃtɛkərkɔmpa'tiːbəl
policy holder	Versicherungsinhaber *m*	fɛr'zɪçəruŋs-'ɪnhaːbər
poor quality	schlechte Qualität *f*	'ʃlɛçtə kvaːlɪ'tɛːt
position, job	Stellung *f*	'ʃtɛluŋ
postage	Porto *n*	'pɔrto
poster	Plakat *n*	pla'kaːt
power supply	Stromversorgung *f*	'ʃtroːmfɛrzɔrguŋ
pre-tax profit	Gewinn *m* vor Steuern *pl*	gə'vɪn foːr 'ʃtɔʏərn
premium	Prämie *f*	'prɛːmiə
price increase	Preiserhöhung *f*	'praɪsɛr'høːuŋ
price list	Preisliste *f*	'praɪslɪstə
price maintenance	Preisbindung *f*	'praɪsbɪnduŋ
price reduction	Preisnachlaß *m*	'praɪsnaxlas
prices	Preise *pl*	'praɪzə
printed letterhead	gedruckter Briefkopf *m*	gə'druktər 'briːfkɔpf
prior sale	Zwischenverkauf *m*	'tsvɪʃənfɛrkauf
pro-forma invoice	Proforma-Rechnung *f*	pro'fɔrmareçnuŋ
probation period	Probezeit *f*	'proːbətsaɪt
to produce, to manufacture, to make	herstellen, produzieren	'heːrʃtɛlən, produ'tsiːrən
producer's price	Erzeugerpreis *m*	ɛr'tsɔʏgərpraɪs
product descriptions	Produktbeschreibungen *pl*	pro'dukt-bə'ʃraɪbuŋən
product liability	Produkthaftung *f*	pro'dukthaftuŋ
production	Produktion *f*	pro'duktsɪ'oːn
production costs	Herstellungskosten *pl*	'heːrʃtɛluŋskɔstən
production period	Produktionszeit *f*	produktsɪ'oːnstsaɪt
production programme	Produktionsprogramm *n*	produktsɪ'oːns-pro'gram
production schedule	Fertigungsplan *m*	'fɛrtɪguŋsplaːn
professional experience	berufliche Erfahrung *f*	bə'ruːflɪçə ɛr'faːruŋ

profit and loss account	Gewinn- und Verlust-konto n	gə'vɪn- unt fɛr'lust-kɔnto
profit margin	Gewinnspanne f	gə'vɪnʃpanə
profit mark-up	Gewinnzuschlag m	gə'vɪntsu:ʃlak
profit sharing	Gewinnbeteiligung f	gə'vɪnbətaɪlɪgʊŋ
profitability	Rentabilität f	rɛntabɪlɪ'tɛ:t
programming language	Programmiersprache f	program'i:rʃpra:xə
to prolong, to extend	verlängern	fɛr'lɛŋərn
prolongation	Verlängerung f (Wechsel m)	fɛr'lɛŋərʊŋ ('vɛçsəl)
promotion (professional)	Beförderung f	bə'fœrdərʊŋ
property	Eigentum n	'aɪgəntu:m
proposal, offer	Angebot n	'angəbo:t
prospectus, catalogue	Prospekt m	pro'spɛkt
proxy	Handlungsbevoll-mächtigte f/m	'handlʊŋsbə'fɔl-mɛçtiktə
public relations	Öffentlichkeitsarbeit f	'œfəntlɪçkaɪtsarbaɪt
publicity agency	Werbeagentur f	'vɛrbəagɛntu:r
publicity campaign	Werbekampagne f	'vɛrbəkam'panjə
publicity expenditure	Werbekosten pl	'vɛrbəkɔstən
purchase	Kauf m	kauf
to purchase, to buy	kaufen	'kaufən
purchase price	Einkaufspreis m	'aɪnkaufspraɪs
purchasing power	Kaufkraft f	'kaufkraft
qualification	Eignung f, Qualifikation f	'aɪgnʊŋ, kvalɪfɪkatsɪ'o:n
quality	Qualität f	kvalɪ'tɛ:t
quality control	Qualitätskontrolle f	kvalɪtɛ:tskɔn'trɔlə
quantity	Menge f	'mɛŋə
quantity discount	Mengenrabatt m	'mɛŋənra'bat
questionnaire	Fragebogen m	'fra:gəbo:gən
quotation	Angebot n mit Preisangabe f	'angəbo:t, 'praɪsanga:bə
to quote prices	Preise pl angeben	'praɪzə 'angeːbən
rail transport	Transport m per Schiene f	trans'pɔrt pɛr 'ʃi:nə
railway consignment note	Eisenbahnfrachtbrief m	'aɪzənba:nfraxtbri:f
random access memory (RAM)	Arbeitsspeicher m	'arbaɪtsʃpaɪçər

range, a wide . . . of	Sortiment *n*, eine große Auswahl *f*	zɔrtɪ'mɛnt, aɪnə groːsə 'ausvaːl
rate of interest	Zinssatz *m*	'tsinszats
raw materials	Rohstoffe *pl*	'roːʃtɔfə
read-only memory (ROM)	Festspeicher *m*	'fɛstʃpaɪçər
real property transfer tax	Grunderwerbssteuer *f*	grunter'vɛrpsʃtɔyər
receipt	Erhalt *m*	ɛr'halt
receipts	Einnahmen *m*	'aɪnnɑːmən
receivables	Forderungen *pl*	'fɔrdəruŋən
receiving order	Konkurseröffnungs-beschluß *m*	kɔn'kursɛr'œfnuŋs-bə'ʃlus
recourse	Regress *m*	rəgrɛs
to refer to	sich wenden an	zɪç 'vɛndən an
(our/your) reference	Diktat-/Akten-/ Bezugszeichen *n*	dɪk'taːt/'aktən/ bə'tsuːks'tsaɪçən
references	Referenzen *pl*	refe'rɛntsən
to refund	erstatten	ɛr'ʃtatən
refund of costs	Kostenerstattung *f*	'kɔstənerʃtatuŋ
to refuse a claim	Beschwerde *f* ablehnen	bə'ʃveːrdə 'apleːnən
regarding, re.:	bezüglich, Betr.:	bə'tsyːklɪç
registered office	Geschäftssitz *m*	gə'ʃɛftszɪts
registered trade mark	eingetragenes Warenzeichen *n*	'aɪngətraːgənəs 'vaːrəntsaɪçen
to regret	bedauern	bə'dauərn
to reject a motion	Antrag *m* ablehnen	'antraːk 'apleːnən
reliability	Zuverlässigkeit *f*	'tsuːfɛrlɛsɪçkaɪt
reloading, trans-shipment	Umladung *f*	'umlaːduŋ
reluctantly	widerstrebend, ungern	vɪːdər'ʃtreːbənt, 'uŋgɛrn
to remind somebody of something	erinnern an	ɛr'ɪnərn an
reminder	Erinnerungsschreiben *n*	ɛr'ɪnəruŋsʃraɪbən
to remit	überweisen	yːbər'vaɪzən
remittance	Überweisung *f*	yːbər'vaɪzuŋ
to rent	mieten, vermieten, verpachten	'miːtən, fɛr'miːtən, fɛr'paxtən
repeat order	Nachbestellung *f*	'naːxbəʃtɛluŋ
replacement	Ersatzlieferung *f*	ɛr'zatsliːfəruŋ
representative, agent	Vertreter *m*	fɛr'treːtər

277

representative on commission	Kommissions- kaufmann *m*	kɔmɪsɪ'oːns- kaufman
to request	bitten, auffordern	'bɪtən, aufɔrdərn
requirements	Anforderungen *pl*	'anfɔrdəruŋən
research	Forschungstätigkeit *f*	'fɔrʃuŋsteːtɪçkaɪt
reservation of title	Eigentumsvorbehalt *m*	'aɪgəntuːmsfoːrbəhalt
result	Ergebnis *n*	ɛr'geːpnɪs
retail dealer	Einzelhändler *m*	'aɪntsəlhɛndlər
retail price	Einzelhandelspreis *m*	'aɪntsəlhandəlspraɪs
return, yield	Ertrag *m*	ɛr'traːk
returnable container	Leihbehälter *m*	'laɪbəhɛltər
revenues	Erlöse *pl*	ɛr'løːzə
to revoke an offer	Angebot *n* widerrufen	'angəboːt viːdər'ruːfən
rise	Gehaltserhöhung *f*	gə'haltsɛr'høːuŋ
road transport	Transport *m* auf der Straße *f*	trans'pɔrt auf deːr 'ʃtraːsə
roll-on/roll-off service	RoRo-Verkehr *m*	roːroːfɛr'keːr
royalty	Lizenzgebühr *f*	lɪ'tsɛntsgə'byːr
to run a business	Geschäft *n* betreiben	gə'ʃɛft bə'traɪbən
sack, bag	Sack *m*	zak
salary	Gehalt *n*	gə'halt
sale	Verkauf *m*	fɛr'kauf
sale on trial	Kauf *k* auf Probe *f*	kauf auf 'proːbə
sale or return	Kauf *m* mit Rückgaberecht *n*	kauf mɪt 'rʏkgaːbərɛçt
sales	Umsatzerlöse *pl*, Verkäufe *pl*, Absatz *m*	'umzatsɛr'løːzə, fɛr'kɔyfə, 'apzats
sales promotional letter	Werbebrief *m*	'vɛrbəbriːf
sales on commission	Kommissionsverkauf *m*	kɔmɪsɪ'oːnsfɛr'kauf
sales potential	Absatzmöglichkeit *f*	'apzatsmøːklɪçkaɪt
sales promotion	Verkaufsförderung	fɛr'kaufsfœrdəruŋ
sales territory	Absatzgebiet *n*	'apzatsgəbiːt
sample	Muster *n*, Probe *f*	'mustər, 'proːbə
sample collection	Musterkollektion *f*	'mustərkɔlɛktsɪ'oːn
sample of no commercial value	Muster *n* ohne Wert *m*	'mustər 'oːnə veːrt
savings/deposit account	Sparkonto *n*	'ʃpaːrkɔnto
scanner	Bildabtaster *m*	'bɪltaptastər

school leaving certificate	Schulabgangszeugnis n	'ʃuːl'apɡaŋstsɔʏknɪs
screen, monitor	Bildschirm m	'bɪltʃɪrm
seaworthy packing	seemäßige Verpackung f	'zeːmɛːsɪɡə fɛr'pakuŋ
second-rate quality	zweite Wahl f	'tsvaɪtə vaːl
secretary (to XY)	Sekretär(in) m/f (von XY)	zɛkreˈtɛːr(ɪn) (fɔn)
security	Sicherheit f	'zɪçərhaɪt
selection of samples	Auswahlmuster- sendung f	'ausvaːlmustərzɛnduŋ
to sell	verkaufen	fɛr'kaufən
to sell as sole agent	vertreiben als Allein- vertreter m	fɛr'traɪbən als a'laɪn- fɛr'treːtər
to sell goods on commission	Waren pl in Kommission f verkaufen	'vaːrən ɪn kɔmɪsɪ'oːn 'fɛr'kaufən
to sell off	ausverkaufen	'ausfɛrkaufən
seller	Verkäufer m	fɛr'kɔʏfər
seller's warranties	Gewährleistungs- pflicht f	ɡə'vɛːrlaɪstuŋspflɪçt
selling conditions	Verkaufsbedingungen pl	fɛr'kaufsbə'diŋuŋən
selling expenses	Vertriebskosten pl	fɛr'triːpskɔstən
selling price	Verkaufspreis m	fɛr'kaufspraɪs
semi-finished goods	Halbfertigfabrikate pl	'halpfɛrtɪçfabriː'kaːtə
to send off, to ship, to forward, to dispatch	senden	'zɛndən
to serve an apprenticeship	Lehre f absolvieren	'leːrə apzɔl'viːrən
service	Dienstleistung f, Wartung f	'diːnstlaɪstuŋ, 'vartuŋ
service manual	Wartungsanleitung f	'vartuŋsanlaɪtuŋ
to set up a business	sich selbständig machen	zɪç 'zɛlpʃtɛndɪç 'maxən
to settle a claim	Schadensfall m regulieren	'ʃaːdənsfal reɡu'liːrən
to settle an account	Rechnung f begleichen, zahlen	'rɛçnuŋ bə'ɡlaɪçən, 'tsaːlən
settlement	Begleichung f einer Rechnung f	bə'ɡlaɪçuŋ aɪnər rɛçnuŋ
share	Aktie f	'aktsiə

share deal	Kauf *m* der Geschäfts- anteile *pl*/der Zielgesellschaft *f*	kauf de:r gə'ʃɛfts- antaɪlə de:r 'tsi:lgə'zɛlʃaft
shift work	Schichtarbeit *f*	'ʃɪçtarbaɪt
to ship, to forward, to dispatch, to send off	senden	'zɛndən
shipment, consignment	Warensendung *f*	'vɑːrənzɛnduŋ
shipping documents	Warenbegleitpapiere *pl*	'vɑːrənbə'glaɪtpapiːrə
shipping marks	Versandmarkierungen *pl*	fɛr'zantmar'kiːruŋən
shop steward	Betriebsratsmitglied *n* (am Arbeitsplatz *m*)	bə'triːpsrɑːt'mɪtgliːt (am 'aːrbaɪtsplats)
short hauls	Güternahverkehr *m*	gyːtər'naːfɛr'keːr
shortage	Fehlmenge *f*	'feːlmɛŋə
to show, to exhibit	ausstellen (Messe *f*)	'ausʃtɛlən ('mɛsə)
showroom	Ausstellungsraum *m*	'ausʃtɛluŋsraum
signature	Unterschrift *f*	'untərʃrɪft
single European market	europäischer Binnenmarkt *m*	ɔyroː'pɛːɪʃər 'bɪnənmarkt
size	Größe *f*	'grøːsə
skid (rollers)	Schlitten *m*	'ʃlɪtən
skilled worker	Facharbeiter(in) *m/f*	'faxarbaɪtər(ɪn)
slot	Anschluß *m* (zum Computer *m*)	'anʃlus (tsum kɔm'puːtər)
software	Programm *n*, Software *f*	pro'gram
sole proprietorship	Einzelfirma *f*	'aɪntsəlfɪrma
solicitor	Rechtsanwalt *m*	'rɛçtsanvalt
solvency	Zahlungsfähigkeit *f*	'tsaːluŋsfɛːɪçkaɪt
to sort	sortieren	zɔr'tiːrən
sound	sicher (Währung *f*, Kredit *m*)	'zɪçər ('vɛːruŋ. kre'diːt)
space, blank	Füllzeichen *n*	'fʏltsaɪçən
special design	Sonderanfertigung *f*	'zɔndəranfɛrtɪguŋ
special discount	Sonderrabatt *m*	'zɔndərrabat
special packing	Sonderverpackung *f*	'zɔndərfɛrpakuŋ
special price	Sonderpreis *m*	'zɔndərpraɪs
specialized fair	Fachmesse *f*	'faxmɛsə
specification	detaillierte Aufstellung *f*	deta'jiːrtə 'aufʃtɛluŋ

to specify the delivery route	Versandweg m angeben	fɛr'zantveːk 'angeːbən
specimen, pattern, model	Musterstück n, Probe f	'mustərʃtvk, 'proːbə
spreadsheet	Kalkulationstabelle f	kalkula'tsiːoːnstabelə
staff, workforce, personnel	Belegschaft f	bə'leːkʃaft
stall, booth, stand	Messestand m	'mɛsəʃtant
stand rental	Standmiete f	'ʃtantmiːtə
stand, stall, booth	Messestand m	'mɛsəʃtant
standard quality	Standardqualität f	ʃtandartkvalɪ'tɛːt
standing order	Dauerauftrag m	'dauərauftraːk
statement of account	Kontoauszug m	'kɔntoaustsuːk
statement of earnings	Gewinn- und Verlustrechnung f	gə'vin- unt fɛr'lustreçnuŋ
statistics	Statistik f	ʃta'tɪstɪk
stipulated	vertraglich vereinbart	fɛr'traːkliç fɛr'ainbaːrt
stock	Lagerbestand m	'laːgərbə'ʃtant
to stock, to store	lagern	'laːgərn
stock clerk	Lagerverwalter m	'laːgərfɛr'valtər
stock control	Lagerbestandskontrolle f	'laːgərbə'ʃtantskɔntrɔlə
stock rotation	Lagerumschlag m	'laːgərumʃlaːk
storage	Lagerhaltung f	'laːgərhaltuŋ
to store, to stock	lagern	laːgərn
to streamline (production)	rationalisieren, modernisieren	ratsıonalı'ziːrən, modɛrnı'ziːrən
strictly confidential	streng vertraulich	'ʃtrɛŋ fɛr'trauliç
subcontractor	Zulieferfirma f	'tsuːliːfərfırma
subject, re (regarding)	Betreff m	bə'trɛf
subject to payment of royalties	lizenzpflichtig	lɪ'tsɛntspfliçtiç
to submit an offer	Angebot n unterbreiten	'angəboːt untər'braitən
subscription price	Bezugspreis m	bə'tsuːksprais
subsidiary	Tochtergesellschaft f	'tɔxtərgəzɛlʃaft
subsidy	Subvention f	zupvɛntsı'oːn
substitute	Ersatzlieferung f	ɛr'zatsliːfəruŋ
superannuation fund, pension fund	Pensionskasse f	pɛnzi'oːnskasə
superior	Vorgesetzte(r) f/m	'foːrgəzɛtstə(r)
supplier	Lieferant m	liːfə'rant
suppliers, contractors	Lieferfirma f	'liːfərfırma
to supply, to furnish a customer with goods	liefern, beliefern	'liːfərn, bə'liːfərn

supply contract	**Liefervertrag** m	'liːfərfɛrtraːk
surcharge	**Preisaufschlag** m	'praɪsaʊfʃlaːk
surtax	**Zusatzsteuer** f	'tsuːzatsʃtɔʏər
to take on, to employ, to engage	**einstellen**	'aɪnʃtɛlən
to take out insurance	**Versicherung** f **abschließen**	fɛrˈzɪçəruŋ 'apʃliːsən
to take stock	**Inventur** f **aufnehmen**	ɪnvɛnˈtuːr aʊfneːmən
to take the goods back	**Ware** f **zurücknehmen**	'vaːrə tsuˈrʏkneːmən
take-over	**Übernahme** f **einer Gesellschaft** f	'yːbərnaːmə aɪnər gəˈzɛlʃaft
tape drive unit	**Magnetbandgerät** n	magˈneːtbantgəˈrɛːt
tape library system	**Magnetband-Bibliotheksystem** n	magˈneːtbant-bɪbliʊˈteːksʏsˈteːm
tare	**Tara** f, **Verpackungsgewicht** n	'taːra, fɛrˈpakuŋs-gəˈvɪçt
tariff zone	**Tarifzone** f	taˈriːftsoːnə
tax	**Steuer** f	'ʃtɔʏər
tax allowance	**Steuervergünstigung** f	'ʃtɔʏərfɛrgʏnstɪguŋ
tax consultant	**Steuerberater** m	'ʃtɔʏərbəraːtər
tax exemption	**Steuerfreibetrag** m	'ʃtɔʏərˈfraɪbətraːk
tax-free	**steuerfrei**	'ʃtɔʏərfraɪ
teleprocessing	**Datenfernverarbeitung** f	daːtənfɛrnfɛrˈarbaɪtuŋ
Teletex	**Teletex** n	'teleteks
telex	**Telex** n	'teleks
temporary staff	**Aushilfspersonal** n	'aʊshɪlfspɛrzonaːl
tender	**Ausschreibung** f	'aʊsʃraɪbuŋ
terms	**Bedingungen** pl	bəˈdɪŋuŋɛn
terms of contract	**Vertragsbedingungen** pl	fɛrˈtraːksbəˈdɪŋuŋən
terms of payment	**Zahlungsbedingungen** pl	'tsaːluŋsbədɪŋuŋən
testimonial	**Zeugnis** n **des Arbeitgebers** m	'tsɔʏgnɪs dɛs 'arbaɪtˈgeːbərs
third-party insurance	**Haftpflicht-versicherung** f	'haftpflɪçt-fɛrˈzɪçəruŋ
tool	**Werkzeug** n	'vɛrktsoyk
total (sum) amounting to DM . . .	**Gesamtsumme** f **über DM . . .**	gəˈzamtzumə yːbər . . .
trade	**Handel** m	'handəl
to trade	**Handel** m **treiben**	'handəl 'traɪbən
trade custom	**Handelsusance** f	'handəlsyːˈzã:sə

trade discount	Handelsrabatt *m*	'handəlsrabat
trade fair	Handelsmesse *f*	'handəlsmɛsə
to trade in	in Zahlung *f* geben	ɪn 'tsaːluŋ geːbən
trade mark	Warenzeichen *n*	'vaːrəntsaɪçən
trade mark-up	Handelsspanne *f*	'handəlsʃpanə
trade payables	Verbindlichkeiten *pl* aus Lieferungen *pl* und Leistungen *pl*	fɛr'bɪntlɪçkaɪtən aus 'liːfərɪŋən, unt laɪstuŋən
trade relations	Handelsverbindungen *pl*	'handəlsfɛrbɪnduŋən
trade tax	Gewerbesteuer *f*	gə'vɛrbəʃtɔyər
trade union	Gewerkschaft *f*	gə'vɛrkʃaft
trader, merchant	Händler *m*, Kaufmann *m*	'hɛndlər, 'kaufman
trading result	Betriebsergebnis *n*	bə'triːpsɛrgeːpnɪs
to train, to instruct	beruflich ausbilden	bə'ruːflɪç 'ausbɪldən
training, education	Ausbildung *f*, Erziehung *f*	'ausbɪlduŋ, ɛr'tsiːuŋ
training courses for salespersons	Schulungskurse *pl* für Verkäufer *pl*	'ʃuːluŋskurzə tyːɪ fɛr'kɔyfər
to transfer	überweisen	yːbər'vaɪzən
transfer of title for the purpose of securing a debt	Sicherungsübereignung *f*	'zɪçəruŋs- yːbəraɪgnuŋ
transit, in . . .	unterwegs, auf dem Transit *m*	untər've:ks, auf de(ː)m 'tranzit
transmission channels	Übertragungswege *pl*	yːbər'traːguŋsveːgə
transport	Transport *m*	trans'pɔrt
transportation insurance	Transportversicherung *f*	trans'pɔrtfɛrzɪçəruŋ
transshipment, reloading	Umladung *f*	'umlaːduŋ
to treat	behandeln	bə'handəln
trend	Trend *m*	trɛnt
trial product sample	Produktmuster *n*	pro'duktmustər
trustee	Konkursverwalter *m*	kɔn'kursfɛrvaltər
turnover	Umsatz *m*	umzats
turnover tax	Umsatzsteuer *f*	umzatsʃtɔyər
typist	Schreibkraft *f*	'ʃraɪpkraft
unanimous(ly)	einstimmig	'aɪnʃtɪmɪç
under patent law	patentrechtlich	pa'tɛntrɛçtlɪç
under reserve	unter Vorbehalt *m*	'untər 'foːrbəhalt
undermentioned	unten erwähnt	'untən ɛr'vɛːnt
to underwrite a risk	Risiko *n* versichern	'riːzɪko fɛr'zɪçərn

underwriter	**Versicherer** *m*	fɛr'zɪçərər
unemployment	**Arbeitslosigkeit** *f*	'arbaɪtsloːzɪçkaɪt
unit costs	**Stückkosten** *pl*	'ʃtʏkkɔstən
unit price	**Stückpreis** *m*	'ʃtʏkpraɪs
to unload	**ausladen**	'auslaːdən
update	**Änderungsdienst** *m*	'ɛndəruŋsdiːnst
user identification	**Benutzeridentifikation**	bə'nutsər-
(user id)	*f*	ɪdɛntɪfɪkatsɪ'oːn
utility	**Dienstprogramm** *n*	'diːnstprogram
vacancy, opening	**offene Stelle** *f*	'ɔfənə 'ʃtɛlə
valid	**gültig**	'gʏltɪç
valuation	**Bewertung** *f*	bə've:rtuŋ
variable costs	**variable Kosten** *pl*	varɪ'aːblə kɔstən
VAT (value added tax)	**Mehrwertsteuer** *f*	'meːrveːrtsʃtɔyər
venture capital	**Wagnis-/Beteiligungs-**	'vaːgnɪs-, bə'taɪlɪguŋs-
	kapital *n*	kapɪ'taːl
via (Dover)	**über (Dover)**	yːbər
to visit a fair	**Messe** *f* **besuchen**	'mɛsə bə'zuːxən
visitor to a fair	**Messebesucher** *m*	'mesəbə'zuːxər
vocational training	**Berufsausbildung** *f*	bə'ruːfsausbɪlduŋ
to vote for (against)	**abstimmen für**	'apʃtɪmən fyːr
	(gegen)	(geːgən)
voucher	**Beleg** *m*	bə'leːk
wage(s)	**Lohn** *m*, **Löhne** *pl*	loːn, løːnə
wage tax	**Lohnsteuer** *f*	'loːnʃtɔyər
warehouse	**Lagerhaus** *n*	'laːgərhaus
warehouse company	**Lagerhausgesellschaft**	'laːgərhausgə'zɛlʃaft
	f	
warrant, warranty,	**Bürgschaft** *f*, **Garantie**	'bʏrgʃaft, garan'tiː,
guarantee	*f*, **Garantievertrag** *m*	garan'tiː'fɛrtraːk
water transport	**Wassertransport** *m*	'vasərtranspɔrt
waybill, consignment	**Frachtbrief** *m*,	'fraxtbriːf,
note	**Begleitschein** *m*	bə'glaɪtʃaɪn
wealth tax	**Vermögenssteuer** *f*	fɛr'møːgənsʃtɔyər
well-founded	**begründete**	bə'gryndətə
complaint	**Beschwerde** *f*	bə'ʃveːrdə
wholesale dealer	**Großhändler** *m*	'groːshɛndlər
wholesale price	**Großhandelspreis** *m*	'groːshandəlspraɪs
without charge	**ohne Berechnung** *f*	'oːne bə'rɛçnuŋ
without obligation	**unverbindlich**	unfɛr'bɪntlɪç
word-processing	**Textverarbeitungs-**	'tɛkstfɛrarbaɪtuŋs-
system	**system** *n*	systeːm

work in progress	**unfertige Erzeugnisse** *pl*	'unfɛrtigə ɛr'tsɔygnɪsə
to work overtime	**Überstunden** *pl* **machen**	'y:bərʃtundən 'maxən
worker participation (in decision-making), co-determination	**Mitbestimmung** *f*	'mitbəʃtimuŋ
workforce, staff, personnel	**Belegschaft** *f*	bə'le:kʃaft
working hours	**Arbeitszeit** *f*	'arbaɪtstsaɪt
working storage (computer term)	**Arbeitsspeicher** *m*	'arbaɪtsʃpaɪçər
works council member	**Betriebsratsmitglied** *n*	bə'tri:psra:tsmɪtgli:t
workshop	**Werkstatt** *f*	'vɛrkʃtat
wrapping	**Umhüllung** *f*, **Verpackung** *f*	um'hyluŋ, fɛr'pakuŋ
write head	**Schreibkopf** *m*	'ʃraɪpkɔpf
write lock, file protection	**Schreibschutz** *m*	'ʃraɪʃuts
to write off	**abschreiben**	'apʃraɪbən
year under review	**Berichtsjahr** *n*	bə'rɪçtsja:r
yield, return	**Rendite** *f*, **Ertrag** *m*	rɛn'di:tə, ɛr'tra:k
zero-rated	**ohne Mehrwertsteuer** *f*	'o:nə 'me:rve:rtsʃtɔyər

3

German–English Listing of Technical Vocabulary

m masculine
f feminine
n neuter
pl plural

Abfuhr *f*	carriage
abheben (vom Konto *n***)**	to draw money (from an account)
Absatz *m*, **Verkäufe** *pl*	sales
Absatz *m*, **Vertrieb** *m*	marketing
Absatgebiet *n*	sales territory
Absatzmöglichkeit *f*	sales potential
Absatzorganisation *f*	distribution network
Abschlagszahlung *f*	payment on account
abschreiben	to write off
Abschreibungen *pl*	depreciations
Absender *m* **einer Sendung** *f*	consignor, shipper
Absichtserklärung *f*	letter of intent
abstimmen für/gegen	to vote for/against
Abzahlungskauf *m*	hire-purchase
Adresse *f*	address
Akkreditiv *n*	letter of credit (L/C)
Aktenzeichen *n*	our/your reference
Aktie *f*	share
Aktiva *pl*	assets
Alleinverkaufsrecht *n* **vergeben**	to grant sole selling rights
Änderungsdienst	update
Anfrage *f*	inquiry
Anfuhr *f*, **Gütertransport** *m*	carriage
Angebot *n*	offer, proposal
Angebot *n* **annehmen**	to accept an offer
Angebot *n* **mit Preisangabe** *f*	quotation
Angebot *n* **unterbreiten**	to submit an offer
Angebot *n* **widerrufen**	to revoke an offer
angemessener Preis *m*	fair price

286

Angestellte f/m, **Beschäftigte** f/m	employee
Anlage f (Anl.)	enclosure
Anlagevermögen n	fixed assets
anmelden (zu einer Messe f)	to apply for space
Anmeldung f	application
Anschluß m (zum Computer m)	slot
Anspruch m	claim
Anstellungsvertrag m	contract of employment
Antrag m **ablehnen**	to reject a motion
Antrag m **durchbringen**	to carry a motion
Antrag m **stellen**	to bring forward a motion
Anzahlung f	down-payment
Anzeige f (Bildschirm-)	display, screen
Arbeitgeber(in) m/f	employer
Arbeitnehmer(in) m/f	employee
Arbeitslosigkeit f	unemployment
Arbeitsspeicher m	random-access memory (RAM), working storage
Arbeitsvorbereitung f	operations scheduling
Arbeitszeit f	working hours
auf Ihre/unsere Kosten pl	at your/our expense
Aufschub m **gewähren**	to grant an extension
Auftrag m	order
Auftrag m **ausführen**	to execute an order
Auftrag m **erteilen**	to place an order
Auftragsbestand m	orders on hand
Auftragsbestätigung f	acknowledgement of order
Auftragsbuch n	order book
Auftragseingänge pl	bookings
Auftragsnummer f	order number
Ausbildung f, **Erziehung** f	education, training
Ausbildung f **am Arbeitsplatz** m	on-the-job training
ausführliche Informationen pl **über**	detailed information about
Ausgaben pl	expenditure, expenses
Aushilfspersonal n	temporary staff
Auskunftseinholung f	credit inquiry
ausladen	to unload
ausländische Währung f	foreign currency

ausliefern, zustellen	to deliver
Ausnutzungsgrad *m*	capacity usage ratio
Ausschreibung *f*	tender
Außenstände *pl*	outstanding accounts
ausstellen	to exhibit, to show
ausstellen	to issue, to make out
Aussteller *m*	exhibitor
Ausstellerverzeichnis *n*	list of exhibitors
Ausstellung *f*	exhibition
Ausstellungsfläche *f*	floor space
Ausstellungsfläche *f* **mieten**	to book exhibition space
Ausstellungskatalog *m*	official (exhibition) catalogue
Ausstellungsmaterial *n*	display material
Ausstellungsraum *m*	showroom
Ausstellungsstück *n*	exhibit
ausverkaufen	to sell off
Auswahlmustsendung *f*	selection of samples
Avisierungsanschrift *f*	notification address
Azubi *m/f*, **Lehrling** *m*	apprentice
Barzahlung *f* **bei Auftrags-**	cash with order (CWO)
erteilung *f*	
Barzahlungsrabatt *m*	cash discount
Bedarfsanalyse *f*	market analysis
bedauern	to regret
Bedingungen *pl*	terms
befördern, versenden	to dispatch, to send off, to ship, to forward
Beförderung *f*	promotion
begrenzte Auswahl *f* **von**	a limited number of
begründete Beschwerde *f*	well-founded complaint
Begünstigter *m*	beneficiary
belasten, berechnen	to charge
Beleg *m*	voucher
Belegschaft *f*	workforce, staff, personnel
Benutzeridentifikation *f*	user identification (user i.d.)
berechnen, belasten	to charge
berechnen, Rechnung *f*	to invoice, to bill
erstellen	
Berichtsjahr *n*	year under review
beruflich ausbilden	to train, to instruct

berufliche Erfahrung *f*	professional experience
Berufsausbildung *f*	vocational training
Beschäftige *f/m*, Angestellte *f/m*	employee
bescheinigen	to certify
beschlußfähig sein	to constitute a quorum
Beschwerde *f*, Mängelrüge *f*	complaint
Beschwerde *f* ablehnen	to refuse a claim
Beschwerde *f* anerkennen	to allow a claim
Bestellschein *m*	order form
Bestellung *f* vormerken	to enter/to book an order
Bestimmungsland *n*	country of destination
Bestimmungsort *m*	place of destination
Beteiligungskapital *n*	venture capital
Beteiligungsunternehmen *n*	joint venture
Betreff *m* (Betr.:)	subject, re (regarding)
betrieblicher Aufwand *m* und Ertrag *m*	operating expenses and income
Betriebsergebnis *n*	trading result
Betriebsratsmitglied *n*	works council member
Betriebsratsmitglied *n* (am Arbeitsplatz *m*)	shop steward
Betriebssystem *n*	operating system
Bewerbung *f*	application
Bewertung *f*	valuation
Bezugspreis *m*	subscription price
Bilanz *f*	balance sheet
Bildabtaster *m*	scanner
Bildschirm *m*	screen, monitor
Binnenmarkt *m*	domestic market
Broschüre *f*	brochure, leaflet
Bruttoertrag *m*	gross profit
Bruttogewicht *n*	gross weight
buchen	to book
Buchhalter *m*	accountant, bookkeeper
Buchhaltung *f*	accounting, bookkeeping
Buchung *f*	entry
Buckwert *m*	book value
Bürgschaft *f*, Garantievertrag *m*	warrant, guarantee
Büroautomatisierung *f*	office automation

Chef *m*	boss
Chefsekretär(in) *m/f*	personal secretary
Container *m*	container
Darlehn *n*	loan
Darlehnsgewährung *f* gegen Forderungsabtretung *f*	factoring
Datei *f*	file
Datenausgabe *f*	output
Datenaustausch *m*	data transfer
Datenbank *f*	data base
Dateneingabe *f*	input
Datenfernverarbeitung *f*	teleprocessing
Datenflußplan *m*	flowchart
Datenübertragungsleitung *f*	communication line
Datenverarbeitung *f*	electronic data processing (EDP)
Dauerauftrag *m*	standing order
Deckung *f*	coverage
Defekt *m*	defect
detaillierte Aufstellung *f*	specification
Devisenabteilung *f*	foreign exchange department
Dienstleistung *f*	service
Dienstprogramm *n*	utility
Diktat-/Atken-/Bezugszeichen *n*	(our/your) reference
direkter Zugriff *m*	direct memory access
Diskette *f*	disk
Diskontsatz *m*	discount rate
Dividende *f*	dividend
Dokumente *pl* gegen Akzept *n*	documents against acceptance (D/A)
Durchschnittsware *f*	fair average quality (f.a.q.)
ehrlich, rechtschaffen	honest
eidesstattliche Erklärung *f*	affidavit
Eigenkapital *n*	equity capital
Eigentum *n*	property
Eigentumsvorbehalt *m*	reservation of title
Eignung *f*, Qualifikation *f*	qualification
eingetragenes Warenzeichen *n*	registered trade mark

Einkaufsbedingungen *pl*	buying conditions
Einkaufspreis *m*	purchase price
Einkommensteuer *f*	income tax
Einnahmen *pl*	receipts
einstellen	to employ, to engage, to take on
Einstellungsgespräch *n*	interview
einstimmig	unanimous(ly)
einzahlen (auf Konto *n*)	pay into an account
Einzelfertigung *f*	one-off production
Einzelfirma *f*	sole proprietorship
Einzelhandelspreis *m*	retail price
Einzelhändler *m*	retail dealer
Einzelverpackung *f*	packaging
Eisenbahnfrachtbrief *m*	railway consignment note
elektronische Post *f*	electronic mail/E-mail
. Telefax	. fax
. Teletex	. Teletex
. Telex	. telex
elektronischer Briefkasten *m*	electronic mailbox
elektronisches Zeichengerät *n*	plotter
Empfänger *m* einer Sendung *f*	consignee
Entlassung *f*	dismissal
entschädigen	to compensate
Entwicklungstätigkeit *f*	development (of a product)
Erbschaftssteuer	inheritance tax
Ergebnis *n*	result
erinnern an	to remind somebody of something
Erinnerungsschreiben *n*	reminder
Erlöse *pl*	revenues
Ersatzlieferung *f*	substitute, replacement
erstatten	to refund
Erstbestellung *f*	initial order
erstklassige Qualität *f*	first-class quality
Ertrag *m*	return, yield
Erwerb *m*	acquisition
Erzeugerpreis *m*	producer's price, factory gate price
Erziehung *f*, Ausbildung *f*	education, training
Etikett *n*	label

europäischer Binnenmarkt *m*	single European market
Exporteur *m*	exporter
exportieren	to export
Exportverpackung *f*	export packing
Facharbeiter(in) *m/f*	skilled worker
Fachmann *m*	expert
Fachmesse *f*	specialized fair
fällig werden	to fall due
Fälligkeit *f*	due date
Faß *n*	barrel
Fehler	fault
fehlerhaftes Material *n*	faulty material
Fehlmenge *f*	shortage
feilschen, handeln	to bargain
Fertigfabrikate *pl*	finished goods
Fertigungslöhne *pl*	direct labour
Fertigungsmaterial *n*	direct material
Fertigungsplan *m*	production schedule
fest anbieten	to make a firm offer
fester Preis *m*	fixed price
Festkomma *n*	fixed point
Festspeicher *m*	read-only memory (ROM)
Festspeicherplatte *f*	hard disk
Filiale *f* Zweigniederlassung *f*	branch
Finanzmittelfluß *m*	cash flow
Finanzplanung *f*	budgetary accounting
Firma *f*	firm, business, company
Firma *f*, in eine . . . eintreten	to join a firm
Fixkosten *pl*	fixed costs
Fließband *n*	assembly line
Fließfertigung *f*	assembly line production
Flugblatt *n*	handbill
flüssige Mittel *pl*	liquid funds
Forderung *f*	debt, claim
Forderungen *pl*	receivables
Forderungsabtretung *f*	assignment of a debt
Forschungstätigkeit *f*	research
Fracht *f*	freight, cargo, carriage
Fracht *f* gegen Nachnahme *f*	freight collect
Fracht *f* inbegriffen	freight included

Frachtbrief *m*	consignment note, waybill
Frachtbriefdoppel *n*	duplicate consignment note
Frachtkosten *pl*	freight/forwarding charges
Frachtrate *f*	freight rate
Fragebogen *m*	questionnaire
freibleibend anbieten	to offer subject to confirmation
Fremdkapital *n*	borrowed capital
Fremdsprachensekretärin *f*	foreign language secretary/ bilingual secretary
Führungskraft *f*	executive
fundierte Branchenkenntnisse *pl*	profound knowledge of the trade
Fusion *f*, Zusammenschluß *m*	merger
fusionieren	to merge
Garantievertrag *m*, Bürgschaft *f*	guarantee, warrant
Gebrauchsanweisung *f*	operating instructions
Gebühr *f*	charge, fee
gedruckter Briefkopf *m*	printed letterhead
Gehalt *n*	salary
Gehaltserhöhung *f*	rise
Gelegenheitsgesellschaft *f*	joint venture
Gemeinkosten *pl*	overhead costs
Gemeinkostenzuschläge *pl*	overhead charges
Gemeinsamer Markt *m*	common market
Gemeinschaftliches Versandverfahren *n*	Community Transport Procedure (CTP)
Generaldirektor(in) *m/f*	chairman/woman
Generalvertretung *f*	general agency
Gesamtkosten *pl*	all-in costs
Gesamtsumme *f* über DM . . .	total (sum) amounting to DM . . .
Geschäft *n* betrieben	to run a business
Geschäfte *pl* tätigen	to do business
geschäftlicher Ruf *m*	business reputation
Geschäftsbericht *m*	annual report
Geschäftsbeteiligungen *pl*	business partnerships
Geschäftsbrief *m*	business letter
Geschäftsentwicklung *f*	development (of business), growth

geschäftsführendes Vorstandsmitglied *n*	managing director
Geschäftsführer(in) *m/f*	manager(ess)
Geschäftssitz *m*	registered office
geschätzter Jahresumsatz *m*	estimated annual turnover
gesetzlich geschutzt	legally protected
gesetzliche Rücklagen *pl*	legal reserves
Gewährleistungspflicht *f*	seller's warranties
Gewerbesteuer *f*	trade tax
Gewerkschaft *f*	trade union
Gewinn *m* nach Steuern *pl*	after-tax profit
Gewinn *m* vor Steuern *pl*	pre-tax profit
Gewinn- und Verlustkonto *n*	profit and loss account
Gewinn- und Verlustrechnung *f*	statement of earnings
Gewinnbeteiligung *f*	profit sharing
Gewinnspanne *f*	profit margin
Gewinnzuschlag *m*	profit mark-up
Girokonto *n*	giro account
Gläubiger *m*	creditor
gleichlautend buchen	to book in conformity
Gleitkomma *n*	floating point
Gleitzeit *f*	flexible working hours, flexitime
Grenzkosten *pl*	marginal costs
Größe *f*	size
große Auswahl *f* von	a wide range of
Großhandelspreis *m*	wholesale price
Großhändler *m*	wholesale dealer
gründen	to establish, to found
Grunderwerbssteuer *f*	real property transfer tax
gültig	valid
günstiger Preis *m*	favourable price
Güteklasse *f*, Sorte *f*	grade
Güter *pl*, Ware *f*, Handelsware *f*	commodity, goods, merchandise
Güterfernverkehr *m*	long hauls
Güternahverkehr *m*	short hauls
Gütertransport *m*, Anfuhr *f*, Abfuhr *f*	carriage
Gutschrift *f* erstellen	to credit
Gutschriftsanzeige *f*	credit note

Haftpflichtversicherung *f*	third party/liability insurance
Haftung *f*	liability
Halbfertigfabrikate *pl*	semi-finished goods
Hallenplan *m*	hall plan
Handbuch *n*	manual
Handel *m*	trade
Handel *m* **treiben**	to trade
handeln, feilschen	to bargain
Handelsmesse *f*	trade fair
Handelsrabatt *m*	trade discount
Handelsrechnung *f*	commercial invoice
Handelsspanne *f*	trade margin
handelsüblich	accepted in the trade
handelsübliche Qualität *f*	commercial quality
Handelsusance *f*	trade custom
Handelsverbindungen *pl*	trade relations
Handelsware *f*, **Güter** *pl*, **Ware** *f*	merchandise, commodity, goods
Händler *m*, **Kaufmann** *m*	trader, merchant
Handlungsbevollmächtigte *f/m*	proxy
Hauptbuch *n*	ledger
Hauptgeschäftsstelle *f*	head office
Hauptversammlung *f*	general meeting
herstellen	to make, to produce, to manufacture
Herstellungskosten *pl*	production costs
hervorragende Qualität *f*	outstanding quality
Huckepackverkehr *m*	piggyback (combined road and rail) service
Hypothek *f*	mortgage
Importeur *m*	importer
Importlizenz *f*	import licence
in eine Firma *f* **eintreten**	to join a firm
in Lizenz *f* **herstellen**	to manufacture under licence
in Zahlung *f* **geben**	to trade in
Industriebetrieb *m*	industrial plant
industrielle Produktion *f*	industrial production
Industriemesse *f*	industrial fair
Industrienorm *f*	industrial standard
informieren	to inform

Inkassobüro *n*	collection agency
interessiert sein an	to be interested in
Inventur *f*	inventory
Inventur *f* aufnehmen	to take stock
Investition *f*	investment
Investitionsgüter *pl*	capital goods
im voraus	in advance
Irrtum *m* vorbehalten	E & OE (errors and omissions excepted)
Jahresabschluß *m*	annual financial statement
Jahreshauptversammlung *f*	annual general meeting of the shareholders
Jurist *m*, Rechtsanwalt *m*	lawyer
Kabelanschluß *m*	cable connection
Kalkulation *f*	calculation
Kalkulationstabelle *f*	spreadsheet
Kanister *m*	metal container
Kapitalertragssteuer *f*	capital gains tax
Kapitalverhältnisse *pl*	capital structure
Kasse *f* gegen Dokumente *pl*	cash against documents (CAD), documents against payment (D/P)
Katalog *m*	catalogue
Kauf *m*	purchase
Kauf *m* auf Probe *f*	sale on trial
Kauf *m* der Einzelwirtschafts- güter *pl* der Zielgesellschaft *f*	asset deal
Kauf *m* der Geschäftsanteile *pl* der Zielgesellschaft *f*	share deal
Kauf *m* mit Rückgaberecht *n*	sale or return
kaufen	to buy, to purchase
Käufer *m*	buyer
Kaufkraft *f*	purchasing power
Kaufmann *m*, Händler *m*	merchant, trader
kaufmännische Angestellte *f/m*	clerk
Kaufvertrag *m*	contract of sale
keine versteckten Kosten *pl*	no hidden extras
Kennwort *n*	password
Kirchensteuer *f*	church tax

Kiste f	case
Klage f einreichen gegen . . .	to bring an action against somebody
Klassifizierungen pl	classifications
Kommissionär m	commission agent
Kommissionskaufmann m	representative on commission
Kommissionsverkauf m	sales on commission
Konferenzen pl	conferences
Konkurrent m	competitor
Konkurrenz f	competition
konkurrenzfähiger Preis m	competitive price
konkurrieren	to compete
Konkurs m	bankruptcy, liquidation
Konkurs m anmelden	to file for bankruptcy
Konkurs m machen	to go bankrupt
Konkurseröffnungsbeschluß m	receiving order
Konkursverwalter m	trustee, official receiver
Konossement n	Bill of Lading (B/L)
Konsortium n	consortium
Konsularrechnung f	consular invoice
Konto n	account
Konto n ausgleichen	to balance an account
Konto n eröffnen	to open an account
Konto n schließen	to close an account
Konto n überziehen	to overdraw an account
Kontoauszug m	statement of account
Konzern m	group, concern
Konzerngruppe f	division
Konzession f	franchise
Körperschaftssteuer	corporation tax
Kosten pl	costs
kostendeckend	cost-covering
Kostenerstattung f	refund of costs
kostenlos	cost-free/free of charge
Kostenvoranschlag m	estimate
kostenwirksam	cost effective
Kreditversicherung f	credit insurance
Kreditwürdigkeit f	credit standing
Kunde m	customer
Kundendienst m	after-sales service
kündigen	to give notice

Kursverlustverischerung *f*	insurance against loss on the exchange rate
kurz-/mittel-/langfristiger Kredit *m*	short-term/medium-term/long-term credit
laden, ausladen	to load, to unload
Lagerbestand *m*	stock
Lagerbestandskontrolle *f*	stock control
Lagerhaltung *f*	storage
Lagerhaus *n*	warehouse
Lagerhausgesellschaft *f*	warehouse company
lagern	to store, to stock
Lagerumschlag *m*	stockturn
Lagerverwalter *m*	stock clerk
Laserdrucker *m*	laser printer
Lastschriftsanzeige f	debit note
Lattenkiste *f*	crate
laufendes Konto *f*	current account
Laufwerk *n*	drive (disk)
laut Ihrer Bestellung *f*	as per your order/in accordance with your order
laut Rechnung *f*	as per invoice
laut Vertrag *m*	as per contract
Lebenslauf *m*	curriculum vitae
Lebenslauf (Kurz-) *m*	personal data sheet
Leerstelle *f*, **Füllzeichen** *n*	blank, space
Lehre *f* absolvieren	to serve an apprenticeship
Lehrling *m*, **Azubi** *m/f*	apprentice
Leihbehälter *m*	returnable container
leiten, verwalten	to manage
Leiter(in) *m/f*, **Geschäftsführer(in)** *m/f*	manager(ess)
Lieferant *m*	supplier
Lieferfirma *f*	suppliers, contractors
Lieferfrist *f*, **äußerster Termin** *m*	deadline
liefern	to supply, to furnish a customer with goods
liefern, innerhalb der Lieferzeit *f*	to deliver within the specified time
Lieferschein *m*	delivery note

Lieferung *f*	delivery
Lieferung *f* durchführen	to effect delivery
Liefervertrag *m*	supply contract
Liquidität *f*	liquidity
Listenpreis *m*	list price
Lizenz *f* erwerben	to acquire a licence
Lizenzgebühr *f*	royalty
lizenzpflichtig	subject to payment of royalties
Lohn *m*, Löhne *pl*	wage(s)
Lohnabrechnung *f*, Personalliste *f*	payroll
Lohnsteuer *f*	wage tax
löschen (Datei *f*)	to erase
Luftfracht *f*	air cargo, airfreight
Luftfrachbrief *m*	air waybill
Lufttransport *m*	air transport
Magnetband *n*	magnetic tape
Magnetband-Bibliotheksystem *n*	tape library system
Magnetbandgerät *n*	tape drive unit
Magnetkopf *m*	magnetic head
Magnetplattenspeicher *m*	disk storage
Mahnbrief *m*	dunning letter/reminder letter
Mangel *m*, Defekt *m*	defect
mangelhafte Ware *f*	defective goods
Mängelrüge *f*, Beschwerde *f*	complaint
Marke *f*	brand
Markierung *f*	marking
Markt *m*	market
Marktforschung *f*	market research
Marktlage *f*	market situation
Marktumfrage *f*	market survey
Maske *f*	mask, picture
Massengüter *pl*	bulk goods
Massengütertransport *m*	bulk haulage
Matrixdrucker *m*	dot-matrix printer
Mehrwertsteuer *f*	VAT (value added tax)
Meister *m*	foreman, master
Menge *f*	quantity
Mengenrabatt *m*	quantity discount

Merkblatt n	instructions, brochure, leaflet
Messe f	fair
Messe f **besuchen**	to visit a fair
Messe f **eröffnen**	to open a fair
Messe f **veranstalten**	to organize a fair
Messeausweis m	fair pass
Messebesucher m	visitor at a fair
Messehostess f	hostess
Messeleitung f	fair management
Messeordnung f	exhibition regulations
Messestand m	stand, stall, booth
Messeveranstalter m	organizer (of a fair)
Messezentrum n	exhibition centre
mieten, vermieten	to rent
Mischung f	blend
Mitbestimmung f	co-determination, worker participation (in decision-making)
Modell n, **Muster** n	pattern
modernisieren	to streamline (production)
Monopolstellung f	monopoly
Montage f	assembly
Montageanleitung f	assembly instructions
Muster n, **Probe** f	sample
Muster n, **Modell** n	pattern
Muster n **ohne Wert** m	sample of no commercial value
Musterkollektion f	sample collection
Musterstück n	model, pattern, specimen
Muttergesellschaft f	parent company, holding company
Nachbestellung f	repeat order
Nachfrage f	demand
Nachfrist f	additional period of time
Nachnahme f	cash on delivery (COD)
Nebenkosten pl	extras
Nettogewicht n	net weight
neuester Katalog m	latest catalogue
Nichtübereinstimmung f **mit Muster** n	non-conformity with sample

offene Stelle *f*	vacancy, opening
Öffentlichkeitsarbeit *f*	public relations
ohne Berechnung *f*	without charge
ohne Mehrwertsteuer *f*	zero-rated
pachten	to lease
Packliste *f*	packing list
Packstück *n*, Kollo *n*	package
Palette *f*	pallet
Papiervorschub *m*	paper feed
Passiva *pl*	liabilities
Patent *n* anmelden	to apply for the patent
Patent *n* verwerten	to exploit a patent
patentiert	patented
patentrechtlich	under patent law
Pauschalbetrag *m*	lump sum
Pauschalsatz *m*	flat rate
Pensionskasse *f*	pension fund, superannuation fund
per Adresse *f* (per Adr.)	c/o (care of)
Personalangelegenheiten *pl*	personnel matters
Personalleiter *m*	personnel manager
Personalliste *f*	payroll
Pfändung *f*	attachment
Plakat *n*	poster
Plattenbetriebssystem *n*	disk operating system (DOS)
platzen	to bounce
Porto *n*	postage
Posten *m* (Ware *f*)	item
Postwurfsendung *f*	mail circular, mailshot
Prämie *f*	premium
Preis *m*, alles inbegriffen	all-in price
Preisaufschlag *m*	surcharge
Preisbindung *f*	price maintenance
Preise *pl*	price
Preise *pl* angeben	to quote prices
Preise *pl* ausgleichen	to adjust prices
Preise *pl* unterbeiten	to beat prices
Preiserhöhung *f*	price increase
Preisliste *f*	price list
Preisnachlaß *m*	price reduction

Preisnachlaß *m* gewähren	to grant an allowance
Probe *f*, Muster *n*	sample
Probezeit *f*	probation period
Produktbeschreibungen *pl*	product descriptions
Produkthaftung *f*	product liability
Produktion *f*	production
Produktionsleistung *f*	output
Produktionsprogramm *n*	production programme
Produktionszeit *f*	production period
Produktmuster *n*	trial product sample
Proforma-Rechnung *f*	pro-forma invoice
Programmiersprache *f*	progamming language
Prospekt *m*	prospectus, catalogue
Protokoll *n* führen	to keep the minutes
Provision *f*	commission
Prozentsatz *m*	percentage
Prozeß *m*, Rechtsstreit *m*	lawsuit, litigation
Prufungswesen *n*	auditing
Qualifikation *f*, Eignung *f*	qualification
Qualität *f*	quality
Qualitätskontrolle *f*	quality control
Rabatt *m*, Skonto *n*	discount
Rate *f*	instalment
Ratenkauf *m*	hire purchase
rationalisieren, modernisieren	to streamline (production)
rechnen	to calculate
Rechner (Taschen-) *m*	calculator (pocket-)
Rechnung *f*	invoice
Rechnung *f* erstellen, berechnen	to invoice, to bill
Rechnungsbetrag *m*	Invoice amount
Rechnungsdatum *n*	date of invoice
Rechnungsnummer *f*	invoice number
Rechnungsposten *m*	item
Rechnungsstellung *f*	invoicing
Rechtsanwalt *m*, Jurist *m*	solicitor, lawyer
rechtschaffen, ehrlich	honest
Rechtsstreit *m*	litigation, lawsuit
Referenzen *pl*	references

Regress *m*	recourse
Regulierung *f* der Beschwerde *f*	adjustment
Rendite *f*	yield
Rentabilität *f*	profitability
Restzahlung *f*	payment of the balance
Risiko *n* abdecken	to cover a risk
Risiko *n* versichern	to underwrite a risk
Rohstoffe *pl*	raw materials
RoRo-Verkehr *m*	roll-on/roll-off service
rückständige Beträge *pl*	arrears
Rückstellungen *pl*	accruals
Rückzahlungstermin *m*	due date
Rundschreiben *n*	circular
Sack *m*	sack, bag
Saldo *m*	balance
Schachtel *f*	cardboard box, carton
Schaden *m*	damage
Schadenersatz *m*	compensation
Schadenersatz *m* verlangen	to demand compensation
Schadensfall *m*	claim
Schadensfall *m* regulieren	to settle a claim
Scheck *m* ausstellen	to draw a cheque
Schichtarbeit *f*	shift work
schlechte Qualität *f*	poor quality
Schlitten *m*	skid (roller)
Schnittstelle *f*	interface
Schreibkopf *m*	write head
Schreibkraft *f*	typist
Schreibschutz *m*	write lock, file protection
Schulabgangszeugnis *n*	school leaving certificate
Schuldner *m*	debtor
Schulungskurse *pl* für Verkäufer *pl*	training courses for salespersons
seemäßige Verpackung *f*	seaworthy packing
Sekretär(in) *m/f* (von XY)	secretary (to XY)
Selbstkosten *pl*	cost price
senden, versenden, befördern	to dispatch, to send off, to ship, to forward
Serienfertigung *f*	mass production
sich an einer Messe *f* beteiligen	to participate in a fair

sich beschweren über	to complain about
sich bewerben um	to apply for
sich selbständig machen	to set up a business
sich wenden n	to refer to
Sicherheit f	security
Sicherungsübereignung f	transfer of title for the purpose of securing a debt
Sitzung f eröffnen	to open the meeting
Sitzung f schließen	to close the meeting
Sitzungen pl	meetings
Skonto n, Rabatt m	discount
Software f	software
Sonderanfertigung f	special design
Sonderpreis m	special price
Sonderrabatt m	special discount
Sonderverpackung f	special packing
Sorte f, Güteklasse f	grade
sortieren	to sort
Sortiment n	range
Sparkonto n	deposit/savings account
Spediteur m	forwarder, carrier
Spediteurübernahme-bescheinigung f	Forwarding Agent's Certificate of Receipt (FCR)
Speicher (Computer-) m	memory
Speicherdichte f	density
Speicherschutz m	memory protection
Spesen pl	expenses
Stammdatei f	master file
Stand m abbauen	to remove a stand
Stand m aufbauen	to install a stand
Standardqualität f	standard quality
Standmiete f	stand rental
Statistik f	statistics
steckerkompatibel	plug compatible
Stellung f	job, position
Steuer f	tax
Steuerberater m	tax consultant
steuerfrei	tax-free
Steuerfreibetrag m	tax exemption
steuerpflichtig	liable to tax
Steuervergünstigung f	tax allowance

stornieren	to cancel
Streitfall *m*	dispute
Streitfallregelung *f*	commercial settlement of a dispute
streng vertraulich	strictly confidential
Stromversorgung *f*	power supply
Stückkosten *pl*	unit cost
Stückpreis *m*	unit price
Subvention *f*	subsidy
Tagesgeld *n*	call money
Tagesordnung *f*	agenda
Tara *f* Verpackungsgewicht *n*	tare
Tarifzone *f*	tariff zone
Tastatur *f*	keyboard
technische Planung *f*	engineering
Teilnahmebedingungen *pl*	conditions of participation
teilnehmen (an einer Konferenz *f*)	to attend (a conference)
Teilzahlung *f*	part payment
Teilzeitkräfte *pl*	part-time workers
Textverarbeitungssystem *n*	word-processing system
Tintenstrahldrucker *m*	ink-jet printer
Tilgungsrate *f*	amortization instalment
Tochtergesellschaft *f*	subsidiary
Transit *m*, auf dem . . ., unterwegs	in transit
Transport *m*	transport
Transport *m* auf der Straße	road transport
Transport *m* per Schiene	rail transport
Transportversicherung *f*	transportation insurance
Tratte *f*	draft
Trend *m*	trend
Typenrad *n*, Schreibrad *n*	daisy wheel
über (Dover)	via (Dover)
über einen Antrag *m* entscheiden	to decide on a motion
überblick *m* geben	to outline
überfällig	overdue
überfälliger Betrag *m*	amount overdue

305

überfälliger Wechsel *m*	bill overdue
übernahme *f* einer Gesellschaft *f*	take-over
Übersichtsplan *m*	floor plan
Überstunden *pl* machen	to work overtime
Übertrag *m*	brought forward (b/f), carry over
Übertragungswege *pl*	transmission channels
überwachen	to control
überweisen	to remit, to transfer
überweisung *f*	remittance
Überziehungskredit *m*	overdraft credit
Umhüllung *f*, Verpackung *f*	wrapping
Umladung *f*	transshipment, reloading
Umlaufvermögen *n*	current assets
Umsatz *m*	turnover
Umsatzerlöse *pl*	sales
Umsatzsteuer *f*	turnover tax
uneinbringliche Forderung *f*	bad debt
unfertige Erzeugnisse *pl*	work in progress
unter Vorbehalt *m*	under reserve
Unter-Händler *m*	negotiator, intermediary, agent
Unternehmensleitung *f*	management
Unterschrift *f*	signature
unterwegs, auf dem Transit *m*	in transit
unverbindlich	without obligation
unvorhersehbare Umstände *pl*	circumstances beyond our control
variable Kosten *pl*	variable costs
Verbindlichkeiten *pl* aus Lieferungen *pl* und Leistungen *pl*	trade payables
Verbraucherpreis *m*	consumer price
Verbrauchsgüter *pl*	consumer goods
Verbrauchssteuer *f*	excise tax
Vereinbarung *f*	agreement
Vergleich *m*	compromise
Vergleich (Konkurs-) *m*	composition
Verjährung *f*	period of limitation

Verkauf *m*	sale
Verkäufe *pl*, Absatz *m*	sales
Verkäufer *m*	seller
verkaufen	to sell
Verkaufsbedingungen pl	selling conditions
Verkaufsförderung *f*	sales promotion
Verkaufspreis *m*	selling price
verlängern	to prolong, to extend
Verlängerung *f*	extension, prolongation
Verlust *m*	loss
vermieten	to rent
Vermögenslage *f*	financial standing
Vermögenssteuer *f*	wealth tax, net worth tax
verpachten	to lease
Verpackung *f*	packing
Verpackung *f*, Umhüllung *f*	wrapping
Verpackung *f* zum Selbstkosten-preis *m*	packing at cost
Versandabteilung *f*	dispatch department
Versandanzeige *f*	dispatch note
Versanddatum *n*	date of shipment
Versandmarkierungen *pl*	shipping marks
Versandort *m*	place of dispatch
Versandweg *m* angeben	to specify the delivery route
Verschuldung *f*	indebtedness
Versehen *n*	error, oversight
Versicherer *m*	underwriter
Versicherung *f*	insurance
Versicherung *f* abschließen	to take out an insurance
Versicherungsgesellschaft *f*	insurance company
Versicherungsinhaber *m*	policy holder
Versicherungspolice *f*	insurance policy
Versicherungszertifikat *n*	insurance certificate
versteckter Mangel *m*	hidden defect
Vertrag *m* abschließen	to contract, to enter into a contract
Vertrag *m* ändern	to amend the contract
Vertrag *m* beglaubigen	to certify the contract
Vertrag *m* ist null und nichtig	the contract is null and void
Vertrag *m* läuft aus	the contract expires
Vertrag *m* stornieren, kündigen	to cancel a contract

Vertrag *m* **verlängern**	to extend a contract
vertraglich festschreiben	to become contractual
vertraglich vereinbart	stipulated
Vertragsbedingungen *pl*	terms of contract
Vertragsbedingungen *pl* **aushandeln**	to negotiate the conditions of a contract
Vertragsdauer *f*	period of contract
Vertragserfüllung *f*	fulfilment of contract
Vertragsfälligkeitstag *m*	maturity date of contract
Vertragsfristen *pl* **für Leistungen** *pl*	deadlines
Vertragshändler *m*	franchised dealer
Vertragsklausel *f*	contract clause
vertragsschließende Parteien *pl*	contracting parties
Vertragsstrafen *pl*	penalties
vertreiben als Alleinvertreter *m*	to sell as sole agent
Vertreter *m*	agent, representative
Vertretung *f* **übertragen**	to entrust a firm with the agency
Vertrieb *m*, **Absatz** *m*	marketing
Vertriebskosten *pl*	selling expenses
Vertriebsnetz *n*, **-organisation** *f*	distribution network
verwalten, leiten	to manage
Verwaltungskosten *pl*	administration expenses
Verzögerung *f*	delay
Verzugszinsen *pl*	interest for default
Vollzeitarbeitskräfte *pl*	full-time workers
Vorausbestellung *f*	advance order
voraussichtliche Entwicklung *f*	expected growth
Vorauszahlung *f*	advance payment
Vorführung *f*	demonstration
Vorgesetzte *f/m*	superior
Vorräte *pl*	inventories
vorrätig haben	to have in stock
Vorsitzende *f/m*	chairperson
vortragen (Saldo *m***)**	to carry forward (the balance)
Wagnis-/Beteiligungskapital *n*	venture capital
Ware *f*, **Güter** *pl*, **Handelsware** *f*	goods, commodity, merchandise
Ware *f* **umtauschen**	to exchange the goods

Ware *f* zurücknehmen	to take the goods back
Waren *pl* in Kommission *f* verkaufen	to sell goods on commission
Warenbegleitpapiere *pl*	shipping documents
Warenpartie *f*	lot
Warensendung *f*	consignment, shipment
Warenverzeichnis *n*	list of products
Warenzeichen *n*	trade mark
Wartung *f*	service
Wartungsanleitung *f*	service manual
Wartungsvertrag *m*	maintenance contract
Wassertransport *m*	water transport
Wechsel *m*	bill of exchange (B/E)
Wechselverbindlichkeiten *pl*	notes payable
Werbeagentur *f*	publicity agency
Werbeantwort *f*	business reply
Werbebrief *m*	sales/promotional letter, follow-up letter
Werbegeschenk *n*	advertising gift
Werbekampagne *f*	publicity campaign
Werbekosten *pl*	publicity expenditure
Werbemuster *n*	free sample
Werbesendung *f*	commercial
Werbung *f*	advertising
Werksleiter *m*	plant manager
Werkstatt *f*	workshop, machine shop
Werkzeug *n*	tool
wettbewerbsintensiver Markt *m*	highly competitive market
Widerspruch *m* erheben	to object to something
wirtschaftliche Lage *f*	economic position
Wirtschaftsprüfer *m*	chartered accountant
zahlen	to pay, to make payment, to effect payment
Zahlung *f*	payment, settlement
Zahlung *f* bei Erhalt *m* der Ware *f*	payment on receipt of goods (ROG)
Zahlung *f* durch Akzept *n*	payment by acceptance
Zahlung *f* durch Scheck *m*	payment by cheque
Zahlung *f* durch Sichttratte *f*	payment by sight draft

Zahlung *f* **durch unwider-** **rufliches bestätigtes** **Dokumenten-akkreditiv** *n*	payment by irrevocable confirmed documentary letter of credit (L/C)
Zahlung *f* **gegen Bankgarantie** *f*	payment against bank guarantee
Zahlungsbedingungen *pl*	terms of payment
Zahlungsempfänger *m*	payee
Zahlungsfähigkeit *f*	solvency
Zahlungsunfähigkeit *f*	insolvency
Zeitungsinserat *n*	advertisement
Zentrale *f*	head office, headquarters
Zentraleinheit *f*	central processing unit (CPU)
Zeugnis *n* **des Arbeitgebers** *m*	testimonial
Zinsen *pl*	interest
Zinseszins *m*	compound interest
Zinssatz *m*	rate of interest
zu Händen von . . . (z. Hd.) *pl*	for the attention of . . .
Zulieferfirma *f*	subcontractor
zum halben Preis *m*	at half price
zum Selbstkostenpreis *m*	at cost
zur Zahlung *f* **auffordern**	to demand payment
Zusammenarbeit *f*	co-operation
Zusammenschluß *m*, **Fusion** *f*	merger
Zusatzsteuer *f*	surtax
Zusätzliche Vergütung *f* **an** **Arbeitnehmer** *pl* **neben Lohn** *m* **und Gehalt** *n*	fringe benefits
zustellen, ausliefern	to deliver
Zuverlässigkeit *f*	reliability
Zwangsverkauf *m*	compulsory sale
Zweifelhafte Forderung *f*	doubtful debt
Zweigniederlassung *f*, **Filiale** *f*	branch
zweite Wahl *f*	second-rate quality
Zwischenhändler *m*	commission agent

4

Index